modern book of
dream
interpretation

cassandra eason's
modern book of
dream
interpretation

quantum
LONDON • NEW YORK • TORONTO • SYDNEY

quantum

An imprint of W. Foulsham & Co. Ltd
The Publishing House, Bennetts Close, Cippenham, Slough,
Berkshire, SL1 5AP, England

ISBN 0-572-03081-9

First published by New Page Förlag Sweden with the title *Drömmar – att välja och tolka sina drömmar*

Published by arrangement with Tönnheim Literary Agency, Sweden

Cover illustration by Jurgen Ziewe

A CIP record for this book is available from the British Library

Please note that dreams about a person dying never mean
they are really going to die. They are just symbolic of
natural change.

Printed in Great Britain by Creative Print & Design (Wales), Ebbw Vale

Contents

The World of Dreams 7

CHAPTER 1 Understanding Your Dreams 11

CHAPTER 2 Celebrity Dreams 23

CHAPTER 3 Learning to Control Your Dreams 27

CHAPTER 4 Exploring the World of Dreams 35

CHAPTER 5 Your Dream Lover 42

CHAPTER 6 Psychic Dreams 51

A to Z of Dream Meanings 61

A 62
B 71
C 84
D 102
E 116
F 125
G 137
H 146
I 155
J 162
K 168
L 174
M 187
N 198
O 204
P 213
Q 225
R 230

S 240
T 253
U 263
V 267
W 272
X 281
Y 283
Z 285

Index   287

The World of Dreams

Long ago, the native North Americans all lived in the same area of land. Day and night, Grandmother Spider Woman, who created humans and animals from clay, wove tiny nets of thread she called 'dream-catchers'. Mothers hung the nets over cradles to ensure that their babies would sleep peacefully as bad dreams would become entangled in the web and only the happy ones would filter through. With the first rays of sunlight, the bad dreams would break free and return to the place of shadows, but the good dreams would sparkle like rainbows and linger all day.

Eventually the native North Americans grew so numerous that the tribes had to disperse in different directions to find new hunting grounds. Grandmother Spider Woman could no longer visit all the cradles to keep her webs in order and so she taught her magical secret to the wise grandmothers who in turn taught their daughters to weave magical webs for their babies, using willow hoops and thread made from animal sinews or cord from plants.

Like Grandmother Spider Woman, grandmothers and mothers all over the world have woven their magic to banish the bad dreams of their families. In Viking lands they would gather amber and create strings of honey-coloured stones, said to contain the power of many suns, to hang at bedroom windows or over cradles to banish fears and night shadows. The *spá-kona* or *völva*, the wise woman of a village, would interpret the meanings of dreams, especially those of women who were regarded as being naturally prophetic. These dreams might offer guidance as to the success of their husband or father's journeys, or offer glimpses of a new land that the family might colonise.

Understanding our dreams

In the modern world too, our dreams hold the keys to our inner world and can often guide us toward the best course of action in our everyday life.

We all dream, although we may not recall many of our night-time visions. Dreams can take us to wonderful places where we can meet old friends, encounter new lovers and talk with our guardian angels. Our dreams can show us new opportunities or solutions to problems that we may have been worrying about endlessly and sometimes dreams can warn us about future hazards or about people who are untrustworthy.

Dreams can be like mirrors of what is happening in our lives. For example, you may dream of floods and drowning when you are finding it hard to cope with money worries or are being overwhelmed by the demands of others in your waking life. Similarly, dreaming of trying to leave an urgent message but being prevented can reflect something you are trying to communicate to someone close. Ask yourself; who is it who may not be listening?

Like a dream detective you can work out what a dream is trying to tell you and take action. And once you have worked through this book, you will be able to take more control of your dreams and start swimming away from that flood for example.

As for all those wonderful dreams of marrying a great man or woman, having a lot of money, mixing with royalty or lying on tropical shores in the smallest of swimwear with the flattest of stomachs, they are all possibilities that can come true in the real world. You may not literally take tea with royalty or marry your favourite celebrity but you can get yourself noticed at work or get a promotion, take a package holiday to Greece or at least enjoy an hour or so in a sauna.

A note about sleep disturbance

If you have small children, work long hours or travel long distances every day to work and then have to do chores when you get home, you may fall into bed totally exhausted. Often you will then toss and turn all night, worrying about what has been left unfinished and anxious that if you cannot sleep you will not be able to face the day ahead. I have done that so many times and then fallen into an exhausted stupor as light breaks, my half-sleep disturbed by strange, seemingly meaningless dreams; snatches of conversation, lights, colours and feelings which were then broken by the crying of an infant or the relentless ring of the alarm clock. This sleep confusion is in fact a very healthy reaction to stress and indicates that our minds are sorting through the actions of the day, filing what can be saved as memories or ideas and discarding what is left.

Some people also suffer from night terrors which occur during a different stage of sleep from normal nightmares. Although night terrors are particularly prevalent in children, adults can also experience them. Usually the dreamer holds no memories of it, only a sense of sheer terror and perhaps the sensation of sleep paralysis. Thankfully, they are quite rare. If you or a child do suffer from nightmares or night terrors, perhaps you might find it helpful to buy a dream-catcher for your bedroom or a net to which you can attach crystals to hang over the bed so ensuring your dreams are good ones sent to you by Grandmother Spider Woman.

Learn to enjoy the night

Make dream time a priority for a while so that you can focus on your dreams. If you are perpetually tired, make sleep a priority for a week or two. Sex can induce wonderful dreams but if you are overwrought and exhausted, all you may want is a gentle cuddle or a night or two alone to recharge your batteries. Dream lovers are far less demanding than real ones at the end of the day (see page 42). Even if you are not exhausted, go to bed really early once or twice a week or spend the odd grey morning or afternoon asleep if you have the opportunity. If you do have a lover, then these siesta times are a good opportunity for a sleep, followed by passion and then more sleep and possibly shared dreams (see page 48).

If you are suffering from sleep disturbances or are just plain worn out, beg, steal or borrow half an hour's sleep during the day (called the power nap and it certainly is a kick start for the afternoon). In warm countries, a siesta after lunch is part of the working day. If you have children, try to get a friend or relative to look after them overnight so that you can get an unbroken stretch of sleep and dream time. You can return the favour for another stressed mother or father.

For quality sleep and dream time

Use these methods to help promote beneficial rest.

- Make sure your bedroom is warm but well ventilated.
- Imitate the birds and animals and make yourself a nest using plenty of soft bedding and cushions.
- Tidy your bedroom, removing old coffee cups, newspapers and washing and put your mobile phone on silent answer – better still switch it off!
- Light rose or lavender incense or burn a relaxing essential oil.

☾ Use subdued lighting. Fibre optic or lava lamps can be very relaxing. If you use a scented nightlight, place it safely in a glass container where it cannot ignite anything, even if it gets knocked over.

☾ Play gentle rainforest, ocean or dolphin music softly in the background of your room.

☾ Lie down on your bed and imagine yourself cocooned and floating on pink fluffy clouds.

When you are relaxed, close your eyes and float on your clouds into sleep, pushing away worries on clouds of their own or release them to float off like balloons. If you find it difficult to drift off, do not consciously try to sleep. Instead, imagine the alarm has just gone off on a cold grey morning and how wonderful it feels to snuggle down under the bedclothes.

At first you may find that your dreams are confused or fragmented as your mind unloads the excess mental load. But as you make sleep time a creative part of your life so you can rest assured that when you wake you will feel restored, refreshed and full of ideas and enthusiasm for the day.

About this book

All of these themes and others will be explored in more detail throughout the pages of this book, as well as the meanings of many different dream images. I have used the actual dreams of people to show how dream work can be helpful. I have also written about creating happy, beautiful dreams, using dreams to answer questions and improve self-confidence and suggested ways of driving away nightmares and insomnia. There are many exercises in the different chapters you can try if you wish to remember your dreams more clearly and explore the dream world.

CHAPTER 1

Understanding Your Dreams

According to dream researchers, we dream approximately five times each night with the first dream being short and occurring in the early part of the night. Our minds tend to use this first dream to sort through the information of the day whereas later dreams, which can last from 30 to 40 minutes, are more creative and involved. It is often these longer dreams which provide the best ways of understanding our hidden feelings and fears about people and situations and for deciding which is the best course of action to take. For instance, we may be feeling pressurised into making a decision about which we are not certain. In our waking time, our intuition or wise inner voice is often a good guide, but sometimes that voice can be drowned out by people telling us what we ought to do or because we are distracted by 101 other concerns, particularly if we are going through a difficult time or are being given conflicting advice. Dreams are therefore a way for us to get in touch with our subconscious inner voice and also of gaining access to information not available to the conscious mind. Our minds possess an unconscious radar that can steer us onto the right path or warn us of potential hazards. When we are asleep the daytime world fades and our bodies are still and the other part of us can emerge.

Once you learn to interpret and trust your dreams, daytime decision-making will become clearer and easier because you will be using all parts of your mind, including the all-valuable intuition that we ignore. Let me give you an example of how a particularly vivid dream helped one woman to see the way forward clearly.

Lindsey was in her forties and married with three teenage children. Sometimes she thought of her husband as a particularly troublesome child since he hardly ever helped her around the house but always demanded her attention.

Although she worked from home as a web designer, Lindsey's family expected her to fit her business around their minor crises and social life. She seemed to spend most of her time acting as a referee in disputes between her husband and the children, both parties throwing tantrums and demanding her support against the other.

One night after a particularly bad argument with her husband, Lindsey had a vivid dream:

> *My deceased father was in the back garden of my home lighting paper and attempting to set fire to the house. I was trying desperately to put out the fire with small bowls of water while persuading the family they were in danger. My father was laughing at my feeble attempts to put out the fires and the children were ignoring me. Then I realised that my father had changed into my husband. Suddenly I gave up. 'Let it burn,' I said and walked back inside. I woke up crying.*

Of course Lindsey wasn't hoping her house and family went up in flames, but sometimes vivid imagery is our mind's way of telling us to wake up and listen to a message we are ignoring, perhaps at the cost of our own health and happiness. On analysing the dream Lindsey recalled that her father had acted in the same uncaring selfish way towards her mother as Lindsey's husband did to her. Her mother had constantly placated him and protected the children from his anger. History was repeating itself and Lindsey's mother had died an unhappy and disappointed woman. Lindsey realised that she had been given the impetus to do something about her situation.

Lindsey was aware that because she had gone back inside the house in her dream, she was not yet ready to walk away from the destructive situation. So she resolved to distance herself gradually from her family, to stop acting as peacemaker and begin to make a life of her own. She is now much happier and goes away for weekends to paint, her favourite hobby. Since she is no longer intervening in quarrels they have actually reduced, as she is no longer the willing audience.

Dreams can also reflect anxieties that we may be repressing which are causing us stress. For example, Margaret was in her thirties and had a very busy life combining her wooden toy business with running a home and caring for her husband and family. She told me:

> *I was trying to get to the airport to catch a plane to go to an important International Toy Fair. In my dream my car broke down and when I tried to dial on my mobile for assistance, I kept dialling the wrong number and could not remember the correct number for roadside help. I realised that I was going to miss my plane and then when I looked in my bag for something, my passport had also gone.*

How well many of us know such nightmare scenarios from real life. When we enact catastrophes in our dreams, our subconscious is telling us that we are losing control of our lives. Missing trains and planes, cars breaking down, losing keys and passports, leaving cases on trains are all symbols that our waking world is spinning out of control. Of course you can't magically create any more hours in the day, but you can take a short break for a few days and prioritise what absolutely has to be done and nothing more. For a while write lists, times and places that cannot be missed and work other commitments around them. In this way, even an anxiety dream can be very positive.

Working in pictures

When we are small children we think in pictures rather than words. This kind of understanding means that rather than reducing our thoughts and ideas to words in order to explain them, we allow the images to expand so they lead easily to other images and can inspire us to try all kinds of new ventures. Of course as adults we recognise that we need words in order to categorise experiences, to communicate with others and to gain information. But in the night time we revert to the ability to create and think in pictures; so when we analyse our dreams we have the best of both worlds.

Let me explain how these dream pictures can bring to the surface those thoughts we push away because they are too difficult to handle, but which may hold the key to long-term fulfilment.

Sanna had been living happily with her partner for a number of years and as they were in their early thirties they were both focusing hard on their careers. One night, Sanna had a particularly vivid dream:

> I dreamt that my partner had died and I was taking his body in a cardboard box on the train to my late grandmother's house. When I got off the train I realised I had the wrong box. When I opened it the box contained meat pies.

The results of eating too much cheese before bedtime? No, a clear indication that like Lindsey, Sanna deep down wanted change in her relationship. The death of her partner in the dream suggested that she was ready to move on to the next stage in their relationship and put the lid on the present phase, however happy. The fact it was a cardboard box with a lid and not a nailed down coffin showed that she was not intending to bury her partner, that is, leave him. Instead, Sanna was going back with his body to a childhood place that represented security and a permanent home where she had been happy, in this case her grandmother's house. When we go back to childhood, if it was happy, it usually indicates that we want to find a missing ingredient in our present life, which for Sanna in this case meant the need to feel settled and secure. A desire for permanence was definitely rearing its head.

The box Sanna picked up by mistake contained what she really wanted instead of a carefree relationship and a high-flying career. Pies are a symbol of home cooking and, in a number of cultures, of fertility, which suggests a solid state of affairs, a settled home, marriage and baking to feed a family. Deep down the dream pictures were saying that her flippant days were coming to an end and were bringing to her attention her desire for marriage, a home, children and possibly grandchildren with her partner.

All a bit much from one dream? Not to Sanna. She considered the dream to be so important that she told her colleagues at work about it and they discussed what it might mean and she continued to talk about it the next day when I met her. When I told her what the dream signified, Sanna told me that her sister was expecting a baby the following month. It is likely her sister's pregnancy triggered off the issue of children in Sanna's life and caused her subconscious to come to the fore to remind her of her own ticking biological clock.

Remembering your dreams

Very vivid dreams like Sanna's do seem to imprint themselves on our memories, as though we have taken a photographic image and we may find ourselves discussing them with friends and family as though they had actually occurred. In psychology this is called the flashbulb memory and is the same as when we recall what we were doing in detail at a particularly significant moment in history, for example when we heard the news of the death of Princess Diana or of the Twin Towers disaster in New York.

But with many other dreams, the details can fade within a few minutes once we start to make the breakfast or get children ready for school. Our memory also has a habit of tidying up details and burying pretty fast the bits your conscious mind does not want you to remember. As a result, if you are going to use your dreams as a source of information, it is important that you remember as many details as possible. The following traditional Hawaiian method is very easy but effective. All you need is a glass of water.

A Hawaiian ritual for remembering dreams

☾ Drink half a glass of water just before sleep, leaving the other half nearby. This is to symbolise entering the dream state.

☾ After you have drunk the water say,
As I drink the water it reminds me that I will recall my dream.

☾ Now settle comfortably into bed, visualising yourself floating on clouds until you have fallen asleep.

☾ When you wake in the morning, drink the other half of the water and say to yourself:
As I drink once more, I recall my dream.

You may also find it helpful to keep a dream journal. You might like to use a folder or notebook with loose pages so that you can add to the book, rearrange the order and start an A to Z dream-meaning section of your own. To do this, rearrange the dream-meaning symbols in your folder every other week into alphabetical order. For ease, you could keep the list on a computer file. At the end of this book I have listed more than 1000 dream meanings to help you get started (see pages 62–286). Keep a notebook and pen at your bedside or, if you prefer, a tape recorder. As soon as you wake, in the night as well as in the morning, from a dream or even a vivid nightmare, switch on the light and write down any details that you can recall. You can include dream characters, feelings, any really important dialogue and possibly a few key words to help you recall the overall impressions when you analyse the dream material later. This need only take a minute or two. At first you may decide to record dreams only at weekends, but if a dream has woken you, scribbling down the details can be settling. Try to do this when you have a bad dream as they are usually important. In contrast, if the dream was good and you want to return to it, picture one of the last or the strongest pleasurable images or scenes or imagine a path leading back to a place in the dream that you liked, such as a sunny corner of a dream garden, a palm tree on a sandy beach or yourself sitting on a throne in a castle. If you do not want to go back into a particular dream however, or you want to calm down from a nightmare, picture yourself floating on pink fluffy clouds, through a starlit sky or enclosed in a warm dark blanket gently rocking in the cosmic cradle. This is also a good way of overcoming insomnia.

Some dream symbols will have special meaning for you and will recur at important times in your life (see also pages 17–19). For example, a beautiful dream butterfly may signify that you are ready for a new stage in your life. Therefore, whenever you dream about a butterfly, you can note in your dream book what is happening in your real life at that time and what you felt in the dream when you saw the butterfly, to promote greater understanding of what is happening to you. One bonus is that once you consciously start deliberately trying to recall and record your dreams, it becomes much easier to remember them.

Understanding the message in your dreams

It is unlikely that you will want to follow up every dream in detail, but if a dream seems significant, especially if you are going through a period of change or uncertainty, to analyse the dream in detail may be helpful in understanding your real feelings about a person or situation.

When you have time, perhaps in the evening, sit quietly by soft lamplight or candlelight and re-read the dream material you recorded that morning or listen to your dream tape.

Look up any basic dream symbols within the list on pages 62–286 if you are uncertain of what the dream images might mean. Now imagine each of those symbols in turn as they appeared in your dream and allow your intuition and imagination to fill in more details and if necessary expand on the setting of the image. For example, if you dreamed of a beautiful golden fish in a lake, allow your imagination to roam beyond the lake, perhaps into a nearby forest. This type of daydreaming is a very good way of drawing out the different levels of your dream. If the dream is still unclear, focus on the feelings aroused in the dream by the main symbols and as you recall them notice how they make you feel. It might be helpful to extend some of the conversations in the dream in your mind and if the dream was unfinished or the actual ending was unsatisfactory, then create an ending. This can often guide you as to what you really want to do or what you feel deep down.

When you have interpreted your dream, add the details to your dream journal giving the date of the dream and any significant events which may be happening in your real life at the time of the dream. Note also the location of each dream. If it is a place from the past, whether your personal past or a past world, it may have special significance to your present situation. Sometimes past dreams represent a re-run of an old situation that needs resolution if you are to move forward. Or, as in the case of Sanna's dream, it may be an indication that you want the security you experienced in childhood or a carefree period if you are feeling tied down by burdens in the everyday world.

You could organise your dreams into categories along with a significant phrase or keyword, for example love, family, falling or wish fulfilment (where you dream of winning the lottery or getting a best-seller published). You will find your own categories emerge quite naturally. Finally, add the main individual key images plus any new insights to the A to Z dream list at the back of your journal.

Recurring dream images

As I mentioned on page 15 most of us seem to have one, or perhaps two, particular images that appear in our dreams over a number of months or even years. These personal images carry a particular message, perhaps advice or a warning that comes from the wisest part of us. Sometimes, the symbol will appear in the everyday world a day or two after a dream, as a way of indicating that the dream did have a special meaning. The psychologist Carl Gustav Jung called this 'synchronicity' or a meaningful coincidence, the same phenomenon that has us meeting someone we haven't seen for years in a totally unexpected place we shouldn't have been in anyway, usually just after we have thought of the person, seemingly for no reason.

Even the most sceptical scientist now acknowledges that incidents are connected in ways we cannot understand. Let me tell you the story of Fatima, a businesswoman I met while I was on a research trip to Cairo. She was totally practical and very intelligent, but had also learned to trust her intuitive side. She described how she first encountered her recurring dream image of a cat. Cats were sacred in Ancient Egypt more than 5000 years ago and were represented by the goddess Bast. Bast is depicted as a cat or in her form of Bastet, a cat-headed goddess. She was believed to be fiercely protective, especially towards women. It may be that Fatima's ancestors once made offerings to the goddess:

> I was with a group of students from Cairo who made a field trip to the temples at Luxor. It was very intense. We were studying hard and often spent the night in temples waiting for lectures that might begin at four in the morning. It could be very strange sitting in those rooms and feeling the old magic around you. After the trip many of us began having dreams about Bast the cat goddess.
>
> At that time I was in a very serious relationship with a man. We were about to get married and had even started choosing the colours of the furnishings for the new home we were about to set up.
>
> I began to have dreams about Bast in her cat form. In one of them, I was in a lift with my partner and I was going to press the button to take us down to the ground floor but a small cat appeared and stopped me. When I put out my hand to press the button, she pushed my arm away.
>
> I didn't know what the dream meant at first and forgot about it. Then it happened again. I dreamed I was walking down the street with my partner and the cat pushed against my legs to stop me walking with him.

I then dreamt I was in a car and my partner had left me there to sleep the night. The cat appeared again and this time she spoke to me and said that she didn't want me to sleep here alone. I told her that I couldn't sleep with her in the car and reached down to throw her out. But when I reached down to pick her up and throw her out of the window, she had changed into thousands of tiny cats. I threw the cats out of the window and they changed into the figure of the man in my life who was running away.

I understood what the dream meant when I did not hear from my partner for weeks and then he suddenly deserted me without an explanation.

Fatima told me that now when she dreams about cats, she usually sees one the next morning and knows that her subconscious is warning her to let her head rule her heart.

As these personal symbols are so significant, I will tell you of another woman I met, Sally, who had a good job in marketing although she wanted to become a nurse. Her fiancé Tim was a senior executive in the same firm as her and wanted her to apply for promotion. Sally said to me:

For a week, I dreamed every night of a hawk trapped in a snare in woodland. I managed to free the bird but I saw that he had lost the feathers of one wing that appeared to be injured. Despite this, the bird flew away and left me feeling very alone.

The weekend after the dreams, Sally and Tim went for a seminar at a hotel in the countryside and again Sally had the dream and woke up early. Unable to sleep, she went for a walk in the woods and found a hawk, not in a snare, but perched on a tree and she could see feathers were missing from its body and it had hurt its wing.

Sally rushed back to the hotel to wake Tim who was annoyed and said that they had to prepare for the morning lectures and did not have time to waste on a stupid bird. Sally went to the reception and asked them to telephone the local vet. She went back and waited with the bird until help came, by which time she was late and Tim had chosen another partner to work with that day.

When they went home, Sally applied for her nursing course and since then she and Tim have split up. Although she was emotionally injured by Tim's controlling manner, like the hawk in the dream she was released to enjoy her freedom. Seeing the hawk in the woods in reality and Tim's negative reaction brought to the surface her true feelings and gave her the courage to follow her own path.

A number of people write to me at my website to ask me the meaning of their dreams and often I find their dreams are alerting them to an issue and empowering them with the ability to overcome obstacles. In this book I will describe a few of the dreams I have received on my website and the advice I offered, so you can see how the basic meanings given in the A–Z chapters can be expanded once you add the context of what is happening in the dreamer's life.

If you want to know more about a dream you can contact me at www.cassandraeason.co.uk.

The wolf dream

Zoe wrote to me after seeing me on the TV series *Loose Women* where I was analysing the presenters' dreams. She told me that:

About three and a half years ago I had a strange experience which I have not forgotten and would like to find some answers to my questions about it. I was at the time in a deeply unhappy relationship with a very manipulative and controlling man. One afternoon, when he was either out or busy upstairs, I decided to do some meditation. I do not know if I fell asleep and what I experienced was a dream, but I felt so different and I felt like I was in control of things. This is what I saw and felt:

I was standing in a wood surrounded by trees and I could see a pack of wolves running towards me. I was stuck to the spot and my heart was pounding(I am afraid of dogs in everyday life). As the wolves got to me they ran around me and I turned and started to run with them, I was now a wolf running with the pack. I could see everything the way they did and from the level they do. We ran on until we reached a small cottage in a clearing. About 30m from the front door in an area where the grass was long there was a circle of flattened grass and in the middle of it was a baby wrapped in a blanket. The pack moved over to it and circled the baby, but then we all turned into women with black cloaks on. One of the women picked the baby up and handed it to me. At that point I came back to the here and now.

That was the only time I had that dream/vision. Since then I have left Mr Manipulative and I now live with my new partner and we have a baby girl who is 15 months old. At the time of the dream, having a child was the last thing on my mind. Having now had a baby I wonder what this dream/vision meant.

This is how I interpreted her dream:

This was a truly wonderful vision/dream. Wolves are a terrific symbol of female power and illustrated that you were in an unhappy relationship and were not able to use your power. The vision/dream was your unconscious mind deciding to run with the wolves, that is, take on your own power. The dark robed women are very mystical. You may have belonged to an order of priestesses in a past life who maybe knew the wonderful art of shape-shifting, which is the ability to change into different creatures. They could have also been representing your wise inner self leading you out of trouble with Mr Manipulative. I believe the vision gave you the strength to move into a new and better life and the baby was your future child that was waiting until it was safe to be born. You must be a very special lady to have what is sometimes called a waking dream.

A war dream

Another common dream image is one of loss, disorientation and combat, as depicted in the following letter I received:

My name is Sue and I am 28 years old. I have a regular dream that I am lost in a huge forest and am running as fast as I can because it is getting dark. I can hear soldiers running after me shooting their guns in the air and I know I will be captured and shot but just before they reach me I wake up.

Sue told me that for the previous year she had been involved with an older married man. He had promised he would leave his wife for her but kept saying she had to be patient until his children left school. Her mother, who knows the family but not about the affair, told Sue that the man's wife was pregnant, although she did not believe it. Sue was afraid the man's wife would find out about her and was worried that his wife really was pregnant and that he had been lying to her. Her letter continued:

How can I stop the dreams Cassandra? I am scared one day the soldiers will kill me and I won't wake up, because each time I have the dream they are getting nearer. I call out for Anthony but he never comes to me in the dream. Please change my name so no-one will know who I am.

This is how I replied to Sue:

Sometimes dreams are telling us what our daytime minds push away. The forest represents your tangled emotions and the difficult situation you are in that involves Anthony's family as well as yours. The soldiers are the fears that one day you will be caught out and then will have to face the disapproval of your mother as well as the hurt of Anthony's wife. It truly is your life and your decision, but I think your dream is warning you that you are giving up a lot to stay with someone who may not be prepared to leave his family. Maybe you need to talk to Anthony about your fears or confide in your mother who may be shocked but who will probably support you, especially if Anthony's wife is pregnant. I think you realise that the fact Anthony doesn't come to your help in the dream may suggest that deep down you suspect if things get difficult he may not choose to stay with you. Be assured that you will always wake up – the shooting you fear is the destruction of your dreams of happy ever afters with Anthony.

Following the family tradition

18 year old Joe sent me a message about his dream, another indication that he needed to make decisions in his life:

Every night for a week I dreamed that I was driving to join the Navy with my Dad, but suddenly the road ahead just disappeared and we were in a field. My Dad was furious, because he said I would be late, but the field was filled with beautiful butterflies and flowers and I just sat there enjoying them although my Dad got more and more furious. Then the road came back and I was so upset. I cried but my father told me not to be soft. I still feel upset when I recall the dream. My father was in the Navy until his retirement and all his family have been. I have got the right grades to be accepted for officer training but I am not as excited as I should be.

This was my response to Joe:

This dream is just your unconscious mind telling you that the road your Dad is driving you along (to join the Navy) is his path but may not necessarily be yours. Maybe you need more time to decide before committing yourself to a career into which you will be tied for a number of years. It may be hard for you to tell your father that you are not sure about your future career, particularly as he was in the Navy and may have strong opinions about it. Enjoying the butterflies and flowers in the dream suggests that you should maybe take a year out and then decide if the Navy is your choice. Do you like nature? Perhaps the dream is also telling you that. The fact you were so upset in the dream and your father did not approve of your crying would suggest that emotions may come hard to your father. You may have learned to repress your very valid emotions. It won't be easy but maybe other family members would help you to choose your own course(which might even after a break turn out to be the Navy).

The runaway car

Things that are particularly worrying us obviously feature in our dreams, and problems with finances can be a real source of stress for many people. Anna was 45 and had recently gone into an alternative therapy business with a woman called Lucy, who was also in her forties. Anna had been renting consulting rooms but Lucy had asked her to become her partner, which involved a large financial commitment on Anna's part. Her only doubt about it was that Lucy had split up with her partner of 14 years and was understandably distressed and staying away from work. Lucy's ex-partner, Simon, also worked as part of the business and when they were both in the office the atmosphere was dreadful – to the point that some clients even walked out. This was not their first split either. Staff had told Anna that it happened about twice a year – and Lucy was still trying to win Simon back. Anna said:

> In the dream I had three times, I was driving along with Lucy in the passenger seat. Suddenly the car got faster and faster and I realised it was out of control. I screamed for Lucy to help me but she was talking to Simon on her mobile phone. Each time I woke just before the car crashed. What was it trying to tell me?

This is how I interpreted Anna's dream:

> The car represented your finances spiralling out of control as you embarked on the partnership, as symbolised by the journey in the dream where you were relying on Lucy for help. However, she was talking to Simon and this was your subconscious telling you that her mind was not on the business. Nor, since this has happened before with Simon, would she be focused when a personal crisis hit again. You were driving the car and not Lucy because it was your decision whether to join the partnership.

CHAPTER 2

Celebrity Dreams

One of the most interesting shows I have analysed dreams for is *Big Brother* because the contestants of the house are filmed 24 hours a day. This means that only when they are asleep can they really allow themselves to express their true feelings. The most interesting dream I analysed belonged to Melinda Messenger during a one-off celebrity series. Melinda is a former model who has become a successful TV personality in the UK, a businesswoman and is now also studying philosophy. She described to her housemates a childhood dream:

> I was on top of a hill in the middle of an old-fashioned battle, with spears being thrown and arrows shooting everywhere. Suddenly I thought: I can see a spear coming towards me and an arrow and I thought: OK jump, this is my dream, jump, and I jumped. I thought this is great! I can control it, and I thought right well, I'll fly down the hill, so I flew down to the bottom. Then I ate a huge bag of candies, every one of them.

Melinda's dream was fascinating because it showed that from an early age she was aware she could control her dreams (see page 37 for a very easy technique to do this). So she was able to jump over the spears and the danger and as a result, at the bottom of the hill, she got all the rewards, as represented by the candies.

This ability to stay in control and not panic has proved a valuable strategy in Melinda's everyday life, because being beautiful and talented, she has suffered more than her share of spears of spite and jealousy that probably started in the playground. In dreams we can rehearse real-life situations and by winning through in our dreams carry that confidence into the waking world.

Series four of *Big Brother* featured ordinary people, many of whom I thought were very strong characters. What was interesting here was that the people who dreamed the most were some of the last to be voted out of the house. I believe this was because they were so aware of the importance of creating a good impression with the viewers who were responsible for voting contestants off, that they monitored their own daytime behaviour most strongly, meaning they dreamed more vividly at night when they were less repressed. For example, Alex, a male model who came third, was very concerned about hygiene and found the lower standards of some of the other housemates very stressful. He had a series of dreams about losing his possessions that were packed in a case and not being able to find his car. This was a typical anxiety dream about the loss of control which is the reality of the *Big Brother* house where *Big Brother* has total control. In contrast, the runner-up, Johnny, a former fireman, was nominated for eviction from the house on more than one occasion and was very anxious about the impression he was creating. He had a dream about standing on a street corner trying to sell a bridle and saddle from his horse and then leaving a club after he had (in his dream) been evicted. The bridle and saddle represented his desire to attain a better life after *Big Brother*, although he did not seem ambitious at all while in the house. It was also interesting to discover that in his dream people would say to him how well he had done and it didn't matter what he looked like as Johnny was always self-conscious when compared with the immaculate Alex.

It was interesting to note that the series winner Kate, now a successful TV and radio presenter, had a lot of dreams including one where she was in a plane while her twin sister was jumping up and down on the wing before the plane exploded. It revealed that Kate was subconsciously very aware that her nice girl image was crucial to gain success with public opinion. The explosion was therefore symbolic of her fear of eviction as she projected her own fears of blowing her chances on to her twin.

In the 2004 series, Stuart, a meek and mild man, had a dream of the very macho and streetwise housemate Victor, being attacked by a killer whale. To me this definitely illustrates pent-up resentment popping up after dark! In contrast, Victor, the supposedly tough guy, had a nightmare of being attacked by the Elephant man. In this context, the Elephant man represented the part of Victor he was trying to hide and the fear that others would see through his cool façade. Obviously the self-styled jungle cat Victor had hidden image problems. Most interesting however, was the beautiful, shapely and intelligent blonde housemate called Vanessa. She dreamed of falling in love with a blind man, to whom of course her looks were not the main attraction and who represented a person she hoped would love her for herself. The dream clearly reflected her problems of not being taken seriously by one or two of the men in the house.

No less challenging for me was to analyse the dreams of the four feisty presenters on the UK ITV magazine programme *Loose Women* who at the start were sceptical, to say the least, but I think their dreams were equally revealing. Kaye Adams the presenter, said:

I dreamt that I was in an earthquake and was holding my young son while I tried to find a safe place to hide in. I ran away from the buildings as the sky above me turned black but when I escaped to the park the ground began to open up and the trees began to fall around me.

To me, this is a typical maternal anxiety dream. With regards to young children there is always the fear that as they grow up we won't be able to protect them from everything and don't know what best to do to keep them from the dangers of life (which in Kaye's dream was symbolised as an earthquake).

The UK TV and radio personality Carole McGiffin, said:

I dreamt that I was having a secret affair with Jamie Oliver (a well-known British television chef) *and that CCTV cameras were recording us while we were on the sofa at his parents' house. This meant that when he came round to my flat, people were looking to see who he was having an affair with.*

I don't believe that this is a surprising dream for an independent and successful woman to have, as it reveals a secret longing to be nurtured by a man (in this instance a chef), but highlights a sense of guilt for what she sees as a weakness. Similarly, Sherrie Hewson, an actress made famous for her role in the world's longest-running British television soap, *Coronation Street,* dreamt of the following:

I was in a glass room and everything outside of it was silver. A little hole appeared in the glass room and a silver bird hopped in.

To me, the bird represented a messenger and the silver that eventually seeped in was her emotional side (as silver is the colour of the moon). It was telling Sherrie to let emotion, however painful, back in her life and to go out and find what she wanted instead of shutting herself away.

Finally, I analysed Claire Sweeney's dream. She is a TV actress and star of London West End musicals and had experienced the classic dream that her teeth were falling out. This has many meanings but in her case revealed that although successful and trying new things she was secretly afraid of failure, of literally biting off more than she could chew. Also, because things were happening quickly, there was a fear of losing her power and success as symbolised by the teeth falling out.

Celebrity dreams are very significant mainly because celebrities usually believe that their public face is very important. Their dreams are therefore a form of release and can allow them to express their real thoughts and feelings. To me this makes them very likeable and human as it shows that whether a person is a television personality, a reality television participant or an ordinary person, we all experience dreams that reveal both our fears and hidden potential.

CHAPTER 3

Learning to Control Your Dreams

People have been inducing beautiful dreams for thousands of years. In Ancient Egypt perfume was used to promote a relaxed state in which people moved naturally from waking to sleep, with enhanced awareness so that dream colours were more vivid, sounds were clearer and feelings were more acute. They believed that during such a dream deities would come to them and bring wisdom (see page 32).

Although in the modern world we would not necessarily want to see the old divinities in our dreams, this ancient method is equally effective for creating harmonious dreams. Perfume dream creation can be practised nightly for a week and thereafter when needed. This will rapidly harmonise sleep patterns if you are an insomniac or will help you to rest if you have experienced a particularly pressurised few weeks. Even if all is well in your life, you can spend a night a week, or whenever you have time, creating a beautiful sleep experience from which you can wake relaxed and refreshed using the techniques below. You will need tealights and a bottle of rose or lavender oil to hand.

To induce soothing dreams

:☾ Switch off your mobile phone, switch off fax machines and do not check your e-mails just before getting ready for bed. It is all too easy to slip back into a social or work mode.

:☾ Have a scented bath or shower, with nightlights illuminating the bathroom.

:☾ Afterwards, when you are wrapped up warmly in your dressing gown, have a herbal or milky drink while you sit in semi-darkness listening to gentle music.

:☾ When you are totally relaxed, light a small scented candle or nightlight in a safe place in your bedroom and sit on the bed facing it, well propped up on pillows.

☾ In the semi-darkness gently smell either a bottle of rose or lavender essential oil, rose or lavender cologne or your favourite gentle fragrance. If you have a glass perfume bottle with a stopper or dropper top you can pour your perfume into that. Less romantic, but just as practical, you could distil the fragrance into an eye dropper bottle.

☾ Take time to imagine yourself in a beautiful rose garden or field of lavender or some other flowery and safe place.

☾ Finally, sprinkle just a drop or two of the scent on your pillow to transfer the experience to the realms of sleep.

☾ Blow out the candle and close your eyes letting yourself step through the flowers in your imaginary garden, through field upon field, until at last you sink down among the fragrant blossoms into the world of dreams.

For children (and adults too) you can buy sleep pillows filled with lavender or camomile flowers to aid rest. Alternatively you can place a drop or two of lavender or camomile essential oils on to an ordinary pillow (it is best for children not to inhale directly) from an oil or perfume bottle. I have a lavender sleep pillow that fits around the neck that can be put in the microwave oven for two minutes to release the fragrance. I bought mine from the Body Shop in the UK but there are similar products sold throughout the world.

The importance of bad dreams

Although good dreams are vital for our well-being, we should not try entirely to eliminate spontaneous disturbing dreams, as they are a very effective way of alerting us to matters in our lives that need attention.

For instance, to dream that a tyre on your car bursts in the fast lane causing an accident, is not a psychic warning of a bad accident. Rather it is a way of telling you things that your subconscious may have picked up on but your conscious mind had not. Maybe one of the tyres on your car needs attention or you haven't checked the tyre pressures for a while due to the million and one other matters clamouring for attention in your life. A disturbing dream can be an irritating but essential message like the one that pops up on your computer reminding you that your virus protection needs updating.

Sometimes, anxiety dreams in which everything goes wrong, can make us look at our hidden fears and worries and can either encourage us to do something about them or realise that they are groundless. For example, Jana had a 19-year-old son called Hans who was training in the catering industry but wanted to travel around Europe with his friends. Jana had experienced a bad dream soon after Hans had told her of his plans.

My son was waiting at a bus stop with all his possessions in a huge sack. Hans told me that he was not taking a travel bag because all his friends were using sacks. I knew that the sack was thin and would split and that Hans would lose his things. I ran into a shop and bought him a whole roll of strong rubbish sacks and then asked Hans if he had any money. He replied that he had only a little. I then looked in my bag and discovered that I only had two notes so I ran to the cash machine before the bus came (which was going directly to Europe from the local stop). But as I put the card in the slot, a woman, who was a character in an Australian soap show who had lost her memory, came up, snatched the card and chewed it with her teeth so it could not be used. Although I am a gentle person, I was so angry that I punched the woman. I then asked my son if he had his cash card but Hans could not find it. How could he go to Europe with no money and with the bus coming over the hill?

No wonder Jana was panicking, anticipating all the reverse-charge calls home demanding she sorted out his crises! Most maternal anxiety dreams have a firm basis in past dilemmas that have needed to be sorted out, so what was this dream telling Jana? She couldn't padlock her son to her side, so she needed to distance herself slightly from him before he travelled so that he learned how to sort out his own problems. He also needed to become more responsible for his own finances instead of relying on her to help him out. Sometimes our children have to learn from their own mistakes.

Turning bad dreams into good ones

Because life is so busy, even the happiest adults may spend their nights chasing and missing dream buses or trains or getting off at the wrong station. Worse still are those dreams where you are being pursued or trying to escape from a monster or falling from high buildings. Falling for example, usually symbolises a fear that we have lost control of our lives, whether it be with regards to money, career or relationships. In contrast, dreams of floating through the air should be viewed positively as they indicate a letting go of anxiety and inhibitions. (see page 37 for advice on how to turn falling into floating or flying dreams).

Similarly, sensitive and imaginative children, especially if there is family stress or problems at day care or school, can fear going to sleep because of what are called 'night terrors'. These can result in the child screaming and pointing at an invisible monster. As a result of uncomfortable experiences, adults as well as children can fear the dark, especially if they are staying in an unfamiliar room or if they have suffered a series of recurring nightmares. However, there are many ways of reducing these night terrors which are simply our own inner fears being projected outwards as dream foes.

Let me tell you about Tricia, for example, who was a single parent in her thirties. In her everyday life Tricia was under a lot of pressure financially. She had a stressful job and was temporarily living in rented accommodation while her divorce was finalised. Tricia told me:

> I kept dreaming, night after night, that a hideous giant was living in my home and while the children and I remained in the house (an old dark one that I did not recognise in the dream) the giant would stay in his room. However, every time the children and I tried to escape from the house, the giant would appear and come after us. He would be wherever we fled to, pulling us off buses or waiting around corners. I really feared that the giant would kill us all but each night, just before the giant seemed about to hurt us, I would wake up screaming.

The giant was, of course, all those gigantic worries piling up that seemed to follow her everywhere, whether she was taking her kids for a walk or trying to make the money stretch to pay the mounting bills. On the positive side however, the giant had never hurt the family, indicating that Tricia had the strength to win through even the worst crisis. Whether you are 17 or 70, single, married, with or without children, I am sure you have all experienced enormous worries. Tricia's situation was made worse by the fact she was sleeping badly and was so tired that her problems seemed to get worse during the day.

She had turned to me for help and we decided to cut the dream giant down to size using the approach outlined on page 31. This works with any bad dream that has a particularly nasty figure featuring in it, whether a mythical one like a giant or demon or an actual adversary, for example your ex-partner's mistress, a bullying employer or a critical mother-in-law. You can also use the technique for less personalised dream enemies, for example a sea that threatens to drown you, a crashing aeroplane or a house fire.

Children who find it hard to talk about night foes can be helped to banish their fears by carrying out this exercise, but may need to do it several times over a number of weeks.

To shrink a dream giant

To banish the giant effectively, you will need a pine, lemon or orange essential oil and some paper and a pen. For children, use a soft bath foam, such as chamomile or lavender as the oils are too strong.
You can use this method to overcome other dreamlike adversaries, simply adjust the pictures and the rhyme below to suit the name of your enemy.

- Sit in a well-lit room about an hour before bedtime.
- Draw a huge figure on a large piece of paper. If you are good with computers you can use a paint or draw programme to create your giant on screen. Clip art usually has pictures of frightening natural phenomena or manmade disasters, but scribbled lines on a piece of paper to represent the terror are just as effective.
- Now begin either to delete or to block out with dark colours, parts of your giant.
- When you have finished you should have a satisfyingly empty screen or piece of paper.
- If it is raining you can leave the blanked-out paper outdoors to disintegrate or destroy it in a basin of water. You may prefer to just throw it away. You can print out the empty computer screen file to discard.
- Have a bath or shower using either pine, lemon or orange essential oils to wash away any remaining fears. These essences are both protective and empowering and are therefore ideal for times when we are trying to overcome an obstacle. For a child he or she can create a rhyme to recite as the water swishes away down the plughole. For example:
  Giant, giant wash away, don't come back here any day.
  Giant, giant out of sight, don't come back here any night.
- As you lie in bed, picture yourself calmly blocking out the giant piece by piece.
- Picture in its place an angel or a kind wise figure who will protect you while you sleep.

Tricia did have the dream once more but this time the giant was human-sized and when he came down the stairs he walked out of the house. I am pleased to say that he never returned.

Dreaming true

At the beginning of the chapter I mentioned the Ancient Egyptians were the first dream experts and directed their dreams not only to bring peaceful sleep but also to find the answers to questions they wanted to know. The creative and inspirational part of the mind is largely unconscious and in sleep we can often find creative solutions to problems or recognise opportunities that our waking brain may not have thought of.

The Ancient Egyptians used a technique called 'dreaming true' and believed if they made the right preparations before sleep then wise deities such as Isis, the Egyptian Mother Goddess, or Thoth, the God of Knowledge, would come to them in their dreams and impart knowledge to them. Like the Greeks, the Egyptians had special sleep temples where people could go to induce special dreams. However, many ordinary people would sit in a cave or dark place and look into the light of a burning oil lamp to relax their mind before sleep.

In the modern world we can best understand the old idea of a god or goddess advising a person in sleep as being a method of tuning into the spiritual and wise part of ourselves that can sometimes only be reached in the sleep state. Some people today, however, ask their special angel for advice (see page 33).

I found the ritual overleaf in a corner of the British Museum in a display case that was being refurbished. The old Egyptian words denote that if you light frankincense in front of a lamp and look at the lamp through the smoke, you should be able to see a deity who will answer your questions in a dream.

You might find frankincense a bit strong to burn in your bedroom at night, so you can substitute it with camomile, jasmine or rose scented candles. There are very safe and pretty glass candleholders available and you can stand your candle or incense in sand inside them if you wish.

If you want to make the experience really magical, you can carve the hieroglyphics (Egyptian letters) below, with a nail file or paper knife in the wax of your candle before lighting it. These symbols roughly translate as *May the God come to me in a dream bringing me wisdom.* You could also inscribe an ankh to symbolise health and long life, a frog for fertility, a scarab for new beginnings or a vulture, the symbol of Mother Isis, to represent protection.

To invoke the knowledge of the deities

You will need a scented candle to complete this ritual effectively. Use this method when you require spiritual guidance while you sleep.

- ☾ Light your chosen scented candle and recite your question seven times softly and continuously.
- ☾ Half close your eyes and look at the candle flames, visualising an angel or the wise part of yourself as a wise man or woman.
- ☾ Ask that he or she will protect you in sleep and answer your question in a dream. If you practice this technique regularly, you may find that you always see the same figure, whether an angel, a nun, priest or an ancient Chinese sage.
- ☾ Recite your question seven times more in an ever-decreasing soft voice until your words fade into silence.
- ☾ Extinguish the candle and then go to sleep, visualising yourself walking towards your angel or guide surrounded by golden light.
- ☾ Your may see your guardian in a dream or you may just be aware of a sense of peace and a feeling of protection.

The answer to your question should come in a dream, perhaps symbolically. If not, repeat the exercise the next night and within two or three attempts the dream answer should come. As you become more experienced in creative dreaming you may not even need to light the candle, just recite the question several times before sleep or write it down and place it under your pillow.

Paul's dream question

Paul was in his forties and was from Sweden. He had been married for 15 years when Helena, a newly divorced woman in her thirties, joined his computer firm and made it clear that she was interested in him. Paul was very flattered as both he and his wife worked long hours and rarely seemed to have any time together. He had started to feel restless and taken for granted when Helena suggested they met for drinks and dinner and weekends away once a month when his wife went to see her mother in another part of the country. Paul hesitated to take Helena up on her offer. Being very sceptical about most spiritual things, Paul decided to write his question down and recite it over and over again before sleep without bothering with candles, incense or what he called spooky stuff. He chose a weekend when his wife was away in case he talked in his sleep.

Although Paul complained about resorting to mumbo jumbo, he did have a very interesting dream involving his mother who had died ten years before. In Paul's context, his mother was a symbol of the traditional values and home life he had been brought up to value. Mothers and grandmothers feature remarkably often in dreams as symbols of our conscience or as a form of security (see pages 143 and 195), whether they are living or deceased.

This is how Paul described his dream:

I was a boy again and my mother was making a meal for the family Midsummer celebration (an important date in the Swedish calendar). *The rest of the family were out putting greenery on the Midsummer tree, but I was bored. I wanted to go sailing with my friends. So I wandered upstairs and saw a large box inside my parents' room. When I looked inside the box it was full of sweets. I dragged the box into my own room and began to eat sweet after sweet, hardly tasting them as I crammed them into my mouth in case my mother came upstairs and caught me. To my horror, I realised the box was half empty. Putting the lid on, I put the box back in my parents' room as my mother called me down for the feast.*

The table was full of my favourite foods but I felt so sick I could not eat anything. Then my father went upstairs and brought the sweets down. When the box was opened it was almost empty and everyone pointed at me. They were furious and started to chase me. The Midsummer tree fell down and everything was spoiled. Then I woke up.

You don't need to have a string of psychology degrees to work out that Paul took the hidden and forbidden candies (the new relationship) because he was bored. He tried to hide the evidence of his misdemeanour by putting the lid back on but he could not enjoy his family dinner (symbolic of his present life with his wife) because he had filled himself on exciting but sickly food (the illicit affair). Could he keep the affair secret in real life by hiding it? In the dream Paul was found out as the sweet thief and was faced with the anger of his whole family. Paul had wanted it all: Helena, his wife and a settled life. However, Paul was not prepared to bring the Midsummer tree crashing to the ground. Whatever the moral issues, Paul realised from the dream that he would not be able to lead a double life and was unwilling to lose his wife and perhaps his home and approval of his relatives. Paul started to avoid Helena, and she started dating another married man in the office.

In the next chapter we will explore how you can become aware you are dreaming while asleep and so can explore the dream world and use it to gain confidence and power in the real world.

CHAPTER 4

Exploring the World of Dreams

What is the world of dreams? Is it created entirely within our heads or is it part of a wider dimension that we can enter in sleep? Throughout the ages and even today in some cultures from Greenland to New Guinea where traditions have remained relatively unchanged for hundreds of years, dream journeys are considered as important as daytime travel. The Ancient Greeks believed the soul left the body during sleep and the Inuits of Hudson Bay, Canada, also say that the soul leaves the body during sleep to live in a special dream world. In parts of Africa, it is believed that dream activities occur during nocturnal travel. In particular, the Zulu people interpret dream images as messages and visions, sent by their ancestors.

The positive purpose of dreams

Even if our minds do not actually move beyond the sleeping body, in dreams we can experience vividly other lands, past periods in history and even the worlds of myth. Put another way, we have access to a whole theme park of scenes and ideas through our mind and imagination that is especially active at night. As we explore the realms of sleep we can overcome fears, anticipate success and wake confident and ready for anything.

On page 23 I mentioned Melinda Messenger, the UK TV personality who could control her dreams and turn them to her advantage even as a child. This ability is a spontaneous one, but can be learned very easily so that you can turn nightmares into good dreams and make any dream-time a pleasurable and creative experience. You can defeat your dream foes, turn danger into adventure and overcome obstacles to experience triumph. In the next chapter I describe how you can even find a dream lover in sleep or, if you are happily in a relationship, can share dreams with your partner.

Finding happiness in dreams

Elaine was inspired to build a better life for herself through exploring her dream world and emerged with a plan for finding happiness. She was in her early fifties and had an important but boring job in a hospital laboratory. She had divorced her husband about ten years previously and lived with her mother and father, having invested her half of the profits from the marital home rather than buying herself a new house. Elaine told me:

> *Every night for about a week, I dreamed of a sunny land with blue skies and orange groves which always had a pathway leading into a walled garden. I felt excitement and a sense of overwhelming happiness but then the dream would fade. When I awoke, I decided I really wanted to go down the flowery pathway as I felt it was significant. So one night, I repeated the words "when I see the path in my dream I will follow it" several times before I went to sleep. I had the dream again but then realised within my dream that I was dreaming. It was such fun being in control so I decided to follow the path. It led to a white-washed apartment block where all the apartments had balconies overlooking a flower-filled courtyard. At the back was another pathway which led to a town square that was brimming with flowers, cafés and laughing people. For the first time in years I felt so joyful. I decided to find an apartment that was for sale. I carried on walking and found one in the apartment block I liked so much. It was perfect, tucked away in a corner with a view over the old church, the distant sea and the mountains. I then looked for an estate agent and found one that was open and before long I was arranging to move in.*

When Elaine woke, the excitement remained with her. The following morning Elaine phoned work to say she would be late, the first time in ten years. She stopped off at the travel agent and booked a holiday in Spain for the following week, to the amazement and relief of her parents who thought she had given up on life forever. Once at work she booked some long overdue leave to the surprise of everyone as all her holidays since the break-up of her marriage had been with an elderly aunt who lived in the countryside.

Elaine stayed in a lovely town in Spain called Nerja and searched the streets and squares till she found an apartment block, not exactly the one in her dream, but one she liked just as much. Before the holiday was over she was negotiating a holiday apartment she could buy to rent out when she was not using it.

Five years on Elaine had enjoyed many holidays in Nerja. She eventually negotiated an early retirement package as she had decided to move out permanently as she had made many new friends and learned Spanish. She also wanted to develop her hobby of painting and hoped to sell pictures in a shop in the square.

The dream wasn't a psychic one in the sense that it predicted the future (see chapter six) but it gave Elaine a chance to rediscover a part of herself that had been buried after her marriage break-up (she and her husband had loved the Mediterranean). Because Elaine was aware she was dreaming she could explore possibilities within the dream scenario. She knew that in the dream she would find an apartment she liked and successfully negotiate to buy it and this gave her the confidence to try it for real.

Using your dreams to improve daily life

If you are aware you are dreaming you can, for example, rehearse job interviews, stand up against bullies and fulfil your wishes. By introducing the relevant people and situations from real life into your dreams and creating a successful outcome to any encounter, you can feel more positive and confident in your waking life. As in the case of Elaine, sometimes opportunities will occur in the dream that can inspire you to try similar tactics in the future. Because it is your dream, you can stage manage, direct the action, write the script and get the starring role!

The psychological name for this process is lucid dreaming and even if there are not any specific issues you wish to tackle, the process of controlling dreams is very empowering. Anything becomes possible in the dream world. You can dive deep into blue oceans without having to come up for air, climb the highest mountain without getting tired, turn falling dreams into floating or flying ones, explore the starry skies or crawl deep beneath the earth. You can question anyone you meet and they will answer truthfully. You can be anyone, do anything, go anywhere and the next morning the power will follow you into work or socially. Bit by bit you will be able to transfer your dream abilities into everyday creativity.

To invoke lucid dreaming

Though you can use the dream plane for rehearsing everyday situations, start with more exotic scenarios to stimulate the all-important imagination and expand your personal horizons of possibility.

☾ Just before sleep, lie in bed and close your eyes. Create your ideal dream, whether it be a tropical shore, a big old house in the country, a castle or palace.

- ☾ Imagine yourself as the central character. Walk through the golden palace rooms or swim with multi-coloured fish beneath the sea. Create a story with yourself centre stage. You may find one particular scene works best to get you into the mood.
- ☾ Now create a single symbol that will remind you that you are dreaming when you see it in sleep. Again, go for something out of the ordinary, for example, a rainbow-coloured bird, a golden peacock or a butterfly with jewels on its wings.
- ☾ Re-run the imagined dream scene in your mind, letting the symbol appear five or six times in different places or sections of the dream. As you imagine the symbol in each setting, say to yourself for example:
  When I see the golden peacock I shall know I am dreaming.
- ☾ When you are ready, drift into sleep and hold in your mind the symbol of the rainbow-coloured bird or whatever exotic image you choose.

The first night you may see only part of the scene you devised or have a different dream and may not recall that you are dreaming. Persevere, however, and before long you will have that wonderful moment when you realise that you can fly over the monster's head or shrink a cheating husband to the size of a mouse before climbing into your luxury car with the hunky chauffeur waiting at the door to transport you into the sunset. Whatever the dream, you will wake up filled with optimism and determination because you took charge.

Other lives and dreams

Many of us dream of a special place that is familiar and yet is not one we have visited in everyday life. It can be disappointing to wake up as usually we experience great peace and happiness in the dream place. These dreams often seem as real as life and may stay with us all day. You may be someone who has the same dream and revisits the same dreamy places regularly to the point that it becomes almost a home from home! Dreams may seem to last for hours as you carry out ordinary tasks or share a celebration but there is nothing spooky about this as our minds can play about with time. After all, when we are daydreaming we can take ourselves back into a scene from childhood as though it were today. Those daydreaming times can sometimes seem to last for hours as we relive events or conversations from many years earlier when in fact we may only have been daydreaming for a minute or two.

Theories of the meaning of other life dreams

Psychological theories sometimes say that we all have common symbols stored within our unconscious memory. The psychologist Jung believed that we all have access to a kind of collective pool of human experience because our brains are wired in the same way the world over. Whether you agree with this or not, we all read stories, watch videos, go to museums or travel to different places and so our minds have a huge database of images to use in dreams. The memory is also remarkably good at tidying up and categorising information so we may not recall exactly where a dream image originates from. It may also cause us to feel that we have experienced a far-off land or time as though we had actually been there when, in fact, the basis of that dream lies within the pictures of a book we once read as a child. Some people, however, do believe that they have lived before and that glimpses of this past world re-emerge during sleep when all conscious blocks have gone.

Another theory, one that seems to make more sense to me, is that we are connected through our genes to our ancestors, some of whom may have come from different lands from the one in which we currently live. You make think this is fanciful but anthropologists tell us that humanity first appeared in East Africa 3.5 million years ago. A mere million years ago humans spread from Africa to Asia and 800,000 years ago, the first humans appeared in Europe and Scandinavia while 60,000 years ago humans went to Australasia. Most of us therefore, have quite a rich genetic heritage so it may not be so unthinkable that in our dreams the memories of our ancestors manifest themselves.

Let me give you an example of a past-life dream and then I'll describe how if you don't dream of past lives or far-off places you can learn to do so and so add another exciting theme to your night time repertoire. Better than a bad night of television!

John was in his forties and lived in Scotland. He had a recurring dream of walking through a town in France, wearing clothes that seemed to come from the eighteenth-century. John said:

> I was always with the same beautiful woman who would wear a big hat decorated with plumed feathers. I was aware that I loved her but I was afraid to ask her to marry me in case she rejected me. We would always go to an archway that led out of the town and I always stopped and felt afraid to go through the gate because I feared that something dreadful would happen to me. I was convinced that I would be killed and I would never see my love again. I would always wake, very frustrated, as my dream always ended at the gate.

Interestingly, John talked about frustration in his waking life. He had a good job in engineering but he wanted to start his own business, although he was hesitating because he feared that it might fail and he would lose everything. It seemed to me that John needed to practise lucid dreaming so that he could walk through the gateway and, if there was someone waiting to kill him, disarm the foe and be free of the fears that were restricting him.

He felt that the woman in the dream was his other half or twin soul and he regretted he did not experience such depth of feeling for his wife as he did for the unnamed woman in the dream. Like a lot of forty-something men, John was feeling he had missed out a bit. If I had been a marriage guidance counsellor, I would have advised rekindling a bit of excitement in his current relationship and talking about his unfulfilled needs to his wife. Instead I thought that if he took a risk to find fulfilment in his work, his desires for perfect love would then, hopefully, be channelled into something more useful and less frustrating.

When I talked to John, he made the connection that Bonnie Prince Charlie had come over from France to Scotland in the 1740s. John decided to try to trace his distant ancestry to see if that would shed some light on the dream. It may have been an ancestor who had experienced a similar dilemma during that time who was speaking to him through his dream. On the other hand, the gate may have simply been a symbol to bring his feelings about his present life to the surface. I therefore also suggested that John tried to locate the town in France and go there to see if the actual place cast up any memories. I never found out if John walked through that gate and outfaced his fears, but I hope he did.

Creating past-life dreams

Choose a period of time to which you have always been interested in that may come from any part of the world. Your choice need not be an exotic location, as sometimes an ancestor from a more local area can provide all kinds of information. If possible, go to places or museums where you can touch, for example, stones or exhibits and artefacts from the past. This will help you to connect and feel enthused for past worlds, especially if history lessons at school were less than inspiring and have left you cold. You can also use holidays as an opportunity for visiting places further away that fascinate you. Greece, Italy and Egypt are all living museums where the past is never far away from the tourist hotels. Collect material of the period that interests you; quite often local or regional museums offer reproduction artefacts for sale. You could also watch videos of films set in the chosen period as well as television documentaries or programmes focused on archaeology or travel. The internet is also a good source of information but you could also read fiction about families who lived in the chosen time and place to submerse yourself in the era. When you are ready and feel you have connected with your chosen period of time and place, try the following method to experience a past-life dream.

To induce a past-life dream

For this you will need a symbol or picture of your chosen era and location. Alternatively, you can use an amber, jade or jet crystal as these are said to contain the power of connection to past worlds.

☾ For two or three nights, about an hour before you go to bed, look through some of the material of your chosen place and time and try to find a character with whom you feel great empathy. It need not be a hero or heroine but someone whose life you understand instinctively.

☾ Before sleep, hold your symbol, picture or crystal. Imagine yourself as the person, with whom you felt a connection, whether fictional or actual. If you have been studying an area where your family lived once or has lived for a number of years there may be a particular family member whose life has similarities to your own. You can picture yourself living his or her life.

☾ Set the symbol, picture or crystal beside your bed and as you drift into sleep walk in your mind through your chosen location or sit on a hill overlooking your chosen scene.

You may find that you need to carry this out for three or four nights before a past-life dream occurs. When you wake, write down the details of your experience and you may find the past world answers a question or helps you to understand and overcome a fear that you have been harbouring in your everyday world. Once you have had a dream, leave it a week or so before you try to create another one. You may find that this time the scene is different, but sometimes they do follow on like a serial.

In time, past-life dreams of different periods may occur spontaneously without any effort on your part. Do not be surprised if when you visit an old place during the day you recognise it from one of these dreams. The mind is far cleverer than we realise and given time much less limited than we may think.

In the next chapter we will look at dream lovers and how you can use the dream world to find or deepen love.

CHAPTER 5

Your Dream Lover

Most people at some time have dreamed of a wonderful lover and of experiencing amazing sex with them in the dream. It may have involved a famous sports person, movie star, music idol or someone whom we do not recognise. You may know the person; your boss, the guy who fixed your roof or a family friend with whom there may have been a slight spark of mutual attraction in the everyday world. Even people with a happy love life and fulfilled sex life in reality can have vivid romantic and passionate dreams of an imaginary lover. Such dreams are normal and healthy, even if the dream is very erotic. They can also have the benefit of spilling over into fulfilling middle of the night or early morning sex with the partner slumbering beside you.

Dream fantasies

If you do dream of making love to a famous or just a highly attractive person, it is what psychologists call a wish-fulfilment dream and what the rest of us regard as a satisfying fantasy, like dreaming of eating a plate of cakes if you are on a diet.

Dream fantasies are just that, fantasies, not an indication that we are going to be unfaithful. Indeed erotic dreams, as well as giving us pleasure, can remind us to possibly lighten up our everyday life or make more time for real lovemaking. If you are currently without a partner, dreams such as these can be an indication that you are ready to meet a new lover; perhaps that hunky builder who has been working outside your office!

Of course, if you practice lucid dreaming (being aware in the dream that you are dreaming, see page 37) there are no limits to the romantic and erotic dream scenarios you can create or develop in sleep. Sharing these dream fantasies by recalling them with a real-life lover can spice up a mundane love life (you can pretend it was happening with them when you describe the dream).

If the person in the dream is someone less famous but known to you and single, such as the guy at work or the single parent who has moved in down the street, the dream may be nudging you towards making the first move.

Identifying a dream lover

The lover you meet in sleep may be someone you do not know and cannot identify, but appears either in particularly vivid dreams or in different dream scenes. Whether or not you practice lucid dreaming, your dream lover may talk to you and be romantic and sensual and so such dreams are usually very fulfilling and empowering (dream lovers are never ever boring or have headaches)!

What is perhaps surprising, however, is the number of people I have met whilst researching my dream analysis work, who have told me that they have met their dream lover in reality not long after dreaming of them and that there was an instant recognition and chemistry. How can this be? If you want to go for the more psychic theory, then the unknown lover you meet in a dream is a real person who is also dreaming of you at that moment and you are drawn together mind-to-mind through telepathic signals in your sleep. Telepathy or mind-to-mind communication is the power that makes us phone our mother the same minute she is dialling our number or contact a friend urgently, yet quite spontaneously, just as, unbeknown to us, they have had a crisis or suddenly need our help.

If you are unattached in real life or unhappy in a relationship you may be sending out these signals in your sleep, which could be answered by someone who is also searching for new love. Even people in reasonably happy relationships may send out love signals in dreams. These entirely harmless dream meetings can inspire people to improve an existing relationship that is basically sound but maybe a bit routine or going through a low patch. You may quite unexpectedly meet your current partner in a dream, make wonderful love or talk and mend a quarrel. The next morning you may well discover that your real partner experienced the same dream and that things are suddenly fine between you.

Translating dream to reality

Dreams can give us clues as to where to find a dream lover in the harsh light of day. Working on the psychologist Jung's theory of synchronicity, which states that all coincidences are not chance but meant to be, our inner radar may guide us to a particular place in the days following a dream at the same time the dream lover is also guided there, apparently by accident. We therefore meet in our waking life through destiny. A dream could also give us a clue as to where we should go to find love, perhaps somewhere we have never visited before; a different holiday destination or a local sports centre that has just opened. From there, it may be possible to discover a new love which we wouldn't have experienced if we hadn't acted on the information disclosed while dreaming. For example, if you had not dreamt of meeting your ideal partner by a swimming pool, you might not have taken as much notice of the person who accidentally splashes water over you while at a swimming pool in your waking life. It may be that because of the dream, you were sending out very positive non-verbal vibes of attraction to this potential and possibly ideal lover. They may also have been dreaming of an ideal mate and when you came along, the two dreams fused into reality.

A more psychological explanation is that we all have a number of potential future partners who could make us happy, though some people are convinced we all have just one twin soul who is totally right. You may, therefore, dream of a person whom your subconscious mind knows would make you happy (a sort of ideal specification) but not necessarily the choice your conscious mind would make. Conscious minds are often influenced more by external beauty or worldly matters like bank balances or success than the factors that make for long-term compatibility or happiness.

Let me give you an example and then I'll describe a way you can try to conjure up your dream lover if all you are dreaming of right now is sorting piles of wet washing or looking for lost car keys in a mountain of clutter.

Finding your dream lover

Samantha was 25-years-old and single, although she had many friends of both sexes. After a series of short relationships, Samantha had felt she was lacking the right person to share her life. One night when she was feeling particularly lonely, she had the following experience:

I dreamt of a tall, blonde man walking out of a grey mist on a high mountain that I recognised as a mountain range near a resort where I used to stay as a child. I followed the man as he climbed down the steep track and as he went into a small hotel called 'The Peak of the Mountain' which had a huge, ruined garden room at the side. I stood beside him at the reception and inquired as to whether there was a room available for the night but I was told that the hotel was full. The blonde man turned to me and introduced himself as Lars. He offered to let me share his room saying that he would sleep on the couch. I accepted and what followed was a wonderfully romantic and erotic encounter but in the morning, when I woke up, Lars was gone.

The dream remained with Samantha all day. Since she had some leave to take, on impulse, Samantha looked on the internet and found a hotel called 'The Peak of the Mountain' in the area she had seen in her dream. She booked a room in the hotel and flew out shortly afterwards. Initially, she was disappointed that there was no sign of a blonde man and no huge, ruined garden room. On the second day, however, she was in the reception booking a mountain walking tour when a blonde man, not quite as tall as in her dream, but with bright blue eyes and a slow sensuous smile walked in. Unfortunately for Samantha there was a spare room so she couldn't offer to share! The man also asked the receptionist about walking trips and Samantha, recalling their closeness in the dream, quite out of character, mentioned she was going on one the next day to a particularly beautiful landscape. It turned out that the man was not called Lars but Sebastian. They had a drink together to plan the next day and this evolved into dinner as it turned out that they not only shared the same interests and humour, but felt like they had known each other for ages. The chemistry between them was definitely working overtime for, by the third night, they were sharing a room. On the fourth morning Samantha asked Sebastian why he had chosen the hotel.

He explained that he had experienced a dream about staying in a mountain resort hotel and of meeting a girl who looked like Samantha. Sebastian had taken sudden leave from his job, as he had been deserted by his lover of five years and was feeling low. He decided he needed to get away. As Sebastian did not know the name of the hotel he had seen in his dream, he went to a travel agent. The agent tried four or five hotels, but as it was very short notice he had difficulty booking a room. He had finally managed to book Sebastian a room at 'The Peak of the Mountain'. Sebastian commented that the hotel looked remarkably like the one in his dream, except that the dream one had a beautiful domed glass garden room.

Whether psychic or not, their dreams brought Sebastian and Samantha together. Curious, they asked the manager about a garden room. They were told that the hotel had once possessed a glass room with a dome at the side but it had been hit by lightning and had been demolished. This seemed to seal their close bond and more than six months later Samantha and Sebastian were still together.

Dreaming of love

There are a number of traditional rituals for seeing a dream lover, who will then hopefully appear in reality soon afterwards. For hundreds, perhaps even thousands of years, young girls and men have called for a lover, known or unknown, to appear to them in a dream. Such rituals may be found in the folk spells of Scandinavia and Western Europe, especially in places such as Scotland and Ireland where Celtic people settled. If you look in my book *Cassandra Eason's Complete Book of Spells* published by Foulsham/Quantum, there is a large section on such rituals. Many were performed the evening before a saint's day, for example St Agnes Eve which falls on January 20th, or in the evening of the day itself. Sometimes rituals have been used to guide young people towards suitable partners. For example, to encourage a girl to dream of the local woodcutter, who may have been interested in her even though she was hoping to marry the local lord's son who had no interest in her. If the ritual worked, the girl would dream of the woodcutter and hopefully realise that even though he could not offer her jewels and silks, he could build her a secure home and would love and cherish her forever. Sometimes dreams can point out the obvious where we may have been missing the point in our waking life.

When these rituals were first devised, people were often more limited to partners from families in local settlements or tribes and couples were often expected to stay together until one partner died. The rituals were therefore associated with first love. Nowadays we can cast round for a dream lover more freely and we can seek our ideal partner on the internet or in different countries as the world is now a much smaller place than it was for our ancestors. Below, I have outlined a few traditional ways of calling a dream lover. They are all are very simple and fun to try.

Traditional dream lover rituals

A Christmas ritual

- Cut yourself a slice of Christmas cake.
- Taking care not to lose your balance, walk up a set of stairs backwards.
- Whilst going upstairs, eat the slice of Christmas cake, catching the crumbs in your free hand.
- Sprinkle the crumbs you have collected beneath your pillow. You should dream of your true love later that night.

A water ritual

:☾ When you are next out for a walk, look for a small piece of wood and take it home with you.

:☾ Fill a tumbler with water and carefully drop the piece of wood inside it.

:☾ Keep the tumbler by your bed when you go to sleep.

:☾ It is foretold that you should dream of falling off a bridge. Don't worry if you cannot swim in your waking life as you should dream that your intended partner will dive into the water and save you.

A wedding cake ritual

:☾ When you are next at a wedding reception, keep a piece of the wedding cake or ask a friend or relative who is going to a wedding to save you some.

:☾ Place the piece of cake underneath your pillow before you go to sleep.

:☾ You should dream of your future husband or wife that night.

A wedding ritual

This is one of my favourite rituals and is best practised on a Wednesday or Saturday.

:☾ Place under your pillow a prayer book opened at the marriage service.

:☾ Bind the page with scarlet and white ribbon.

:☾ Tie a sprig of lavender or a red rose on to the page that says 'with this ring I thee marry'.

:☾ You should dream of your own wedding and see the identity of the groom (or bride).

The Scottish poet Robert Burns had a favourite dream ritual that he described in a poem called Halloween. He advised:

Eat a salted herring just before bedtime and your true love will bring you a drink of water (or something stronger) in a dream.

Wells and sacred lakes have also been used to call lovers in sleep. One recorded case is that of a nineteenth-century servant girl, from Yorkshire in England, who visited the Fairy's Pin Well, so named after the custom of dropping pins in the water as an offering to the fairy that lived in the well. The girl drank water from the well and asked the fairy to bring her a dream of the man she would marry. As tradition demanded, she fell asleep by the well whereupon she dreamt of one of her would-be lovers dressed in wedding finery bringing her a wedding ring and sweeping her off to enjoy feasting and revelry.

Modern dream techniques

If you don't have a well nearby, you can just as easily use a lake or river and like the people of old make a wish and sleep near the water, for example in a tent. You might even discover your potential lover is staying next-door the following morning! If none of these work, follow this adaptation of another old custom:

A modern ritual to call a dream lover

For this you will need a white candle, a mirror and a brush. The ritual is best practised when there is a crescent moon, but you can also work it during any night between the crescent and the full moon. You may even be rewarded by moonlight shining in the mirror on the nights closest to the full moon.

☾ Light a white candle and sit in semi-darkness in front of a mirror in your bedroom. Brush your hair a hundred times before bed, while gazing into the mirror through half-closed eyes.

☾ As you brush, recite over and over again very softly:
In my dreams come to me, a lover true, so that I may see.
My lover true, I do entreat, show me the place where we shall meet.

☾ Blow out the candle and as you do so, stare at the mirror. You may see a faint image of your future love in the glass. If you do not see anything, let your imagination build up a picture in your mind.

☾ Lie in bed with your eyes closed, imagining the mirror and your lover within it smiling at you.

If you do not dream of your lover, repeat the ritual nightly until the full moon, then wait for the next crescent moon before beginning again. Do not be surprised, however, if you see in the mirror or the dream someone with whom you have worked with for a while or a friend of a friend. Often we fail to realise that our future partners may be present friends or colleagues.

Sharing dreams with your partner or current lover

Linda had been married for 40 years and her husband Bill was about to retire. Linda wanted to go to Spain for the winters as many of their friends did so that they could enjoy the sunshine and outdoor life all of the year. However, Bill had his golf and drinking friends in Britain and did not see why Linda and he should uproot, just when he had more free time to spend with them. He refused to discuss moving or even to look at the brochures Linda had collected for long holidays in Spain. Linda was upset Bill was not as enthusiastic about Spain as she was. Then one night she says:

I dreamed I was at the airport with all my cases and was waving to Bill as I went through passport control. I didn't feel scared although in my everyday life I rarely go anywhere alone. Bill looked very unhappy but for once I didn't feel guilty and I had no intention of turning back. I dreamt that as the plane took off and flew through the air, I saw golden birds flying through the clouds through the plane window. I felt totally at peace with myself.

When she woke up, Linda told me that Bill had been watching her. He asked her, 'You wouldn't really go without me would you?' Linda was surprised at the question. He eventually admitted (rather embarrassed) that he had dreamed about Linda catching a plane to Spain and leaving him behind. 'You didn't even turn round', he said indignantly.

Linda explained gently that much as she loved him, she would go alone if necessary even for a few weeks to get away from the winter cold and damp that made her arthritis so bad. Because she had been so happy in her dream, she had realised Spain was important to her and since she had friends there she knew she would cope. All their life she had done what Bill wanted and this had eaten away at her self-confidence, but she now felt able to start being more independent again. No more was said, but that morning she caught Bill looking at the brochures and eventually he suggested they went to Spain just for a fortnight to see how they liked it. So your dreams about a partner do not have to be erotic or romantic in order to overcome a relationship obstacle.

Developing shared dreams

Linda and Bill's dreams were quite spontaneous, but you can develop shared dreams with a lover quite easily. If you have a sensitive lover he or she may be happy to try the exercise on page 50 with you. If a partner is sceptical or uncertain about unconscious realms, try working alone a few times until you are confident. After a few sessions you may find that your partner will report a powerful dream about being with you and even describe the same landscape you saw in your dream. This is because the telepathic bond that causes shared dreams is rooted in love and shared lives. Use these dream meetings to strengthen a relationship that may be going through a tricky patch, to heal a quarrel or even just to talk to your lover on a deeper level while asleep.

A pre-sleep ritual to share a dream with a lover

Work on a night when you do not have to get up early the next morning so you can lie in bed and either talk to your lover or muse to yourself. If you are working on dreams together, go to bed early and lie by candle or moonlight touching hands lightly, creating in words a joint dream setting. It can be as exotic as you like or perhaps a favourite place you both enjoy going to for a holiday or walking. If your lover is not present hold a photograph of him or her, or a gift that they have given you and evoke in your mind their voice, fragrance and touch.

- ☽ Blow out the candle if you used one and close your eyes, maintaining light hand contact either with your lover or chosen item. Whisper softly or say in your head over and over again, *I'll see you in my dreams.*
- ☽ Concentrate on your chosen dream scenario, imagining you both together. Even if alone whisper repeatedly, *I'll see you in my dreams.*
- ☽ As you fall asleep, whether together or alone, hold the picture of your lover and yourself in the dream place in your mind.

When you wake, talk about your dreams to your partner, even if you and your partner do not recall sharing a dream. We have a number of dreams a night, any of which might contain symbols relating to the relationship. Besides, talking about the dreams you had can open channels of meaningful communication.

If you dreamed of a lover, but were working alone, write down as much detail as you can about the dream. Focus on the positive aspects as you may have reached your lover telepathically in the dream.

Developing your relationship through dreams

If you have to spend many nights apart, you can talk without fear in dreams and can communicate over hundreds of miles, make love and share time in your prearranged dreamscape. Even if you are temporarily in a different time zone, remember that an afternoon nap can coincide with a lover's bedtime.

Try to make time once a week or fortnight for joint or individual dream work to focus on the relationship. It may take months of patience before you fully interact with a lover in dreams but each shared recollection, however fleeting, will open doors between your hearts.

CHAPTER 6

Psychic Dreams

In the previous chapters I described how in dreams the barriers of time are not so fixed as they are in the day. Our minds can therefore give us warnings or advice in sleep about possible future events in our lives which we should approach with caution. Take, for example, the story of David. He told me:

I had a dream in which a car came out of a field and smashed into our family car. I told my wife when I woke but I was not worried as I was not anticipating to use the car that day. However, unexpectedly I was asked to make a journey and we set off in the car. I came to a field and recognised it from my dream. I told my wife that this was the place where the accident had occurred, but she reassured me that there was no other traffic around. At that moment a car came hurtling out of the field and I swerved into a ditch to save my family. I believe this was because I was more alert due to my dream the night before.

David was fairly certain when he woke that his dream referred to an event that would happen quickly and so he trusted his forewarning. These premonition dreams are different from nightmares or anxiety dreams, which are probably just a result of feeling jittery in your everyday life. True predictive dreams have been described as more real than even a vivid dream and remain with you long after you would have forgotten an ordinary dream. The dream scene in premonitions is usually three-dimensional, very detailed and when you wake from it, you are fully awake and not at all sleepy or confused. You may only have one of these true warning dreams in your lifetime, if at all. Sometimes these dreams may just be indicating that your subconscious mind has noticed a tyre needs changing or a service of the brakes is overdue. The more you trust your dreams the more control you can gain over your life.

Mothers and predictive dreams

From my own research I have discovered a marked increase in significant dreaming among pregnant women and new mothers. These dreams tend to be far more vivid than dreams experienced at any time since childhood and usually concern the unborn infant or one in the first weeks of life. Often they are a way in which the unborn child can connect with its mother during sleep. They can be very reassuring if you are anxious about the pregnancy or are so busy you feel you rarely have time to sit and relax with your unborn child.

Tracey who lived in Redhead, Australia, wrote to me and said:

My normal dreams in life have never come true, but the two concerning my unborn children did. With my first pregnancy I dreamed three times that my baby would be a boy, blonde, born two months early and perfectly all right. I told myself not even to think about this, as two month premature babies aren't always perfectly all right. However, Simon was born at 33 weeks, blonde and healthy.

Before I knew it, I was pregnant a second time. This time I dreamed that I had twin girls called Jill and Sarah. Later in the pregnancy I was looking at some ornamental pottery babies and kept being strongly drawn to the sets of twins. At 14 weeks gestation twins were confirmed and I said they would be two girls. Sure enough, we now have Beth and Sarah. My husband didn't like the name Jill.

Tracey's first dream prepared her for an early baby and the second for twins. In sleep we can pick up all kinds of helpful information and in Tracey's case her dream proved she was in touch with her babies on an intuitive level.

Such experiences are not at all spooky, but confirm the natural psychic powers that we all have which are most easily expressed in sleep when we are more inclined to listen to our inner voice.

Let me now tell you about Linda. Linda's pregnancy dream also correctly predicted the sex and looks of her unborn child. But there was a vital difference. Her son Ivan was adopted.

I met Linda and Richard, who come from Oklahoma, when I went to Los Angeles to make a programme on maternal instinct in NBC's *Unsolved Mysteries* series. Linda told me about a vivid dream she had experienced that she described as more than just a dream, in which she was in a labour ward:

It was so real I could almost touch the pregnant woman, a blonde, fair-skinned lady. I watched her baby being delivered and it was a dark-skinned, dark-haired boy. The moment was incredibly moving and I was convinced I was witnessing an actual birth. Then I was in my bedroom, wide awake. I noted down the date and the time, as I thought I had somehow witnessed the birth of the child of a neighbour who was pregnant at the time. However, it turned out that my neighbour had not given birth. I told Richard, my husband, about the dream and we discussed what it might mean. We were trying to adopt a baby at the time and when we were eventually given Ivan, he was indeed the child whose face I had seen so clearly that night. The date and time of his birth exactly coincided with my dream. I knew that I had witnessed his birth for a reason, I think to confirm the rightness of the adoption.

Sadly, Ivan's mother died and I was sent some photographs from her family for Ivan. I discovered that she was the fair-skinned, blonde-haired woman in my dream and I felt very close and loving towards her as we had shared such a precious moment.

Richard said that for him, his wife's dream drove away any doubts he might have harboured about the adoption as he now knew that Ivan was meant to be theirs. He felt this bonding helped them through the daily problems of bringing up the child. Conventional scientific research lacks the tools to explain this phenomenon so we can only speculate about why Linda's dream was so uncannily accurate. Did she somehow telepathically tune into her prospective adoptive son in her dream at his moment of birth, as one might suddenly come across a distant and unfamiliar radio station? Or was the source of the dream the boy himself, calling out to a mother who would bring him up, as his own mother could not keep him?

Perhaps we shouldn't worry about the hows and whys but accept that dreams are very wonderful gifts that remind us that there is far more to us than the busy frantic people we sometimes become in the daytime.

Trusting psychic dreams

If you experience any dreams or nightmares that seem to predict events, note down any dates and times and how you felt in the dream and after it. Trust your instincts. If, for example, you dream that something bad will happen if your kids go to a certain place the next night, ask yourself if you always feel like that when they go out alone or late at night. Does this occasion feel different and is that why your subconscious is warning you in the dream? Did the dream make you feel general unease when you woke or was there a definite urgency in the dream making you think to yourself during the day, 'No, they must not go'?

If you decide you are feeling generally anxious about their safety, maybe you should review any arrangements so that your kids can contact you if there is a problem and then you will not worry so much. Dreams can, as I said, suggest there are details in our daily world that need checking or revising. However, if the nagging feeling still won't shift, say so and offer alternative arrangements. Maybe you could ask to change transport arrangements or timings or go another day. You may never know that you were right to delay or change a route, but you could have averted a disaster.

Seeing angels in dreams

I believe we all have a guardian angel looking after us from the moment of birth, perhaps even before, although if you choose not to contact him or her, you will not be troubled. Indeed, some early Christian sects claimed that each of us had a twin soul angel who was with us before birth and stayed with us into death and who would come to us at any time when we called them during our lifetime. This personal guardian can be regarded as a best friend who is always available, always forgiving and leads us gently to greater spiritual awareness and right action.

Children are frequently aware of a personal angel but their presence and awareness may fade as they grow up and get preoccupied with other issues. It is possible that we can reconnect with our guardian angel through dreams. It could happen spontaneously at a time when we are worried or going through a period of change.

For example, Maria was a single parent in her thirties and after her design business collapsed, due to her lack of customers, she had struggled to rebuild a new business. After two years of endless work she finally started to break even but still had to do all the work herself, as she could not afford to pay anyone to help her. As she had young children, much of the accounts and web page work had to be done after the children were in bed. After many sleepless nights Maria was weeping with exhaustion in her office and said aloud:

I cannot go on. Please someone help me.

Maria was too tired even to go to bed and fell asleep in a big chair in her office room. She told me that:

Almost immediately I seemed to be walking on soft, fluffy clouds and wandering through gardens filled with flowers of all colours. I could hear music and smell beautiful fragrances. I felt something brush against me. It felt like soft-feathered wings and as I stumbled along still feeling tired, I felt myself lifted and held aloft by golden wings. Suddenly, a soft voice spoke to me. It said, 'Maria, if you ask I will help you. But you are tired and now you must sleep. Help will come, I promise.' A golden light then surrounded me as I sank back exhausted onto a mound of soft petals. The last thing I remember being aware of, before I drifted off into pastel-coloured light, were the wings holding me, as though I were a baby.

When Maria woke, it was late in the morning and she leapt up in horror. The children did not answer her call. Then she saw a note. Her eldest son, who was ten, had got the other children ready for the school bus and had even tidied round the house, a miracle in itself. That afternoon she then had a phone call from a local college saying they were looking for placements for design students who would work for her for a very low wage in return for the experience. That evening her cousin Liz, who lived about five hundred miles away, phoned to say that she was between jobs and wanted to get away from her home city for a while. She said that she would be happy to help Maria with the children in return for a room, food and the use of the car sometimes.

A coincidence? Maria believes it was her angel who sent help and since then whenever she has dreamed of her angel good things have come into her life.

Encouraging angelic dreams

If you have never dreamed of your guardian angel or never encountered one, you can try the following methods. Even if you do not believe in angels, you can regard an angelic visitor as a higher and wiser part of yourself whose uplifting presence and good counsel can give advice and help in dreams.

To call your guardian angel

Use the ritual below to call on the help and guidance of your personal angel. All you need is a golden candle.

- Just before you go to sleep light the candle in a safe place and look into the flames.
- Let your eyes half close and see the aura of the candle expanding to fill the darkness.
- Close your eyes, open them, blink and smile.
- You should see your angel smiling back at you from the light, radiating an all-encompassing love and protection.
- Touch your heart with your right hand and the angel will touch his or hers with the left, so establishing the sign you can make unobtrusively in times of need of angelic guidance in your daily life.
- Blow out the candle, touch your heart once more as you lie down on your bed.

☽ Picture the golden glow and your angel leading you into sleep and protecting you in your dreams.

Any night you wish to dream of your angel, touch your heart and ask your angel to visit you and bring you wise advice or inspiration. Some people sleep with their hands crossed across their chest if they want an angelic dream.

As you drift into sleep, you may see your special angel smiling and enfolding you in gossamer wings. You may also be aware of the angelic presence fleetingly when you open your eyes in the morning. If you carry out this ritual regularly, you will find that you see your special angel in more detail in your dreams and may learn his or her name.

This is a lovely ritual for children to work if they suffer from insomnia, hyperactivity or nightmares, but be sure to take the candle away so that they are not tempted to try to light it again if they wake in the night.

The angel in the crystal

Another effective method to call your angel into your dreams is to use a crystal. Choose rutilated quartz containing golden filaments, a moss agate, white satin-like selenite, a piece of uncut amethyst, rose quartz or amber. Alternatively, use a clear crystal sphere or a crystal pyramid. Work preferably on a moonlit night. If the moon is not shining, light a silver candle which is the symbolic colour of the moon.

☽ Hold your crystal so that you can see the moon or candlelight reflected in it.

☽ As the light moves within or on the surface of the crystal, you may see your angel briefly within the crystal.

☽ Imagine you are breathing in silver light slowly and deeply. With each out-breath, visualise the light expanding within the crystal so that the angel fills the crystal.

☽ Blow out the candle if you used one and place the crystal beside your bed (or in the moonlight if it is shining) while you sleep.

☽ Close your eyes and imagine the angel walking out of the crystal, getting larger and clearer until he or she is human size (or perhaps slightly taller).

☽ The angel should talk to you in your dream and may perhaps take you on a special journey to a beautiful land.

Children usually love this ritual and feel safe from night terrors with their crystal angel near their bedside. You can let them choose their own special angel crystal which need not be at all expensive and can be especially useful if you or they have to be away from home at night.

Ghosts in dreams

The most common contact with deceased family members comes via dreams. It is nothing to be frightened of if a beloved grandmother or grandfather comes to you in sleep and talks to you or cuddles you if you are lonely or sad. It may be the mind's way of healing grief due to the death of a loved one. If your relation died some years ago, such a dream will recall memories of the love and reassurance they offered you in their lifetime, perhaps when you were a child. However, some people believe that the soul lives on after death and can speak to us in dreams. They are convinced that the bond of love is so great between husband and wife, parents and children, grandparents and grandchildren of any age, that deceased relations can return to us in our dreams to offer us comfort, advice and reassurance. These experiences are usually positive and afterwards the majority of people say that they feel a great sense of peace, especially if the person died suddenly or after a prolonged illness in which they suffered a great deal of pain.

Of course, if such dreams would spook you then you will not have them, for our minds (and some say our deceased relatives), would not allow you to be distressed. But let me tell you about the kind of dreams I mean such as the one Jenny experienced. Jenny cut and styled my hair when I was in London about five years ago and told me the following story:

My parents had been decorating my teenage brother's room and one night I had a dream in which two older, dark-skinned women came up to me. I recognised one of the women to be my late grandmother. The women were telling me to wake up quickly as there was great danger. I woke up straight away and immediately saw smoke pouring into my room from under the door. I left my room and saw that my brother's mattress which had been accidentally propped up against a lightbulb had started to smoulder. I knew that there were gas cylinders kept downstairs so I rushed to wake my mother who rang the fire brigade just before the line went dead. Later, when we were all out of the house and safe, my mother asked me what it was that had woken me in the first place. I told her about the women in my dream and when I described them I discovered that the second, unknown woman I had seen had been my other grandmother who had died before I was born.

Few of us will have dreams with such a dramatic effect as Jenny's. For most of us, visits from relatives or friends are simply loving experiences. In some instances, people may wake and be aware, for example, of the fragrance a late grandmother used to wear. Such dreams can be immensely healing.

For instance, Lucy's mother died suddenly in a road accident when Lucy was working away from home. At the funeral Lucy stood in the graveyard and felt utterly lost. She could not even connect with the memory of her mother and vowed never to return to the cold and bleak graveyard. She returned to her family home but still felt as though her mother was totally gone from her.

That night she lay staring at the ceiling of her childhood bedroom until at last she drifted into a restless sleep which led to a waking dream, that is, a dream that was so vivid, Lucy thought she was awake. Lucy says:

I found myself back in the churchyard but it was early morning and just beginning to get light. The flowers that people had laid on my mother's grave had already died and I began to cry. Then suddenly I felt myself being held by my mother. I could feel the soft wool of her sweater and she smelt of lilacs. I cried out 'where are you?' but I couldn't see her. Then I heard her laugh softly and she said, 'not here, in this cold place. Go to where we were happy. Go to the swing in the garden by the lilac bushes. I am there when you need me.' And then she was gone.

Lucy woke from the dream feeling more at peace and in the early morning went down the garden to the swing where her mother had played with her as a child. The swing was moving gently in the early morning breeze and though the lilacs were not blooming, there was the unmistakable fragrance her mother had loved so much. Suddenly in the middle of her grief Lucy was filled with momentary joy and felt light expanding all round her and she said, 'thank you, Mama!'

Thereafter whenever she came home for a holiday, Lucy went to the swing and knew her mother's love had not gone.

Recreating the memory of loved ones in dreams

Although such dream contact is normally quite spontaneous, you can promote the closeness of a beloved mother, grandmother, grandfather or partner and talk to them in sleep. Of course you may prefer to keep your memories unchanged and not want to dream of family members who have died, although some people like Lucy find psychic dreams supportive. They can be especially healing on anniversaries or at key times such as the birth of a child when the relative would have joined the celebrations.

If you decide that you would like to experience a psychic dream, try the following method. Even if you do not see the deceased person in your dreams you should wake with a great sense of peace.

To call a dead relative or friend

During the morning or afternoon you have chosen to try for a psychic dream, buy some pink or green nightlights and visit a place where you and the deceased person spent a happy time together such as a local beauty spot, a place in the garden where they loved to sit and talk with you, or a favourite café. Take with you a small symbol of the person whom you have lost like a photograph, a scarf, a much-read book or a piece of jewellery. This artefact may have belonged to the deceased person or it could be a gift that he or she made to you that was special, not in monetary terms, but offered and accepted in love.

- As you hold the object, speak in your mind words of love and recall a shared joke or special moment you both enjoyed in the chosen place.
- Notice any special fragrances and take something scented away from the place as a link, such as a fragrant flower, coffee beans, pine needles or a small piece of seaweed from the shore, the scent of which recalls the memory of happy times.
- That evening before you prepare yourself for sleep, light a small pink or green nightlight. Pink and green are the colours of family, love and devotion.
- Set the fragrant symbol near your bed (you can strengthen the scent with a fragrance you associate with the deceased, such as a pot of coffee).
- Play some gentle music that you and the person who has died shared as a special melody. As the tunes unfold, imagine again in your mind the familiar voice joining in with the words or humming the tune.
- Hold the object and ask softly if the loved one will come to you in a dream. Blow out the light and place the object by your bed.
- As you drift into sleep, recall the voice talking softly to you about everyday events.

You may dream about the person in quite an ordinary context, in their home or yours or in the place you visited to remember him or her. In the dream you may not see the figure clearly but may feel aware of the presence or a golden light. Sometimes the dream may take days or weeks to come, so be patient, for I believe love does last forever.

Developing your dream work

In the next section of this book I have written more than 1000 dream meanings that you can use as a key to unlock the meanings behind your dreams. These can be combined with your own personal A to Z symbol list if you keep a dream journal. The dream meanings are only basic explanations as your dreams are uniquely your own. It may be that after dreaming and later in the day when you replay a dream in your mind, that only then will you understand quite clearly what your inner voice is trying to tell you.

The Chinese believed that darkness and night, as expressed in their symbol yin, was a seamless cloak that enveloped all. There are no limits to the ways you can explore and use the world of dreams. Like Grandmother Spider Woman weaving her dream-catchers, the wise Viking women using dreams as guides or the young village girls dreaming of love, your dreams are as important a part of you as your daytime powers. Trust your dreams and let them show you possibilities you had not considered. I wish you happy dreams and even happier waking.

A to Z of Dream Meanings

Refer to this comprehensive dictionary by looking up the image most prominent in your dream to find out what your subconscious is trying to tell you. In some dreams, there may be more than one image that impressed itself on you. If so, think about the relationship between the images and how that impacts on your personal interpretation.

As I mentioned on page 15, you may find it helpful to keep a dream journal which covers what is happening in your waking life as well as the dream images you experience at night, so that you may be able to better understand the guidance your subconscious is offering at night.

Abandonment

If you find yourself abandoned it means there is something or someone in your present situation that is making you feel insecure.

If you are abandoning other people, you may have an unacknowledged resentment toward a present relationship.

Abbey

This suggests you need some quiet time for reflection and indicates you may be wondering about the meaning of your life and how to find more personal fulfilment.

Abroad

To be on holiday or living abroad, if pleasurable, suggests a widening of horizons and a desire for new experiences.

If you feel lost in a foreign city or amongst hostile foreigners, you may be fearful of unfriendly influences or people who may be trying to come into your social circle.

Abscess

You are very resentful about an injustice but are trying to keep your feelings inside, which is making you feel bad within.

See also **boil**

Absent friends

This can be an indication of telepathic communication. You may hear from absent friends soon or should contact them. You may find that they also dreamed of you on the same night or experienced similar dream symbols.

See also **friends**

Abyss

If you are falling into an abyss, you may be feeling that you want to let go of some part of your life where you have taken on too much responsibility.

Academic lessons

English: You need to write, whether it be a novel or just to update your CV.

Geography: You need to check travel plans carefully.

History: You require traditional advice about a matter, especially with regards to justice.

Mathematics: You need to pay closer attention to your financial affairs.

Religious studies: You need to develop spiritually.

Science/technology: You will need to be logical to solve a problem.

See also **classroom, desk, examination, exclusion, school** *or* **teacher**

Accident

If you are involved in an accident, this is a warning that you should be careful of your health and avoid carelessness in the area shown in the dream. For example, if you dreamt of a road accident check your tyre pressures, etc.

If family or friends are involved, you may be very anxious about their welfare or feel guilt, whether valid or not, for neglecting them.

See also **disaster** *or* **flare (distress)**

Acorn

This is a symbol of fertility and predicts prosperity will come into your life. It may also denote that any projects you start now will succeed and grow over the months and years.

Actor or actress

If you are starring in a production, you may be wanting more recognition for your hard work and talents from those around you.

If you forget your words, you may be worried about others finding out about your inadequacies.

See also **play** *or* **theatre**

Adolescent

If you are a young person in the dream there may be a part of yourself that you need to find again or you may simply need to have fun or relax.

If you are dealing with one or more difficult adolescents in your dream, there may be people in your life who are behaving immaturely, whatever their age.

See also **independence**

Advice

If you are receiving wise advice in your dream, you may need to act on it or seek expertise in real life.

If you are the one giving the advice there may be something you need to say but have been holding back. This could be due to a fear of looking as though you are interfering.

Aerial

If a car or television aerial or satellite dish is working well, you are in touch with the feelings and thoughts of others.

If an aerial is broken or out of tune, others may be avoiding discussing important issues or not giving you the full picture.

Aerobics

Moving in harmony suggests that you are in tune with others. If you keep getting the movements wrong it could be that others may be giving you conflicting messages or that you are feeling unnecessarily inadequate as others boast of their achievements.

Aeroplane

If you are flying in a plane you may have a desire for distant travel or to move away from what is restricting you.

To dream of a plane crash can indicate fears of failing in your day-to-day work.

If you are the one flying the plane it shows you have the power to succeed if you let go of your fears. It can also indicate that your love or work life will take off in a big way before long. You may also go on a journey in the near future.

A jet plane can signal a sudden surge of power or success. You may soon win a competition or lottery, possibly with a travel prize.

See also **airport, flying, parachute** *or* **travel**

Air

Enjoying yourself in the open air indicates you should spend more time on leisure or that you would benefit from going to new places.

If the air is polluted or foggy, it indicates that others are stifling your creativity or freedom.

Airport

Waiting to catch a plane says that you are about to embark on a new stage of your life or should seize a new opportunity that will soon come your way.

To miss a plane or to experience delays symbolises frustration at other peoples' behaviour or illustrates that your own fears are holding you back.

See also **aeroplane** *or* **flying**

Alcohol

To enjoy alcohol says that you are ready to shed your inhibitions and do what you want.

If you are drunk then you may feel that you have lost control over your life, especially in relation to others in a particular social setting.

See also **beer, drinking, drunkenness, keg, liqueur** *or* **wine**

Alien

A friendly alien represents original ideas you have that could succeed if you put them into practice. It may also symbolise that you are ready to act independently.

If the alien is hostile you may be feeling left on the periphery, misunderstood or lonely.

Extra-terrestrial dreams can sometimes be out-of-body experiences or simply a sign that you need to develop a part of yourself that has been lost while caring for others.

See also **space**

Alligator

You need to watch out for fast-talking people who could steal your money or confuse you.

If you are chased by an alligator, you should be cautious around a new friend who may try to involve you in risky situations.

See also **crocodile**

Alphabet

If particular letters form initials, try to work out who they refer to. If you cannot, watch out for a significant person entering your life with those initials.

If letters of the alphabet fall around you, you may feel there is never enough time to talk to people or to a particular person to whom you have much to say.

Altar

If you are praying at an altar or building one of your own, it can denote that your spiritual and psychic powers are beginning to emerge.

If there are many people at the altar, you may feel that others are ignoring your inner needs.

If there are ancient priests and priestesses near to the altar or you discover that you have taken on the identity of a priest or priestess, this could be a past-life dream.

See also **church** *or* **sacrifice**

Amber

To dream of this beautiful honey coloured stone indicates that love or personal happiness will enter your life. As it is a gem of great antiquity, you should find that this love or joy will be everlasting.

See also **jewellery**

Ambush

If you are setting up an ambush, you may be planning a form of retaliation as a result of double-dealing or spite at work, which has angered you.

If you are the one who is ambushed, you may fear that you will be caught out over past minor indiscretions such as an unpaid bill.

Amplifiers

If your conversation is being drowned out by loud music, people are not listening to you and you need to be more forceful.

If you are speaking or singing loudly, you will succeed in persuading others to agree with you.

Amputation

This is never a warning that you are going to lose a limb. Instead, an amputation can represent leaving behind a situation or relationship that has become destructive.

For an adolescent, this can be a sign that they are ready to leave home but are feeling nervous.

Anaesthetic

Being given or being under anaesthetic can indicate a desire to escape from painful problems or difficult people.

To dream of waking while under an anaesthetic during an operation and feeling unable to move, suggests you are feeling powerless to escape from hurtful comments or people.

See also **hospital** *or* **operation**

Ancestors

To dream about your ancestors, for example, a beloved grandmother, can be very reassuring if you are feeling sad or lonely and need a reminder that love never dies.

If you dream about old quarrels with a deceased relative, perhaps an unkind relation, it may be time to talk about them to a sympathetic friend and then let the past and guilt go.

Anchor

If an anchor is steadying a boat, then there is someone close to you or someone coming into your life soon who will bring you emotional security.

A broken anchor indicates you are fearful of betrayal from someone you trust.

See also **boats**

Angel

Guardian angels often appear in dreams and you may see the same angel regularly. Guardian angels show that you are protected even if you feel alone.

See also **ethereal being** *or* **heaven**

Anger

To express anger in a dream is very positive and is often a rehearsal for an event in the days ahead.

To be on the receiving end of anger suggests you may feel afraid of expressing your true feelings in a situation you would like to alter.

Animals

Domestic animals indicate that you are moving into a more settled period in your life.

If you are struggling to look after a lot of animals or your home is being invaded by stray cats or dogs, then you have too many demands on your time.

Unusual creatures are usually a bad sign, especially if they attack you.

See also individual animals, **reptile, traps, wild beasts** *or* **zoo**

Antiseptic

See **disinfectant**

Ants

Ants crawling everywhere in your home and over food means that you are feeling overwhelmed by a lot of small issues or problems that have built up and you may be feeling as though you cannot get away from them, even at home. Ants can also indicate minor health worries.

See also **insects**

Anxiety

Anxiety dreams where you lose luggage, miss trains, get stuck in traffic or end up late for appointments, are a simple sign of overload in your everyday world and of trying to keep to impossible work schedules.

Ape

To see a small ape cling to a tree is often a warning sign as it is regarded as a symbol of deceit. It could mean that someone close to you is being false and may cause you unpleasantness.

See also **animals** *or* **monkey**

Apple

A ripe or golden apple is a symbol of fertility and love. It can also be a sign of continuing good or improving health.

A rotten apple or one with a worm inside suggests that someone near to you is being false.

See also **fruit**

Arch

This can indicate a joining together, such as marriage, or may indicate a long-term relationship or reconciliation.

If you are walking through a tall archway, promotion or recognition should come into your life within a week or so.

Archaeologist

This is often symbolic of a need to find an answer to a dilemma that is similar to one you have resolved in the past.

If an archaeologist finds something of interest, it can mean that you will be given, or will find, a very old but cheap item that will be of greater value than you may think.

See also **fossil**

Army

A marching army suggests you should prepare for a change, possibly in the form of unexpected visitors.

An invading army means that you are feeling overwhelmed by others demanding your time and attention.

If you are in the army, it is a sign that you need more excitement in your life.

See also **kit, officer, soldiers, tank (army), uniform, victory** *or* **war**

Arrival

Arriving after a journey suggests that you are very close to succeeding in an area of your life .

It may indicate that in a relationship you and your partner are becoming closer (especially if you arrive with your lover in the dream).

If unexpected visitors arrive, it may be a premonition that the people in the dream will turn up at your door within a week of the dream.

Arrow

Shooting arrows and hitting a target indicates success and shows that if you aim high, you will achieve your goal very soon.

If people are shooting arrows at you, it could mean that a spiteful colleague, neighbour or family member may be trying to undermine your confidence.

See also **quiver**

Artist

If you are the artist, it means you have creative talents that you should put into practice.

If you are the one being painted you will soon get the recognition you deserve.

See also **tattoo**

Ashes

Ashes from a fire show you have regrets from a past relationship.

Ashes in a funeral urn mean you need to grieve for something that has gone wrong.

See also **cremation** or **phoenix**

Assassin

If you are being stalked, there may be someone spiteful in your life who is seeking to assassinate your good name.

If you are killing someone, it is a sign that you need to be ruthless to survive your present situation or demands.

Asthma

If you are unable to breathe in a dream (even if you do not actually have asthma) this suggests someone is stifling you.

If you dream of a child or family member having asthma, you may be trying to take too much control of their lives because you think they will make mistakes.

See also **suffocation**

Attack

If you are attacking a person or a place, you may need to defend yourself against spite or jealousy.

If you are being attacked you may be feeling vulnerable to unfair criticism and should protect yourself by moving away from the situation, rather than fighting back.

Attic

If the attic is dusty and crowded with junk, it is time you cast aside regrets and guilt from the past.

If there is something scary in the attic, there are legal or money matters you need to tackle.

See also **house**

Auction

Bidding for goods or a house in an auction means you should maybe think about taking a risk, whether with your job or in a relationship in order to make a great gain.

See also **house**

Autumn

This is a sign that you need to settle an injustice or claim an outstanding debt that is owed to you.

See also **leaves**

Axe

Chopping something with an axe indicates you have great strength and the potential power to act with courage. If you are wielding an axe you may need to be very assertive to get bullies to back down.

B

Baby

This is a sign of abundance and prosperity and can also indicate the success of a recent venture. If you are trying for a baby it can be a premonition of a future child.

See also **birth, labour, pregnancy, quads, quintuplets** *or* **twins**

Back

If you have back pain or have injured your back quite seriously, it denotes that you have been trying too hard to hold back your feelings of frustration or anger.

If you are stabbed in the back you should be wary of false friends and jealous colleagues.

Backwards

Walking backwards or dreaming of a scene that is running backwards indicates that you are impatient with the inertia or uncooperative attitude of others who are holding you back.

If you are retracing your steps you already have the answer to an important question, but have to acknowledge it.

Badge

If it is a badge of an organisation or an award, it indicates that you will soon get official recognition, perhaps at work or from within your local community.

Bag

If your bag is overflowing and messy, you are trying to keep too many people happy.

If you lose or drop your bag and the contents spill out, you are worried about people finding out about a secret.

Bait

If a fish is taking your bait then you will find happiness in love or success in a financial matter very soon.

If you see baited animal traps you may fear that someone is trying to trick you.

See also **fishing**

Balcony

If you are watching others from a balcony, you will soon get a promotion or enjoy success at work.

When a balcony breaks it means that someone's promises to you may not be fulfilled.

Ball

If you are joining in with a ball game, it indicates that you are secure in your present situation and relationships.

If you are standing and watching from the sidelines, you may be feeling excluded from other peoples' happiness.

Ball and chain

This is symbolic of being held back by people or responsibilities that are not easy to shed but which need discarding. You have an unfulfilled desire to travel.

Balloons

This denotes celebrations and happiness with regards to family or close friends.

A flying balloon or a hot air balloon indicates a desire to travel and be free from restrictions.

A deflated or broken balloon indicates disappointment and shattered hopes in someone you trusted.

Bandage

If you are putting the bandage on someone, it indicates you may be called to mend a family quarrel.

If you are the one being bandaged, you may be accepting a situation you do not really want.

Bank

This symbolises security and confidence in the practical or material aspects of life.

If you dream of a successful bank robbery, it denotes that a risky idea may lead to a great advantage.

To be overdrawn, meet an angry bank manager or take part in a failed bank robbery, suggests that your stressful attitude is stopping you from working out a realistic solution to your financial problems.

A bank vault full of money means you are (or will be) owed money from people who will be unwilling to pay it back.

An empty bank vault indicates that you may find your bank is obstructive about giving you a loan.

See also **money, safe** *or* **saving**

Bank of river

Deep or steep river banks may suggest you are holding back your feelings, especially with regards to love or sexuality.

Crumbling banks or falling down into a river indicates that others are pressurising you emotionally to go against your better judgement.

Banners

Banners promise victory in a long-term aim or desire and indicate that you will gain public recognition or approval.

Banquet

If dieting in your waking life, this can be a compensatory dream for what you are denying yourself.

If you are enjoying a banquet and are not dieting, the dream is saying that you will have more than enough money in the future. It can also mean that you should relax and enjoy sex more.

Baptism

Watching a childhood baptism reflects that you are responsible for children or for someone who is ill and vulnerable and that this is worrying you.

If you are being baptised, it can represent surrendering to a deep love or a determination to follow a career or course in life that is spiritually rather than financially fulfilling.

Barrel

See keg

Barrier

If barriers are protecting you from a crowd or from flooding water, it means you need to keep your defences up in your everyday life to avoid being carried along with the opinions or choices of others.

If you are stuck behind barriers and are prevented from joining a procession or getting to where you want to go, you may be experiencing a problem with figures of authority or the law and may need to seek help.

Basement

This symbolises the unconscious mind and all the things we have buried there such as old guilt, regrets and bad memories. Some of these issues may be creeping back into your mind and so you need to throw them away in your dream and your life.

Basket

A full basket symbolises a gift or a welcome addition to the family whether a baby or through marriage or remarriage.

An empty basket suggests you are giving too much time and possibly money to particular family members.

Bat

A bat says you need to trust your intuition. It also represents the need to look at and talk over hidden fears of attack or your own negative feelings about something.

See also **animals**

Bath/bathroom

There is something or someone in your life who needs to be removed or left behind so that you can feel free again.

If you can't find a bathroom in your dream but need one, you are afraid that people will see through your public façade and realise you are not as efficient or as clever as you seem.

Battle

If you are on the winning side, it means you should press ahead with demanding what you need or fighting an injustice.

When you are afraid in the battle or are losing, then you may be backing the wrong cause or person.

See also **fighting** *or* **war**

Beans

Eating beans is an indication of prosperity coming to you in an unexpected way.

See also **food**

Bear

If the bear is friendly, it indicates you have the strength to win through any obstacles and you may discover an unexpected ally in the near future.

A fierce bear means you are being bullied (maybe emotionally). If you can, try to defeat the bear in the dream as that will show you have the courage to win through.

See also **animals** *or* **wild beasts**

Beard

If someone you recognise grows a beard in your dream they may be hiding something from you in real life.

A false beard says that you should not take a new acquaintance or colleague at face value. Do not confide in him or her until you are sure they are trustworthy and reliable.

Bed/bedroom

Being comfortable in bed during a dream is a wish-fulfilment dream. It suggests you need to relax and rest more.

Having sex in bed says that you have, or will have, a secure and fulfilling relationship.

Being ill in bed means you are worried about missing out on an event or decision concerning you.

See also **quilt**

Beer

This is an indication of impending celebrations, which could mean an improvement in your social life and possibly new friends.

See also **alcohol**

Bees

Bees are a sign of profitable activity and also of communication regarding family matters. They can be a sign of rich and harmonious relationships and even births or marriages in the family that have not been announced, but which your psyche has picked up on a very deep level.

A swarm of stinging bees refers to a possible spiteful attack, perhaps from an older matriarchal figure.

See also **animals, honey** *or* **insects**

Beetle

Beetles crawling everywhere can mean you are worried that you have been careless or left necessary work undone. You may also be worried you will be criticised for not being caring enough towards your partner, family or work by an unfair relation, colleague or neighbour.

See also **animals** *or* **insects**

Beggar

If you are helping a beggar, you should be careful not to fall for too many hard luck stories in real life.

If you are the beggar or are frightened by a beggar, it means you are feeling insecure about losing everything, not necessarily financially but maybe in emotional terms.

See also **homelessness** *or* **tramp**

Beheading

This is actually a good dream as it is a sign that you will soon be able to cut off contact with a person or situation that makes you feel unhappy.

See also **death/dying** *or* **execution**

Bells

This can mean an imminent celebration, marriage or surprise announcement from someone close to you that will make you very happy. It can also symbolise good news from overseas or from long-distance relatives.

See also **church**

Belt

If a belt is too tight, it shows that you are feeling restricted by the pettiness and narrow-mindedness of someone at work or home.

If you lose your belt and your clothes do not fit, you are worried about keeping up appearances.

Bereavement

This is never a prediction that someone is going to die. If you are bereaved in a dream, you may be feeling anxious or angry about a family member's welfare. Depending on the circumstances you may be feeling guilty for feeling this way.

See also **burial, cemetery, coffin, cremation** *or* **death/dying**

Betrothal

See **engagement**

Birds

Like bees, flying birds are an indication of good news, especially from overseas or regarding people you have not heard from for a while.

An unhappy and/or caged bird symbolises your own hidden fears of being trapped in a relationship.

Birds that are attacking you or others symbolise gossip and petty spite from colleagues.

See also individual birds, **animals, feathers, nest** *or* **worm**

Birth

If you are not pregnant, but dream of giving birth it is a sign that your financial prospects should improve. Sometimes it can be an indication that you may become pregnant in the near future.

If you are already pregnant and dream of a difficult birth, you may be expressing fears about becoming a mother. In contrast, if you dream of an easy birth, it is usually a rehearsal for the real event and a sign that you are feeling relaxed about it.

See also **baby** *or* **pregnancy**

Black

If everything is totally black around you or you are driving along in the countryside and your car lights fail, for example, you may be feeling as though you are losing your way in life and have no time or energy to enjoy yourself. Usually this dream is a sign of stress and a warning that you should try to relax more.

Black is also a sign that you may need to grieve for someone or something that you have lost. In Ancient Egypt, black was the colour of rebirth so you should try to focus on any new beginnings that may follow on from a difficult ending.

See also **blindness, colours** *or* **darkness**

Black hole

If you are falling into it, you are feeling that you want to let go of some part of your life where you have too much responsibility.

Blindness

If you are blind in a dream or cannot see properly, it usually means that you are worried that someone is not telling you the truth and that you may be walking blindly into trouble. This can also be an anxiety dream about the future and symbolises a fear of being confronted by unknown forces or circumstances.

See also **black** *or* **darkness**

Blockage

If pipes or your toilet is blocked in a dream, it means that you are worried about your feelings, especially anger, bursting out.

If a road is blocked and you cannot get to your destination, this is another anxiety dream denoting that you have too much to do and not enough time.

Blood

If you are bleeding from a wound you may be feeling drained of natural energy.

If you were afraid of the blood, especially if someone close to you was bleeding, you may be afraid that something important in your life is slipping away from you.

To dream of menstrual blood is a good sign and promises good health and energy. It also indicates that you are a very sexually attractive person.

Blue

This is the colour of leadership and therefore suggests that you should think about applying for a promotion.

If you see a blue mist, it can be a sign that you are a natural healer.

See also **colours**

Boats

This dream brings promises of unexpected travel or holidays. To see yachts or ships, in particular, is a sign that you would benefit from more recreational activities and some relaxation. Boat dreams can also mean that you will soon resolve a quarrel or get on better with someone who has caused you problems.

If you are steering a yacht or small boat, it can indicate that the future launch of a small, independent venture or company will be successful.

Missed or sinking boats indicate fears of change.

See also **anchor, cabin, cruise, harbour, lagoon, lake, lifeboat, navy, oar, overboard, overturn, quay, river, rowing, sailing, sea, shipwreck** *or* **travel**

Body

If you have a slim and fit body in a dream, it can be a sign of wish fulfilment or simply an indication that you are comfortable with how you are and have good self-esteem. If you are aiming to improve your shape in your waking life, this dream is a good sign of success

If you are ashamed of your body or other people are being horrible to you about your figure, you may be worried about creating a good impression with other people. There may be a critical person in your life who tries to control you by making you feel unhappy about your shape.

Boil

If the boil was running pus and blood, you may encounter unpleasant things in the near future.

To dream of boils on your forehead can indicate someone close to you is sick.

See also **abscess**

Bomb

If you were the one detonating the bomb, it can mean you need to release pent-up negative energies or attack an unjust situation.

If you or your home are being bombed, you may fear an out of control situation or someone's hostile or aggressive attitude towards you. It also signifies repressed and negative emotions that you try to hide, even from yourself, should be expressed.

See also **disaster, dynamite, explosion, keg** *or* **terrorist**

Bones

A pile of bones after a good dinner means you are very sensual and able to enjoy life to the full.

A pile of human bones suggests that you are worried about the decline of a relationship.

See also **skeleton**

Book

If you are reading and discover some important facts in a book, it means you will be able to find the answer to any question or problem you have by seeking advice from an expert. Sometimes it is possible to remember what we read when we wake and this can be of benefit in real life.

An open book represents a new opportunity through learning or success with a legal matter. A closed book can indicate that your usual sources of help seem unavailable or people in authority are proving obstructive. Someone may be harbouring a secret you need to know.

If you are writing a book you may have much to say and maybe you really should write a book.

See also **library, page (book)** *or* **reading**

Borders

If you are trying to escape a situation by crossing the border of a country, you are feeling stifled by your work or home life but are afraid to say or do anything about it.

Crossing borders while on holiday in a dream indicates unexpected travel opportunities coming your way.

Bored

Being bored in a dream indicates you need to find new friends and take up new activities.

Dealing with bored children signifies that you try to please others too much.

Boss

A dream where you are the boss signifies a future promotion or business success.

If your boss is praising you or offering you more money, it may be a wish-fulfilment dream, but it can also mean that your efforts at work have been noticed.

An angry or bullying boss means you need stand up for yourself and not give into people because they shout or make a fuss. This can also indicate you are worried about getting into trouble with officials.

Bosses can also represent mothers or fathers.

See also **office** *or* **work**

Bottle

If a bottle is full, you should pour your energies and talents into a new challenge or avenue.

If the bottle is empty, you may be feeling exhausted and need to take care of yourself more.

Bottles in general indicate that good news is coming your way.

Box

A box generally signifies that you may soon receive a gift.

An empty box shows that someone close has revealed a secret they should have kept.

A closed box advises you not to tell any secrets except to trusted friends and family.

Boy

If you recognise the boy, this indicates that a male child is giving you cause for concern.

If you do not recognise the boy it suggests that you need to try something a little adventurous to bring excitement into your life.

See also **children**

Bracelets

To be given a bracelet as a present from someone you know, indicates that the giver wishes to become closer to you.

If a bracelet feels tight, it suggests that you are feeling restricted by a situation or relationship.

If you lose a bracelet, it can be a sign that someone close to you is reading your letters or e-mails without your permission.

To own an ankle bracelet means that you can trust your partner to make a right decision.

If an ankle bracelet is too tight it can be a sign that you are being coerced into making a decision that is not in your best interests. It can also mean that a relationship or friendship is limiting your freedom.

See also **jewellery**

Bread

Eating bread says that money and good fortune will come into your home.

Making bread can indicate that you are being asked to do more than your fair share of the domestic chores and childcare.

See also **flour, food** *or* **loaf**

Breasts

Having beautiful naked breasts is a sexual dream and indicates that you are ready for a fulfilling relationship.

Breastfeeding a baby shows that you are a loving, caring person and can be a premonition of pregnancy.

Being ashamed when your breasts are suddenly exposed signifies fears of letting go sexually.

See also **body**

Bride and/or bridegroom

If you are in a relationship and dream of being a bride or bridegroom to someone who is not your real-life partner or to someone you do not know, it indicates that you need more commitment or romance in your current relationship. If unattached you may, in the time-honoured tradition, be dreaming about a future partner who may be known or as yet unknown to you, except in dreams like these.

See also **veil** *or* **wedding**

Bridge

A bridge can represent a period of transition or a change in your life. It can indicate a new closeness with someone you were previously estranged from, a reconciliation of old quarrels or the finding of a new love partner from overseas.

Broken

Breaking something in a dream, whether accidentally or deliberately, suggests there is something or someone in your life you would prefer not to be there. If something precious is broken, you may be afraid of someone close betraying you or of someone you love moving away.

Broom

Sweeping up can represent a desire for change in your life.

Riding a broomstick through the sky says you have psychic or healing powers you perhaps do not use or are not yet aware of.

Brother

Whether or not you have a brother, a brother figure is a positive male symbol and indicates that a helpful man of similar age and status will come into your life in the near future to protect you.

See also **family**

Brown

This is the colour of the earth and is a sign that you need to ground yourself and be more careful with your finances and other important aspects of your life.

See also **colours**

Bubble

If you are in a bubble or surrounded by bubbles floating in the air, you have every reason to be optimistic as happiness is due to come into your life.

If you felt trapped inside a bubble you are unable to influence events and feel helpless watching as others make mistakes that will affect you.

A bursting bubble talks about a disappointment that you haven't come to terms with.

Buddha

This is a very spiritual dream that indicates emerging healing powers. It also signifies that you have great wisdom and compassion that attracts all kinds of people to you for advice and reassurance. Maybe you should develop this ability professionally.

Buildings

Sometimes buildings symbolise the physical self, so the kind of building and its condition can indicate hidden feelings and desires.

Tall buildings indicate ambitions yet to be fulfilled, while official buildings symbolise bureaucratic, tax or legal matters that need sorting. Burning buildings show a desire to get rid of something that is holding you back and a ruined building indicates you feel worthless or are being manipulated by others.

Bull

This is a symbol of power for both men and women. It can signify male potency and great passion in a woman. It is generally a good sign for a man who wants to father a baby.

A charging bull represents powerful feelings and sexual desires that need to be expressed.

See also **animals**

Bully

If you recognise the bully from real-life then the dream is presenting you with an opportunity to stand up to them and overcome them.

If you do not know the bully, it could be a sign that you are worried about a proposed change in your life. Ask yourself if you are being coerced into it for someone else's benefit.

If you are the bully, you may be feeling timid in your everyday life and your subconscious is telling you to stand up for yourself more.

See also p 31 on how to cut a giant (or bully) down to size or **cruel**

Burden

If you are carrying a heavy burden, it means that other people are demanding too much of you.

If you put a burden down this shows you are ready to take a stand and will refuse to support others financially or emotionally without appreciation. It can herald the end of a difficult period.

Burglar
If your home was being burgled, you may feel that outsiders are intruding upon your private life or that an outsider is posing a threat to an important relationship.

Burial
This is never a prediction of death. Instead it represents the need to bury a bad habit, a destructive relationship or an unfulfilling path through life.

If you are burying someone, you need to resolve unfinished business or quash old resentments that are lurking in the background.

See also **bereavement, cemetery, coffin, death/dying, funeral, grave** *or* **undertaker**

Burn
If you are burned, you may be afraid that you are getting into a situation or relationship too deeply or quickly.

See also **fire** *or* **flames**

Bus
This represents daily routine, so if there are delays or you miss a bus, you are doing too much at home and would benefit from some help.

If the bus is going to travel a long distance, it may represent a desire to move home or make changes within the home and family.

See also **indicators** *or* **vehicle**

Butterfly
This is a universal symbol of rebirth and regeneration. It represents the need to enjoy present happiness without worrying about tomorrow. It can also indicate a rebirth of hope and trust after sorrow.

A trapped, torn or dying butterfly can represent fragile hopes and a sense of frantically trying to hold on to a rapidly changing situation, actual loss or grief.

See also **animals** *or* **insects**

Buttons
Missing buttons on clothes says that there are many small irritations in your personal life.

If the buttons are undone and reveal too much of yourself, you may feel that your self-control is slipping and you are in danger of saying what you really feel, which may actually be beneficial.

C

Cabbage

A single cabbage often represents a person you know, whom you are wondering if you can trust. If the cabbage is healthy then the person is trustworthy but if it is rotten the person may not be reliable.

A lot of cabbages in a field is a sign of coming wealth.

See also **food**

Cabin

To be safe in a ship's cabin on a calm sea is a sign that money worries or legal matters will be resolved in your favour.

To be in a cabin on a stormy sea says you may be clinging emotionally to a person for the wrong reasons.

See also **boats**

Cable

A strong cable that holds something securely is a reassurance that your life is secure.

If the cable is very thin and weak you should take care that you are not putting too much faith in a person or situation that appears to be trustworthy but really is not.

A breaking cable says that you may need to support someone close if they are let down in the near future.

Cactus

A cactus in a dream can suggest you need more space in your personal and emotional life. It can also represent an irritating or irritable colleague at work who keeps invading your space.

If you hurt yourself on a cactus, you may need to step back from a potential quarrel between two people you know well, probably at work.

See also **plants**

Café

Relaxing in a café means that you will have the chance to relax more in the near future or may receive an unexpected invitation to a social event. This dream is telling you to make more time for your friends.

Cage

Caging a fierce animal says that if you are brave enough you can overcome any opposition or anyone who is bullying you.

A bird or small animal in a cage can be a reflection of your own feelings of being trapped by a particular situation or person.

Cake

Eating cakes is a sign of prosperity, fertility and a happy family life.

Baking cakes (unlike bread) says you will have unexpected visitors or an invitation to a party in the near future.

A wedding cake suggests that if you are not married you will be soon or, if you are already married, that someone close to you will soon wed.

See also **flour, food** *or* **icing**

Calculator

If you see someone you know using a calculator, they may have a calculating, colder side you may not have realised.

Using a calculator yourself means you will be successful in a business or money venture as long as you check your calculations and make sure the idea will work beforehand.

Calendar

A calendar on a wall with lots of marks on it says you need to work out what your priorities are which may mean starting to say no to people who always ask you for help.

An empty calendar says you are waiting for something to happen and should do something about it in everyday life to hasten the event.

An old calendar from years ago means that you need to leave some part of the past behind that still troubles you.

See also **forgetting**

Calling

If you hear someone calling to you in a dream but you cannot see them, it is your subconscious telling you that you need to listen to your own inner voice, rather than what others are saying to you.

Camel

One camel suggests that you need to conserve your money and also your energy.

A number of camels are an indication of improved finances, maybe through an unexpected windfall or small legacy.

See also **animals**

Camping

A happy camping trip says that work may be stopping you from having fun.

A bad camping holiday shows you want more from your life than what is on offer.

See also **holiday** *or* **tent**

Cancer

This is not a warning that the dreamer has or will develop cancer but an indication that there is unresolved bitterness, resentment or an obsession that is taking over your life. It should be noted that fears about the health of oneself or someone close usually surface at a time of personal insecurity.

See also **disease** *or* **illness**

Candles

If you are lighting a candle, this is a good symbol of light coming into your life and signifies a solution to a long-standing problem.

Birthday candles herald a pregnancy or celebration such as an engagement in the family.

A candle that keeps going out, is too dim to shed light or in a frightening setting, can refer to a fear of being shut out of a close friendship or relationship. It can sometimes be a warning that you are getting over-tired.

See also **illumination** *or* **wax**

Candy

See **sweets**

Cannibalism

This indicates a fear of being eaten up, whether by the demands of others or by negative feelings such as jealousy or resentment. The dream usually helps to relieve those feelings.

See also **dismemberment**

Canoe

Paddling a canoe along a river or lake shows that you are very self-sufficient and do not need the approval of others.

If the canoe tips over, you may have to suffer jealousy from a relation, colleague or neighbour.

Cap

Wearing a cap like a baseball cap signifies that any work you have finished recently will be greatly admired and this should ease pressure on you.

A cap pulled over your eyes says that you are afraid to slow down and have fun.

A cap over someone else's eyes says that they are quite uptight and may be hiding resentment regarding your popularity.

Captivity

This is a sign that you are being unfairly restricted with regards to a particular matter. Generally, captivity indicates that you need to spread your wings, either by looking for a new job or house or by going on holiday for a while.

See also **cell, chain** *or* **prison**

Car

A car represents ourselves as we go about the world in our daily lives. The type of car and the way it is being driven can indicate a variety of issues. For instance, if you are the one driving this is an indication that you are in control of your life. If you are in a fast car you secretly desire to have more excitement in your life while a family car means that family life is important to you and that you possibly want to have children. An expensive luxury car says that you are ambitious while a broken down car reflects your fears that things will go wrong in your life or in the life of whoever is sitting in the car with you.

See also **indicators, overturn, parking, parking ticket, race (motor), travel** *or* **vehicle**

Car park

This is a dream about safety. If you lose your car or park in a dark frightening place, the dream can reflect your general concerns about safety when you travel. Maybe you need to revise or update your precautions to remove what may be a real anxiety.

See also **parking**

Cards

Playing cards says that you need to take a chance in your life.

If you are gambling for money it indicates your need to take a business risk.

If you are winning at cards it means the risk should pay off very soon. Only if you are losing is it a warning you should be careful with your money.

See also **gambling** *or* **tarot**

Carnival

This symbolises the coming of happiness, celebrations and parties into your life. It can sometimes be a sign that you will become more involved in your local community and can be a prediction that your family will win a prize.

See also **event, party** *or* **procession**

Carriage, horse and

Being driven in an old-fashioned horse and carriage may be a past-life dream.

If you are wealthy and sitting in a very ornate carriage it is a warning that you must not lose touch with old friends while a broken or old carriage says you should not let anyone discourage you, especially regarding travel plans or work related issues.

See also **travel**

Carriage, train

Watching the scenery as it goes by indicates that you will soon go on a journey or holiday, although not necessarily by train.

If you cannot open the door of a carriage to get out, it means that events in your life are going too fast for you.

Being threatened by a stranger in a railway carriage says that you may not be happy about plans you have made for the future or about a particular friend.

See also **travel**

Carrot

Cooked or raw carrots are a sign of good or improving health.

A mouldy or dry-tasting carrot says that you should look hard at the small print of offers, as they may not be to your advantage.

See also **food** *or* **vegetables**

Cart

If a horse is pulling the cart it means that you can expect people to be unusually co-operative and helpful in the days ahead, so push ahead with projects.

An empty cart warns that you are giving too much to others emotionally, practically or financially.

A cart with a broken wheel or axle says you may experience temporary delays with regards to plans.

Casino

This represents a need to experience excitement and unpredictability. If you have taken a risk in real-life and win in the dream casino, it is a good omen for a successful outcome.

See also **gambling** *or* **roulette**

Castle

If you own the castle, then your financial position and career are safe or will become more secure in the future.

If you are a child, guest or servant of the owner of a castle, you will meet (or already know) a powerful person who will be able to offer you help and protection in the future.

A ruined castle symbolises a longing for the security you may have had in the past.

A castle under siege reflects that you feel others are trying to invade your privacy.

See also **crown, fortress, keep** *or* **royalty**

Castration

This is a male anxiety dream that can occur when a man feels threatened by a powerful woman. Problems with a possessive mother can also be expressed like this, especially if the man is about to leave home or get married.

Cats

This is a very ancient symbol of psychic power and magic which indicates that you should trust your instincts regarding people and situations. The image may also indicate a spiritual awakening.

A hissing or scratching cat can represent fears of hidden spite and gossip among people at work or jealous family members.

See also **animals**

Cave

This is a very old universal symbol of the womb that represents future conception, pregnancy and the birth of both ideas and children.

If someone you know was emerging from the cave, it may be that you are worried about them moving away from you.

Being trapped in a cave suggests you are being stifled from emotional pressure, possibly from an over-protective mother.

See also **echo** *or* **grotto**

Celebrities

You want recognition for what you do, whether from your family or boss at work. It can also mean that you have a talent you could develop that would bring you money and success.

If you are talking to or spending time with an idol it means you should not be afraid to develop your own ambitions.

If are mobbed by fans in a dream, it is an indication you may enjoy future recognition and success if you do not hold back from trying to fulfil your ambitions.

See also **fame**

Cell

Being imprisoned in a prison cell shows that you would like to escape from the pressures of your life or from a person who is trying to bully or manipulate you.

If it is the cell or quiet room of a monk or nun you would benefit from peace and quiet for a while and possibly advice from a wise outsider.

See also **captivity**

Cellar

A dark and frightening cellar of a house represents your hidden fears . You might learn what these buried fears are from the objects or even people (or ghosts) you see in the cellar.

Cello

If you are playing well, it means that you are in tune with your intuition and can trust your judgement.

If someone is playing badly, you should be wary of a troublemaker who acts as though they are your friend.

See also **music** *or* **musical instruments**

Cemetery

A cemetery has more to do with memories than death/dying. If you dream of a well-cared-for cemetery it is therefore a sign that you have happy memories of a person whom you believe has gone out of your life forever, but who may return.

A neglected cemetery says you should write to old friends or contact them as they are missing you.

See also **bereavement, burial, coffin** *or* **funeral**

Cereal breakfast

Enjoying breakfast cereal in a dream is a promise of a trouble-free day ahead.

To spill cereal says that you will have to check the details and times of, for example, a planned journey, in order to avoid delays or minor mishaps.

See also **food**

Chain

Golden chains can indicate a happy marriage or links with others that will bring happiness or an advantage in business.

If you are trying to break free from chains you may have outgrown a relationship or situation.

See also **captivity** *or* **jewellery**

Chair

A comfortable chair says you need to take time to relax and rest and maybe see friends.

Being offered a chair says you should take any offers of advice that are given to you.

A chair that breaks when you sit on it says that an offer you may receive is not necessarily reliable.

Chariot

Riding along in a Roman or other old-fashioned chariot in a victory parade can be indicative of a past-life dream. It can also be a sign that you have every reason to feel confident about the future.

Riding in a chariot in battle says that you should not worry about the spite or gossip of others as you have many people who respect you and will defend you.

Chase

If you are being chased by a person he or she usually represents a problem which you are trying to move away from.

If you are chasing someone else, you may have been trying too hard to succeed on their terms. To stop this you need to realise that you don't need their approval.

Being chased by an animal or group of animals says that you are trying to ignore your own strong feelings, maybe with regards to love.

Cheating

If someone else is cheating on you, whether in love, money or business in a dream, you should examine your fears in the light of day and if they still seem valid you should maybe investigate.

Cheating in an examination means you feel uncertain of your own abilities and powers of persuasion. To be caught cheating in a dream means you are feeling insecure and are worried that others would not like you if they knew what you were really like.

See also **infidelity**

Cheese

Although said to cause nightmares, eating cheese in a dream means that your domestic life is or will become very settled and that people in your family will get on much better than in the past.

See also **food**

Cherries

Cherries symbolise love and sexuality and indicate a blossoming relationship or one that you should encourage. It is generally a good sign if you want a baby.

See also **food** *or* **fruit**

Chess

Are you winning the game? If so, it is a good sign that you will negotiate a tricky situation or win a war of words.

If you are losing or are checkmated, you should beware of a person who will try to manipulate you while seeming to be your friend.

See also **games**

Children

If you are a child in the dream you may want to shed some of your current burdens in real life or express your real self.

If you are caring for children and do not want to, someone in your real life is being childish and demanding too much of your attention.

If you want to have a child, and dream of children, you may become a parent before too long.

If you lose a child, whether your own or an unknown child, you may be anxious that you have taken on responsibilities you cannot handle properly.

See also **boy, family, girl, grandchildren, infant, nursery (infant)** *or* **young**

Chimney

If the chimney is smoking, it is symbolic of your desire for home comforts or a friendly welcome by family.

If you can see smoke going upwards straight ahead, prosperity and good luck will come to your home.

A chimney without smoke can indicate that there is a family quarrel or domestic issue that needs sorting.

See also **house** *or* **smoke**

Chips, potato

See **crisps**

Chocolate

This is a pure wish-fulfilment dream which symbolises pleasure with regards to food, drink and sex. This is an excellent indication that you are in tune with your feelings. Chocolate can also indicate that special treats, exciting sex or maybe even a touch of luxury, will come your way soon.

See also **food** *or* **sweets**

Church

A church denotes forthcoming marriages or births in the family and increasing good fortune.

To be alone inside a quiet church says you would benefit from some quiet to gather your thoughts before making a decision.

A church vault represents the importance of tradition. It can foretell a christening or wedding in the family or that someone in the family will begin to study religion or history.

See also **altar, bells, cross (religious icon), gargoyle, mass, priest** *or* **vicar**

Cigarettes

See **smoking**

Circle

Circles are a wonderful symbol of love, happiness and success. If two circles are joined like chains this is an indication of marriage or a union of love.

A broken circle is not a bad omen but says that new people are coming into your family or social circle. If you are divorced it can be indicative of remarriage.

Circus

If you are enjoying watching a circus performance it means you are in harmony with those around you and reflects that this may be a good time for family matters and reunions, maybe with someone from your childhood.

If you are performing in the circus, it might be a sign that you need a more fulfilling job where you can show off your talents.

If an animal escapes or you are unhappy about the animals being used (which may be something you feel strongly about in everyday life) you may lose your temper or need to set others right. It can also indicate a love interest outside of marriage.

See also **clown** *or* **juggler**

City

This symbolises new opportunities coming your way, possibly in the form of a new house or career change. The image of a city symbolises that joint ventures are favoured.

To be lost in a city can mean that you are feeling worried about going to a big event or about being ignored by an official organisation you are trying to deal with.

Classroom

Being in a classroom as a pupil signifies that you will soon have the chance to learn a new skill or will succeed in any tests or interviews that may be coming up.

If you are having a bad time, then you should not let other people try to make you feel stupid in order to boost their own ego.

See also **academic lessons, desk, examination, exclusion, school** *or* **X**

Clock

If you hear a clock chiming it means that the time is coming when you will be able to fulfil an important need or wish.

A stopped clock says that there may be minor delays to your plans.

See also **pendulum**

Clothes

Buying new clothes implies a desire to change your image.

Wearing the wrong type of clothes to a party or for work can mean that you are afraid of disapproval.

Torn clothes indicate that petty spite or gossip is worrying you more than you perhaps care to acknowledge.

See also **costume, dressing, elegant, iron (clothes), tailor, underwear** *or* **washing**

Clouds

White fluffy clouds means that doubts or obstacles you have been experiencing should clear soon.

Storm or fast-moving clouds say that a confrontation or change you have been dreading will actually clear the air and improve the atmosphere at home or work.

See also **sky**

Clown

Someone close to you may be hiding unhappiness behind a smiling exterior. A clown can also be a warning not to take risks or act foolishly in an attempt to please other people.

See also **circus, fool** *or* **jester**

Coconut

Coconuts are symbolic of fertility and prosperity. Picking or eating coconuts indicates an opportunity to make money or, if you want a child, to get pregnant.

See also **food** *or* **fruit**

Cocoon

A butterfly emerging from a cocoon brings with it the promise of a new beginning and the renewal of hope.

If you are wrapped in a cocoon (maybe under blankets or a duvet) and feel snug and warm, you need to think about how to tackle a problem or situation you are ignoring.

Coffee

Drinking coffee often foretells a house move or holiday that will bring you happiness.

Coffee beans mean you should watch your finances while coffee grounds or instant coffee indicate good luck and increased money.

See also **drinking**

Coffin

Like other death symbols a coffin is not a premonition that someone is going to die. The symbol of a coffin is actually a positive sign of laying aside old quarrels, either with the person in the coffin or, if it is your own coffin, the need to put the past behind you in order to let old resentments or guilt go. Coffins can also mean a return to health for you or a family member.

See also **bereavement, burial, cemetery, death, funeral** *or* **undertaker**

Collar

A collar that is too tight means that someone is stopping you from saying what you want or is trying to stifle your ideas.

Colours

Bright colours in a dream mean that there is happiness coming your way whereas dark dull colours can indicate that you are feeling depressed or drained of energy and need to spend more time enjoying yourself and avoiding difficult people.

See also under individual colours

Column of numbers

These represent the need for organisation or the use of logic in your life.

See also **numbers**

Column of people

Marching in columns or rows says it would benefit you to go along with official policies or the majority view, even if your ideas are different.

Column of stone

A tall column promises success in return for your efforts. It is also a symbol of male sexuality.

Comet

If a sudden and unexpected opportunity to shine comes your way, it should be seized as it may be short-lived.

See also **space**

Composer

Some people actually hear new tunes in dreams and if they can reproduce them in the morning, can play or even sell them. To dream of composing music says you have many creative talents you could develop successfully.

See also **music**

Compost

See **manure**

Computer

Using a computer, whether or not you actually own one, says that any form of communication you have received recently should be kept carefully in order to resolve a possible future dispute.

A working computer means that you should be logical in order to make any decisions.

A crashed or broken computer says that if a particular person is being unhelpful or unresponsive you should bypass them.

See also **e-mail, novel, office** *or* **web (internet)**

Con-man

You know deep down that someone who has made you a good offer or promised you a great deal is not going to fulfil their promises.

Contamination

You may fear that a family member or partner is being badly influenced or ill-advised by someone outside of the family.

Contamination also indicates a fear that events beyond your control may prevent you from doing something, for example going on holiday. This is actually quite a common anxiety dream.

Continent

Travelling to another continent denotes either a chance to expand your business or an excursion overseas. It can also signify that someone living abroad may contact you, possibly with a good idea or with an offer of help.

See also **foreign** *or* **travel**

Cooking

To enjoy the experience of cooking is a very positive sign with regards to fertility, happy families and permanent love. However, if the kitchen is a mess and everything is burning, it means that someone is interfering in your domestic life and should be told to leave you alone.

Corn

Eating or cooking sweetcorn signifies a new or restored friendship and a small amount of money coming your way.

Popcorn is a fun symbol that means you need to take a day off and act as childlike as possible (within reason!)

If a person you know is eating popcorn, this is a warning that you should not take their promises too seriously.

Corn, field of

This is a very old symbol of future prosperity and fertility. It can sometimes be a sign of pregnancy, prosperous investments or success at work.

Corner

If you cannot see round a corner, it means you are afraid for the long-term future of a project or relationship.

If someone is hiding round a corner, check the details of any plans you have recently made for hidden costs or problems.

Costume

Dressing up in a fancy dress costume means you are worried about someone finding out about a personal secret or weakness. To dream of someone you recognise in fancy dress costume can suggest you have doubts about their actions or intentions.

See also **clothes** *or* **tailor**

Counting

To be counting money is a sign that you need to take time to consider all the options and factors before making a decision or a major purchase. You need to watch out for money draining away on small expenses.

See also **debt** *or* **money**

Countryside

A day in the countryside can be a compensatory dream to make you feel better if you have been feeling stressed. If the countryside is in decay, it means you are worried about someone spoiling a special event or relationship.

Court of law

This indicates a fear about dealings with officialdom, such as the tax office. There is an unconscious need to speak out without losing your temper about unfair treatment from people at work or at home.

See also **divorce court, judge, jury, lawyer** *or* **oath**

Court of royalty

If you are made to feel welcome in a court, this shows that a meeting with your boss or older relations will go well.

If you are being excluded from court this can mean that someone else is being unfairly favoured in your family or at work.

See also **royalty**

Cow

A cow indicates a period of peace in your life and a gradual increase in prosperity.

An unfriendly herd of cows indicates that a family member is trying to bully you into agreeing to a plan you do not like.

See also **animals, dairy** *or* **milk**

Crab

A crab coming out from under a rock means that any illness or problems you or someone close to you have been experiencing are coming to an end.

A crab scuttling under rocks says that you or someone close is finding it hard to express love, perhaps because of a past betrayal.

See also **animals**

Cream

This is a dream that promises good or improved health or pleasure in your family life or with a lover. Sour cream however, says that someone is jealous of your domestic happiness.

See also **food**

Creeping

If you are creeping along a floor, you may be trying to avoid an argument where you know the other person will be very angry although you are in the right.

If you hear someone creeping up towards you, this is a sign that you are worried about being caught unprepared.

Cremation

This is never a sign of impending death/dying. It actually represents an inner desire to clear up misunderstandings and start anew in a relationship. If this is not possible, you should draw a line under the past and move on.

If you are the person being cremated, it means that you want to change your image but are afraid to do it. Go for it!

See also **ashes, bereavement, funeral** *or* **undertaker**

Crescent moon

See **moon**

Criminal

To be threatened by a criminal means you are worried about a money or property venture.

If you are the criminal you may need to take an unconventional approach to a problem and maybe take a risk.

See also **prison, thieves** *or* **violence**

Crisps

Eating crisps in a dream is a good sign that new friends or seeing old ones will bring you great pleasure and fun.

If you are cleaning up spilled potato chips, other people are having fun while you seem to be taking all the responsibility.

See also **food**

Crocodile

Being threatened or attacked by crocodiles represents a primitive fear of being affected emotionally by others.

The crocodile is also a negative phallic symbol so you may be angry with a lover or not enjoying sex.

See also **alligator**

Cross (religious icon)

This symbol means that you are protected and you should not fear danger. Sometimes the icon of a cross can also be a hint that you should give up a bad habit that is bad for your health and well-being.

See also **church**

Crossed out

If something is crossed out in a dream it suggests possible delays and obstacles. It can also be indicative that you are having secret doubts about a venture or relationship.

See also **dates**

Crossroads

This marks a turning point in your life involving choice. If the signs are clear, you should make a fast decision. If however, the sign is broken or there is no signpost present, you should wait until you are more certain and look for guidance. The actual places marked may be of deep significance.

Crow

This is a warning so check your facts and figures about a new venture before acting. It can also mean that money you have forgotten about may suddenly reappear.

See also **animals**

Cruel

If someone is being cruel to you, there may be something about them that secretly worries you. If you do not know the people, you may be worried that a family member is being bullied or that your home is not secure.

See also **bully**

Cruise

Enjoying a cruise is a sign you need relaxation and a holiday.

If you feel unhappy on a cruise you may be worried regarding plans to spend a long time with relations, especially in-laws or prospective in-laws.

See also **boats** *or* **travel**

Crutches

If you are on crutches you may be worried about depending on someone else too much.

If you dream of someone else using crutches, you are taking too much responsibility for their happiness.

See also **injury**

Crowds

This is a sign that you are feeling lost and easily influenced by other people. Holiday or fair crowds suggest you would benefit from some superficial fun.

Crown

Being given a crown promises major success or financial improvement within a year.

If you dream of someone else being crowned it means that you may be asked to prove your loyalty to a friend or to your work.

See also **castle** *or* **royalty**

Crying

This may reflect a disappointment or sorrow that you need to express. If you are comforted then the dream says you need to talk through your fears.

If a friend or family member is crying, you may need to ask tactfully if they are unhappy in real life and then offer support as the dream may be a telepathic signal of hidden distress.

Crystal ball

If someone is telling your fortune it is a sign that you feel that other people are influencing what should be a personal decision.

If you are the person reading the crystal ball, you should try and make a note of what you see as the images may be important. You should trust your intuition the day following the dream.

See also **fortune teller**

Cup

This is a very old symbol for sexual commitment and bliss. It can also reveal hidden desires and emotions in love.

Curtains

Drawn curtains are a sign of domestic happiness and promises increased togetherness, maybe in the form of setting up home with a lover. Looking in through a curtained window says that you need emotional commitment from a relationship.

D

Dagger

This is a symbol of power that indicates your wishes will be granted. If you are threatened or stabbed with a dagger, beware of treachery or malice from someone who is over-friendly towards you.

See also **knife**

Dairy

If you see cows being milked or you are making cheese or butter, it means you need to challenge people who are taking advantage of your good nature.

If you are in charge of a dairy or own one, you should expect to receive a regular increase in money.

See also **cow**

Dam

A dam filled with water means you should try to save money.

A burst dam means you are bursting with resentment at keeping quiet regarding a matter that angers you.

Damage

If someone gives or sells you a damaged item it is a sign that you may be feeling resentful towards someone who is not giving you their full attention or devotion.

If you damage property it means that something or someone is stopping you from making changes in your real life.

See also **destroy**

Damp

Feeling damp or being out in damp weather indicates that someone is draining you of energy or is being unenthusiastic about an idea of yours.

Damsons

See **fruit**

Dancing

This is symbolic of happiness in love, romance, a coming celebration or gift.

If you are left without a partner, you may be feeling suspicious with regards to the attention a real-life partner may be showing someone else.

See also **nightclub**

Danger

Try to remember what happened when you felt the danger as, for example, a car crash might mean you should check your tyres. If you manage to escape from danger it means that your worries about a problem in your waking life are unfounded.

Darkness

If you are happy about being in the dark, you should withdraw from a difficult situation.

If you are fearful of the dark you should share your worries with someone close to you as that will help them to disappear.

To move from darkness into light means that you will be given an unexpected opportunity to show off your talents.

See also **black** *or* **blindness**

Dates (on a calendar)

To dream of a particular date in the future means that something significant may happen to you when the date occurs in your waking life.

A crossed-out date in the future says that anything planned for that day may be cancelled or postponed.

See also **crossed out** *or* **diary**

Dates (fruit)

This is often a sign of love, sexual satisfaction, pregnancy or a welcome birth for you or someone in your family. Dates are also a symbol of prosperity, especially concerning invested money.

See also **food** *or* **fruit**

Dawn

This is always a positive sign that the following day should be better than the day before. It is generally a promise of new beginnings, whether in love, career or hope.

See also **sky**

Death/dying

This is actually a positive omen which indicates a new beginning, whether it be recovery from an illness or a fresh new episode in life. It is usually a sign of good fortune after a period of negativity.

Sometimes, to dream of death/dying indicates that a relationship or job has come to a natural conclusion and you need to move on.

See also **beheading, bereavement, burial, coffin, execution, funeral, killing, mourning, obituary, skeleton, suffocation, suicide** *or* **widowed**

Debt

Paying off your debts indicates recovery from an illness or crisis.

If you dream of getting into debt, this can reflect actual money worries, anxiety or unnecessary guilt about others.

See also **counting** *or* **money**

Decay

Decaying buildings suggest the dreamer is clinging to the past while decaying fruit or vegetables promise an improvement in health or finances.

See also **teeth**

Decorating

Painting a house or room says that there are changes you would like to make with regards to your home or family life.

See also **home** *or* **house**

Decorations

Christmas or festival decorations herald a coming celebration regarding good news or the return of a family member.

Deep

Deep water or a deep ravine that you are forced to enter is a sign of fear with regards to a commitment, either in love or sexually. If you manage to swim through the water or cross the ravine, this means that your fears are groundless.

See also **descent, diving, lagoon, lake, river** *or* **sea**

Deer

To have a deer come close to you is a sign of family reconciliation or the making of peace with a friend.

To see deer running away is a warning that you will need to be very tactful when dealing with an oversensitive family member or colleague.

See also **animals, elk, fawn, stag, venison** *or* **wild beasts**

Delays

Transport delays, especially during an important journey or just before a holiday, are simply anxiety dreams about the incompetence of others who hold you back from achieving your targets.

See also **detour** *or* **travel**

Demons

To see lots of little black demons is symbolic of your own irritation with a person or situation you are having to keep secret at the cost of your own well-being and stress levels. Seeing demons is sometimes a warning of over-indulgence.

See also **devil** *or* **incubus (male sexual demon)**

Den

An animal den can represent your hidden feelings, especially sexual ones. If you have made yourself a den or refuge at home, it can be a sign that you need to withdraw from the demands of others.

Dentist

This denotes a fear of being hurt or left helpless by official changes or decisions. It can also be a sign of reluctance to deal with official, legal or tax demands.

Depression

Being depressed in a dream means that you may not be as happy about a present offer or relationship as you think, but it can indicate that new love or opportunities for happiness are coming your way.

Deputy

Depending on how you feel about a new deputy, whether it be disappointment at being passed over for the promotion or a feeling of being second best, it can be a sign that it will take time for you to realise your ambitions.

Descent

To feel excitement as you descend in a plane or walk down a mountain indicates you may soon have the opportunity to travel or will be given an opportunity from afar.

If you feel fear while you descend, it indicates that you are worried that feelings of passion or love will not last.

If you are feeling reluctant to descend, it means that you are living beyond your means.

See also **deep**

Desert

This can be indicative of a forthcoming business trip or a journey to see long-distance relatives.

To be caught in a sandstorm or find yourself lost in the desert says that you are not getting the support you need from others and feel isolated as a result.

See also **dunes, oasis, sand** *or* **travel**

Deserted

To find yourself in a deserted place means that you may need to go it alone with certain projects or ideas.

If a lover or your family desert you, you may unconsciously have a fear of infidelity or old family alliances are threatening your happiness.

Deserter

If you desert the armed forces, a big organisation or maybe close family, it could be a sign that people are trying to force you to conform to their ideas.

If you help someone to desert their responsibilities, it is a sign that your commitment to your workplace or family may be tested.

Desk

A school desk says that you are not being taken seriously and feel resentful of this.

A tidy office desk promises that you will get your business or financial affairs under control very soon.

See also **academic lessons, classroom, examination** *or* **school**

Desperation

Putting pressure on yourself to succeed or escape by any means possible is indicative of a frustration or worry that you have not discussed with others.

Destroy

This is a stage further than mere damage. It illustrates that you feel incredibly strongly about a matter or person and are prepared to risk everything for them.

If you feel that someone else is being destructive, it means that you may need to stand up to a person in real life who could be difficult about your future plans.

See also **damage**

Determination

This is an excellent dream and is often a rehearsal for real-life situations and means that you should be able to succeed in whatever venture you choose to undertake.

Detour

Taking a detour to avoid delays or danger is very positive and shows that if you adapt your plans in your waking life you will succeed.

To dream of an endless detour that takes you further and further away from your destination indicates that you must avoid being distracted by others.

See also **delays** *or* **travel**

Devil

Young girls and women sometimes dream of being attacked sexually by the devil. It is nothing sinister, but a sign of awakening sexuality.

To dream of being pursued or trapped by the devil says that you are in denial with regards to your negative, and perfectly justifiable feelings, about a person or situation.

See also **demons, hell** *or* **incubus (male sexual demon)**

Dialling

If you are trying to dial a number on a phone and keep getting it wrong, forgetting it or it is engaged, it is an indication that you are worried that you cannot persuade someone to change their behaviour or listen to your feelings.

See also **engaged, mobile phone** *or* **telephone**

Diamonds

Dreaming of diamonds is a sign that a prospective investment or financial outlay needs closer scrutiny before you decide to go ahead.

See also **gemstones** *or* **jewellery**

Diary

If you dream that your diary is full of appointments it is a sign that your life is becoming too stressful and you are anxious that you will not be able to fulfil all of your commitments.

An empty diary is an anxiety dream centred on a fear that you will not get an invitation or a date that you long for.

See also **dates (on a calendar)**

Dice

You may be worried about the trustworthiness of a person or the reliability of a job offer. If the throw of your dice means you win a game, it means you can take a risk in real life.

Digging

To dig for treasure or gold says you may be expecting too much from someone close to you.

To dig soft soil promises that efforts now will bring rewards in the future but to dig hard soil says some secrets are best left covered up.

See also **earth**

Dinosaur

You or a person close to you may have ideas that are outdated and need to be re-thought.

If you are attacked by a dinosaur, it means that someone's narrow-minded attitudes may be affecting the way you live your life.

Dirty

A dirty house reflects that someone's critical behaviour is worrying you.

If you are covered in dirt you may not be certain about committing yourself sexually in a relationship.

Disappearing

If people disappear in your dream it is an indication you fear a relationship will not last.

If children disappear it is a reflection that you feel overburdened by the welfare of others.

If you disappear, you may be insecure about yourself and have low self-esteem.

Disaster

Major disasters are very rarely a premonition as dreaming of, for example, plane or train crashes, is usually an expression of hidden fears regarding events beyond your control. You may also be afraid of something happening that will spoil your happiness at a future event.

A minor disaster is a sign that you are trying to do too many things at once or trying to please too many people at the expense of your own peace of mind.

See also **accident, bomb** *or* **earthquake**

Discovery

Discoveries in dreams usually mean that your subconscious is trying to alert you to an issue that you have been ignoring or trying to deny.

Disease

You may fear that you or family members are being contaminated by negative people or influences. You may also be feeling unhappy with your life and need to make changes.

See also **cancer, gangrene, illness, invalid, measles** *or* **rabies**

Dish

Being given a dish of food is a prosperity dream while serving people from a dish says that you are giving too much of yourself to others.

To break a dish indicates that you are contemplating a change to your domestic life.

Disinfectant

Disinfecting your home or yourself is a way of trying to eliminate bad influences or critical relations who are invading your personal space or trying to turn someone against you.

Dismemberment

This is a very ancient dream that is associated with shaman or magical leaders of tribes. On no account is this a premonition that you will die or lose limbs, rather it is a sign that a major change in attitude or priorities is taking place inside you.

See also **cannibalism**

Diving

Diving into deep water shows a release of inhibitions.

To dive in order to rescue someone from the water says you may be called upon to support a friend or relation who has not yet admitted they are in trouble.

See also **deep, lagoon, lake** *or* **sea**

Divorce

If you are unhappily married in your waking life, this can be your subconscious telling you it is time to think about leaving. However, divorce usually indicates a role change within a relationship or signifies that a third party, maybe a child, elderly relation or friend, may soon be moving into your home or will have a marked influence in your life.

Divorce court

A disapproving person, usually older, is trying to cause trouble in your relationship or is competing for attention or affection.

See also **court of law** *or* **judge**

Doctor

This is usually a sign of improving health but can sometimes show that you are feeling neglected and vulnerable and want to feel cared for. This is a common dream for carers who give so much of themselves but may not receive similar attention.

See also **hospital, operation** *or* **x-ray**

Documents

Signing documents means that you are ready to make a major change or commitment but want a guarantee.

To lose documents can mean that you are being pressurised into changes about which you are uncertain.

To find documents in a dream can be an indication of where you will find lost or missing documents in real life.

Dog

This is often a symbol that a loyal friend will give you the support you need and is also a sign that you need to learn to trust your instincts.

A dog running towards you indicates a reunion with an old friend.

A ferocious dog can represent a fear of hostility, especially your uncontrolled anger and aggression.

See also **animals** *or* **tail**

Dolls

Dolls are associated with childhood or children so to dream of playing with dolls (even if you do not have children) is a sign that deep down you want a baby.

To dress a doll means that you or someone close to you is being manipulated and feel helpless to stop it.

See also **playing (children)** *or* **toys**

Dolphins

This is a wonderful dream that symbolises healing, which may be taking place either emotionally or physically within you. It can sometimes be a sign that you have healing powers that could be developed.

See also **animals** *or* **wild beasts**

Donkey

A heavily loaded donkey is a warning that you should not take on the burdens of others.

To ride or lead a donkey indicates that you should be patient with a person who is proving to be stubborn.

See also **animals** *or* **wild beasts**

Door

An unfamiliar door is a sign of new opportunities.

If the door is old-fashioned and you manage to open it and walk through, it may lead to a past-life dream.

A familiar but closed door means that you are being made to feel unwelcome by relatives or that people are making it difficult for you to progress at work.

See also **handle, keyhole** *or* **lock (door)**

Double

Seeing double in a dream or having double the money you asked for means that rewards will be greater than expected both financially and in terms of success.

To meet your double shows that someone at work may be taking credit for your efforts or stealing your ideas.

Dove

A single dove indicates that a recent quarrel will soon be mended.

To see a flock of doves is a sign of family happiness and of love with a special person.

See also **animals** *or* **birds**

Dragon

This is a great symbol of your power, future success, healing, psychic abilities and passion. To see a fire-breathing dragon that is destroying all in its path can represent your own repressed desires for major change in your life. It can also be a sign of sexual frustration.

See also **mythical creatures**

Dragonfly

A dragonfly over water or settling on you promises good news from overseas.

A dragonfly in your home indicates that family or friends may outstay their welcome in your home.

See also **animals** *or* **insects**

Drain

Water pouring down a drain can be a warning that others are draining your resources both practically and in terms of energy.

A blocked drain can say that you are repressing feelings that would be better expressed openly. You may also be trying to hold on to a situation or person unwisely.

Drama

To be in a theatrical production or to be involved or witness someone causing a fracas, means that you or the other person being dramatic feels very strongly about an injustice in real life. You may also be repressing feelings of frustration and anger.

See also **theatre**

Drawers

If you are opening a drawer you are being unwisely tempted to reveal a secret.

To close a drawer says that you need to put off a decision for a while.

A drawer that is too full to shut properly represents stress or a minor illness.

Drawing

A beautiful drawing shows that you are in control of your life and that your perspective on an issue is the correct one.

A drawing that goes wrong or does not resemble the subject indicates that you are concentrating too much on detail and not looking at the wider issues.

See also **painting (picture)**

Dreaming

To know you are dreaming enables you to control the dream which can enable you to defeat monsters, rehearse situations and gain power (see page 37). To dream that something good was just a dream may mean you are having doubts about promises that have been made to you.

Dressing

Dressing for a special occasion says you are concerned about making a good impression upon someone new in your life.

If your clothes do not fit or you cannot get dressed properly, it means you are anxious about not fitting in with your family or at work.

See also **clothes**

Drinking

Drinking alcohol alone in a dream means you are eager to learn a new skill.

To drink with someone indicates that you want to become friends or maybe a lover of the person with whom you are drinking.

To drink tea or coffee promises a social gathering and new friends.

Drinking water says you should listen to your inner voice.

See also **alcohol, coffee, drunkenness, keg, liqueur, milk, nightclub, tea, thirsty, vice** *or* **wine**

Dripping

A dripping tap or guttering says that someone, perhaps a child or partner, is trying to wear down your resistance to what you know is a bad idea. You should be very careful if you are thinking about giving into them.

Driving

If you are driving then you are in control of a particular situation and should not let others try to take over or change your mind about a certain issue.

If the brakes fail or a vehicle goes out of control while you are in it, you should be careful about letting others spend your money.

See also **travel**

Drop

Look closely at what you drop in your dream as it may symbolise something or someone you would secretly like to get rid of.

Drowning

Although this is a frightening dream, if you do not actually drown it means that you are ready to make a major commitment or take a financial risk that could pay dividends.

If you do drown, it is either a past-life dream or a sign that you are overwhelmed with responsibilities and commitments and need to reassess your priorities.

A child drowning may represent a growing fear that you cannot protect your own children as they become more independent.

See also **lagoon, lake, river, sea** *or* **water**

Drum

The sound of battle drums is a warning that you should not ignore family resentments as they may result in a quarrel unless they are resolved immediately.

To see drums in procession announcing the coming of someone important means that a new venture should be successful.

Drunkenness

If you enjoyed the sensation of being drunk it could be a sign that you may want to shed your inhibitions and be more sexually adventurous.

If the drunkenness provoked hostility or had destructive results, this can represent a fear of losing control or a desire to say or do something which could have negative consequences.

See also **alcohol** *or* **drinking**

Duck

This signifies domestic happiness and the arrival of a new member of your family, whether through a new relationship, a marriage or a birth.

See also **animals** *or* **birds**

Duel

Fighting a duel with swords or pistols means you are harbouring resentment toward someone close to you that you have not brought into the open for fear of destroying the friendship or relationship.

Duet

Singing a duet is a sign of finding love or, if you already have a partner, of increased and permanent harmony.

See also **music** *or* **singing**

Dumbness

Not being able to speak or to cry out for help in a dream, indicates that someone close to you is ignoring your protests and you feel frustrated that they are not taking you seriously.

Dump

Rubbish on a dump means that people are denying their responsibility for a difficult situation or letting you sort out their problems once too often.

See also **junk**

Dunes

Climbing sand hills and then looking out to sea means you are coming to the end of a difficult phase.

If you keep slipping and falling down the dunes it means that what you want from life seems to keep slipping from your grasp. However, if you keep persevering, you should achieve your goal eventually.

See also **desert** *or* **sand**

Dusk

Dusk says that you are aware that a particular situation or relationship has almost run its natural course but you are reluctant to let go for fear of being alone.

Dust

A room of objects covered with dust means you have been ignoring your own needs and desires for far too long. You may also be feeling guilty about not contacting a particular old friend or relation for a while.

Dwarf

A dwarf, especially a mythical one in a cave or guarding treasure, indicates that you are having problems with someone who is either making you feel small and stupid or who is mean with money or practical help.

See also **gnome**

Dynamite

This usually indicates that any new ideas or suggestions you have will take off.

If an explosion has terrible consequences, it means you are facing a potentially explosive family situation which will not be resolved easily.

See also **bomb**

Eagle

The eagle is thought to be the king of the birds and a symbol of the sun and fathers. To see an eagle flying high means that your ambitions will be realised while a nesting eagle says that an older or overly dominant man is standing in the way of your happiness, success or promotion.

See also **animals** *or* **birds**

Ear

This is a sign that you should listen to advice before making any change to your life. Make sure you avoid gossip, however fascinating, for you could be the next target.

Earrings

This is a sign that you need to listen carefully to what people are saying in order to discover what is beneath the surface meaning.

If the earrings contain jewels it means your opinions will be heard.

To lose an earring means that you will only hear half a story.

See also **gemstones** *or* **jewellery**

Earth

Looking down on the earth from space may be indicative of an out-of-body dream, mind travel or emerging psychic abilities.

To dream of soil says that you prefer to seek a practical solution to difficulties rather than hoping for a miracle.

See also **digging, land** *or* **mud**

Earthquake

This is often an indication of insecurity in a relationship or work situation based on warning signs you may have missed on a conscious level.

Collapsing buildings can indicate that there may be a financial problem you will need to face.

If you escape from an earthquake, you will be offered changes that will improve your lifestyle.

See also **disaster**

East

If you are due to travel eastwards and dream of seeing the sun rising in the east, it is a sign of new beginnings.

An east wind means you need to face the reality of a situation or unpleasant facts.

Easter

Buying chocolate rabbits or eggs to celebrate Easter is a sign that a plan or new relationship will be successful.

See also **egg**

Eating

To enjoy eating means you are relaxed about your body and sexuality.

To feel guilty about eating means that you are suppressing your real feelings or denying yourself something.

Ebb

If the tide is going out it is a sign that you need to let go of an unrealistic idea or unsatisfactory relationship.

To dream of a ship going out on the ebb tide means you could do with a holiday to temporarily escape problems in your life.

See also **boats** *or* **sea**

Eccentric

If you or someone else is acting or dressing oddly in a dream, it is a sign that you want to be unconventional and take a risk, even if others are advising you against doing so. It can also be our subconscious telling us that the least likely course of action, or seemingly less attractive option, will prove to be the best one.

See also **freak** *or* **unusual**

Echo

If you are in a place filled with echoes, you may be feeling that no-one is really listening or taking notice of you.

If people are echoing your words, someone in your waking life might be stealing your ideas or taking the credit for your work.

See also **cave**

Eclipse

This is symbolic of your personality or talents being overshadowed or belittled by others.

See also **moon** *or* **sun**

Editor

If a person is editing and correcting what you have written, you may need to tackle someone who is reporting what you say in an exaggerated fashion that may cause you trouble.

Eel

A wriggling eel indicates someone in your life who is trying to get out of a promise they have made to you.

If you have caught an eel on a fishing hook, beware of an unreliable person who has just entered your life.

See also **animals**

Efficiency

If you dream of being very efficient and organised it is a sign that you could soon be offered a promotion. It can also indicate that an important event you have been organising will be a great success.

Effort

If your efforts are appreciated in a dream, you will succeed in a matter that has been worrying you.

If you are unappreciated in the dream, it means you are wasting your time making an effort with the person or people you are dreaming about.

Egg

This is an excellent symbol of fertility which is good if you want to get pregnant or are about to launch a new business or creative venture.

See also **Easter**

Elderly

To become or already be old in a dream is actually a positive omen indicating that you will have a long and happy life.

Dreaming of old people, whether or not you know them, is a sign that you should let the past go and move on.

Election

If you are voting in an election it is indicative that you need to talk about a worry regarding a friend or family member, even though it may not directly concern you.

To dream of winning an election says that you are more popular than you think.

See also **government** *or* **politician**

Electricity

If you dream about electricity lines or pylons, it is symbolic that you will require help from other people to succeed.

A power cut is an indication that a source of income may be temporarily cut off.

Electric shock

This is usually a sign of an unexpected but advantageous change in direction after a sudden setback.

Sometimes this can be your subconscious warning you to check the wiring or the safety of a particularly troublesome appliance.

Elegant

If you are dressed smartly, you may soon get invited to an unexpected special party or social event.

If everyone around you is dressed elegantly and you haven't made a similar effort, it is a sign that someone close to you is trying to undermine your confidence.

See also **clothes**

Elephant

This indicates a wise person will enter your life who will be able to give you support in fulfilling an ambition.

If the elephant is frightening, you may have a huge and very daunting task ahead of you and need to tackle it bit by bit.

See also **animals, ivory** *or* **wild beasts**

Elevator

See **lift**

Elk

If the elk is friendly it means that you will have help to bring a plan into action.

A charging elk indicates that someone is ignoring your feelings and pressing ahead anyway with an issue you disagree with.

See also **deer**

Elusive

If someone is avoiding you or you have lost contact with somebody, it means that you have hidden doubts regarding a relationship or promise that has been made to you.

Elves

Elves that are surrounded by light or wearing light-coloured clothes are traditionally a very magical sight and a promise of excitement and new experiences coming into your life. They can also indicate that small children will bring you joy.

Elves in dark clothing are traditionally labourers that gather treasures. It is therefore usually a sign that you may have a small windfall or bonus related to your hard work in the past or from forgotten investments.

See also **mythical creatures**

E-mail

This is a sign that you are feeling overwhelmed at work. If you receive an e-mail you have been waiting for in real life, you may receive it the following day as you could have been psychically linked to the sender while asleep.

See also **computer** *or* **office**

Emeralds

To dream of emeralds means that love will find you.

A broken or tarnished emerald is a sign that you need to put a stop to someone who is abusing you emotionally.

See also **gemstones** *or* **jewellery**

Emptiness

If you dream of empty cupboards or of an empty bank account, you have been allowing people to drain you financially or emotionally.

An empty room or place suggests that it may be time to seek new friends and places to fill gaps left by a recent loss in your life.

Emu

Emus are usually a sign of imminent foreign travel. They can also indicate unexpected visitors or new acquaintances from abroad, especially from the southern hemisphere.

See also **animals** *or* **wild beasts**

End

To come across a dead end is a sign that a relationship or job is going nowhere and that your efforts would be put to better use somewhere else.

Ending

If your dream has a happy ending, you don't need to worry about the person or matter you dreamed about beforehand.

If your dream ends on a sad note or you wake before it has concluded properly, you may need to focus on your own happiness for a while rather than others.

Engaged

If you keep getting the engaged tone when trying to phone someone, your dream is telling you that you may be relying too much on the opinion of the person you are trying to contact.

If you are trying to contact a doctor or the emergency services, you have hidden fears regarding the health of a family member or yourself. There may also be safety issues at home you should double-check.

See also **dialling** *or* **telephone**

Engagement

If you dream of accepting a proposal of marriage you have stronger feelings for a partner in your waking life than you perhaps care to admit. If you do not know the person who proposes, they may come into your life within a month.

See also **marriage**

Engine

If you or someone close to you is trying to fix a broken car engine, it can be a warning that you should check the mechanics of your car before an imminent journey.

To see a train engine means you may soon go on a journey to see friends or relatives who live in a different part of the country.

English lesson

See **academic lessons**

Entrance

This depends on what kind of entrance you or someone else makes in the dream. Generally, an entrance represents your hopes or fears for the future. Therefore, to make a spectacular entrance to a place indicates that your efforts or talents will get recognition.

Envelope

To receive an envelope means that you should receive good news.

If you receive a tax or official looking envelope, this is your subconscious reminding you to respond to any urgent financial or business letters.

See also **letter, mail** *or* **postman**

Eruption

A volcanic eruption indicates that you are worried about the suppressed fury of someone who tries to control you or that your own patience, possibly with that person, is coming to an end.

See also **volcano**

Escalator

To go up an escalator indicates a smooth and more prosperous period in your life.

To go down an escalator means you regret leaving a place or person more than you perhaps realise.

A broken escalator illustrates a problem within a relationship that you need to sort out.

See also **stairs**

Escape

To escape danger is a sign that your worries about the future are unfounded.

If a pet escapes it is a sign that you have too much to do and are worried that you are not taking care of everybody properly. This is a typical female anxiety dream.

Estimate

If an estimate for building work or car maintenance, for example, is too high, you may be feeling that you are putting more into a particular relationship or situation than you are getting out of it.

Ethereal being

A floating being, whether an angel, fairy or nature spirit, is an indication that your subconscious mind is trying to tell you something. It may even be that an actual angel has tried to contact you so you should make the time to be reflective and listen to what they may have to say to you.

See also **angel, fairy, ghost** *or* **spirits**

Evening

Evening time in a dream says you have nearly come to the end of a difficult situation.

To spend a happy evening with friends is a reminder that you should make more time to see them, especially if old or absent friends appear in the dream.

Event

To attend a big gathering means you may soon be invited to an event which will bring you opportunities.

If an event goes wrong, especially if it has been organised by you, it is a sign that you are trying to do too many things at once.

See also **carnival, party** *or* **picnic**

Evergreen

An evergreen tree says that a relationship will be long lasting and happy. This is also a good sign if you are worried about the health of older relations.

Ewe

A female sheep, especially with lambs, means that you are rightfully concerned about your family, especially with regards to any children, and should continue to help them through a worrying time.

See also **animals, lamb** *or* **sheep**

Examination

If the dream referred to a medical examination, you may be worried about your health or your subconscious is reminding you that a check-up is overdue.

If you dream of a school examination, you may be afraid that you know far less than other people at work or in social circles.

See also **classroom, desk, school** *or* **X**

Excitement

If you are excited about going to a place or meeting someone, any future visit to that location or person you dreamed about should prove to be fortunate for you.

Exclusion

If other people are excluding you from a situation or conversation it is a sign that you are feeling isolated through no fault of your own in your waking life.

To dream of a child being excluded from school or friends' outings may mean that you are picking up on a child's unspoken worries about bullying.

See also **classroom** *or* **school**

Excrement

Dreaming about excrement is an indication that money is coming your way.

Execution

If you are the person who is executed it means the time has come to put a stop to a situation that is worrying you greatly.

If you are watching an execution, it signifies that a long-drawn out matter will be resolved.

See also **beheading, death/dying, gallows** *or* **noose**

Exit

If you cannot find an exit to a building you may have become too involved in the worries of others and need to find a way out.

Expensive

If everything in a shop or restaurant is too expensive for you, it could be an indication that you may be worried about taking on a new financial commitment.

If you receive an expensive present, the person who gave it to you should praise you or declare love for you soon.

Explosion

If you caused the explosion it means that you should express your feelings about unfair treatment or others' selfishness towards you.

If you are running away from an explosion, your worries about work or money are building up and you need to seek wise advice.

See also **bomb**

Extra-terrestrial

See **alien** *or* **space**

Eyes

This is a symbol that means you should trust the evidence of your own eyes and not rely on what people tell you. It is often an indication that you should double-check any contracts or official documents carefully.

See also **optician**

F

Face

To see a happy face indicates new friendships and a warm welcome in a new place or situation.

An angry face is symbolic of confrontation. If you recognise the angry person it is a warning that he or she may be hiding negative feelings.

Failure

To experience failure in a dream symbolises your inner fears of not living up to the unrealistic expectations of others. It can also highlight fears of falling ill and of not being able to do tasks. This is usually a sign that you need more rest and relaxation.

Fainting

This is your mind's way of alerting you that you are doing too much and will make yourself ill if you do not slow down and take care of yourself.

If a family member faints, it could be a sign that they have been indiscreet or are in the process of considering an unwise action.

Fair

This is a sign that pleasure will come into your life soon.

If you win a prize at a fair it means you will be lucky in love or will come into money very soon.

To experience an accident or fright on a fairground ride means that other people are taking over your life and you know deep down you need to stop them before you get hurt.

Fairy

This is a very magical dream that says your secret wishes should soon come true. If the fairy conveyed a message to you, heed it as it should help you to solve a long-standing problem.

See also **ethereal being** *or* **mythical creatures**

Fairy story

This is a sign that children will bring you great happiness, whether they are your own or someone else's. This is an excellent dream to have if you want to become pregnant or are expecting a baby as it promises a happy outcome.

Falcon

If you see a falcon in your dream it promises career or business success.

If you use the falcon for hunting you should be careful not to be too over-assertive regarding a work matter.

See also **birds** *or* **wild beasts**

Falling

This is one of the most universal dream symbols and scenarios. At its most positive, falling represents the letting go of inhibitions and of opening the self to new experiences. This is a particularly good dream to have if you are planning to have (or are involved) in a sexual relationship.

If you hit the ground, it signifies fears of losing control. You should examine dreams such as this carefully as they can offer hidden signs of valid, but possibly unacknowledged, worries.

See also page 37 for advice on how to turn falling dreams into floating or flying ones.

Fame

If you dream of talking to famous people then you will enjoy an increase in fortune or recognition.

If you are the famous person in the dream you should definitely push ahead with a venture which you have been holding back as creative, work or personal success is assured.

See also **celebrities**

Family

If you dream of your own family, the dream scene may tell you something which otherwise would have remained hidden.

If you belong to another family it may be a past-life dream or may indicate that new members will be coming into your family.

See also under individual family members, **children, hugging, pregnancy** *or* **relations**

Fan (electric)

This symbolises that it is time to reduce the pressures in your life or to take the heat out of a particular confrontation within the family or between friends that is unlikely to be otherwise resolved.

Fan (traditional)

You should be wary of flattery that may mask malice.

Fat

If you dream that you are very fat but are not worried by this, you should soon have an increase in prosperity.

If you are unhappy in the dream because you are fat, you may be afraid to let go of your inhibitions or act unconventionally because of what other people might say.

Father

Whether or not your father is alive, if the relationship with the father figure is good in the dream, it indicates you need reassurance and advice from a wise father figure.

To dream of a forbidding, stern father or the disapproval of authority figures such as bank managers or taxmen, indicates there are unnecessary restraints on your spontaneity and you need to assert yourself.

See also **family** *or* **parents**

Fawn

A fawn with its mother can reflect a desire for a family or a more settled way of life.

To see a fawn alone, or in danger, expresses fears about your children or your own vulnerability especially about being left alone.

See also **animal, deer** *or* **wild beasts**

Fear

If the fear is unknown, invisible and stalking you, it means that you have hidden doubts or fears about a person or plan.

If you are afraid for yourself or your family about a real-life danger or enemy, the dream is a sign that you are worried about your home and family security and need to tighten this to reassure yourself.

Feast

See **banquet**

Feathers

If the feathers are being worn by someone you recognise from your waking life, it is an indication that you feel they are being inconsistent, unpredictable and possibly cowardly.

See also **birds**

Feet

Feet, whether your own or those of others, represent freedom from restrictions and the opportunity to travel.

Feet that are cold or injured indicate you are worried about being trapped in a situation. If a child has injured feet, it can be symbolic of parental anxieties, for example, about a child going off alone or away from home.

Dirty feet are a sign that you wish to be more spontaneous while infected feet suggest that someone in your life is trampling on your feelings.

See also **shoes**

Fence

If you are outside a fenced off area and trying to get in, it is a sign that you feel you are coming up against many obstacles in your waking life.

If you are within a fenced off area it can indicate that you are concerned about security in your home.

If you see a broken fence, it is a sign that you need to resolve a quarrel.

See also **railings**

Ferry

See **boats**

Fighting

Whether you are fighting a battle or just one person, it means you need to stand up for what you believe in.

If you dream of losing a fight, it shows that you are afraid of a confrontation, although by avoiding the inevitable you are causing yourself more distress.

See also **battle** *or* **war**

Figs

These are symbols of love, sexual satisfaction, pregnancy and a welcome birth for you or someone in the family. They are also a symbol of prosperity, especially concerning money that has been invested.

See also **food** *or* **fruit**

Fine (money)

If you are fined for speeding in your car or get a parking ticket it is a sign that you are possibly taking one too many risks in your life.

See also **parking ticket**

Fine (weather)

Fine weather in a dream signifies calm and happy times ahead. It is a good indication of happiness, if not good weather itself, if you are planning an outing or holiday.

Fire

To light a fire means that you need to take the initiative regarding a job as others will not do it for you.

To witness something being ravaged by fire shows that you have a deep fear that particular thing will be destroyed in your everyday life by the interference or ill intentions of others.

See also **burn** *or* **flames**

First

If you come first, either in a race or competition, you should acknowledge your ambitious side and not stand aside for others.

Fishing

To dream of fish or fishing is a sign that answers are being purposely kept from you and people are skirting around issues that are important to you.

To catch a big fish means that you may win a prize soon.

See also **bait, herrings, salmon, sea, tank (fish)** *or* **worm**

Fist

If you or someone else is waving a fist in a threatening way, it means that you may be afraid of a bully or of your point of view being undermined by a dominant boss or relative.

Flag

This symbolises your need to show courage and to gain support for a new plan.

A ripped flag says you are supporting the wrong side in an argument.

Flames

If you are surrounded by flames, it may be a past-life dream or a fear that a situation or relationship may not work.

See also **burn** *or* **fire**

Flare (distress)

Sending up a distress flare indicates you need to talk through your worries with someone.

If you see a distress flare and go to the rescue, a family member may ask you for help soon.

See also **accident**

Flat

A comfortable and pleasant flat symbolises security.

If the flat is dirty and noisy, it means that your home life is being invaded by outside interference.

See also **home** *or* **property**

Fleas

If there are fleas on you or in your home, it may be symbolic of parasitic people taking advantage of you. There may also be a lot of minor worries in your life that are preventing you from relaxing.

See also **animals** *or* **insects**

Flies

If flies swarm around you or are crawling on food, it means that you may be afraid of petty gossip or jealous people spoiling a relationship. You should try to avoid these people.

See also **insects**

Floating

This is symbolic of overcoming difficulties to find personal harmony. Floating can also indicate an increase in personal power.

If you find yourself floating with a partner it can be a sign of sexual bliss or an out-of-body experience.

Pregnant women frequently experience this as they connect with their unborn child floating in their womb.

If you find yourself floating through total emptiness this can echo a sense of isolation in real life.

Floodlights

Floodlights suggest that there are matters you need to bring out into the open. They also indicate that you are worried someone is not telling you the truth.

Floods

If floods surround and trap you, it means that you are being swamped by other people's emotions or demands. It may also be a sign that you are feeling repressed or helpless.

See also **leak, wading** *or* **water**

Floor

Floors tend to represent the more basic aspects of our life such as food and shelter. If you slip it means you need to take your time completing paperwork to ensure you do not lose important documents due to rushing.

If you are cleaning or mending a floor it means that your money situation will improve or a house move will be financially beneficial.

A dirty or cluttered floor says that you have too many things to sort out in your head and need to go back to basics.

A laminated or polished floor suggests that your path through life will become easier over the next few weeks.

Flour

A jar or bag of flour indicates you have, or will attain, a happy and secure family life. Usually it is an indication of a desire to settle down.

Flour that is mouldy or crawling with insects is symbolic of jealousy in your home life. You should take care not to let it affect your happiness.

See also **bread** *or* **cake**

Flowers

Flowers, especially roses, are the ultimate symbol of love and romance. Therefore, to walk through a garden of flowers, even alone, suggests that if you are not involved in a relationship you will soon find romance.

A bouquet suggests you may have a hidden admirer or will soon receive an unexpected gift from a friend.

Dying flowers is a warning that friends who may seem to be good company are not actually that loyal.

See also individual flowers, **garden, garland, nursery (botanical)** *or* **plants**

Flute

If someone you recognise is playing the flute, it shows that they have touched you deeply and you can trust them with your feelings.

If you are playing the flute it means that you are seeking a deeper relationship with a lover or good friend.

See also **music** *or* **musical instruments**

Flying

This is often associated with sex even though dreams of flying are also a sign of astral or out-of-body experiences and can be very empowering.

If you experience a gentle landing, new opportunities and a growth in passion will be yours.

A difficult landing means that you are fearful a plan will run into difficulties. If you are afraid of flying generally, this is simply an anxiety dream not an omen.

See page 37 for further information on flying dreams
See also **aeroplane** *or* **airport**

Food

If you have plenty of food in a dream you should not need to worry about your future security.

If you don't have enough food, you may be feeling starved of approval or affection from people who should be more supportive towards you.

See also under individual foods, **hungry, meal, obesity, picnic, ripe, rotting, sausages** *or* **sweets**

Fool

If you or someone else is acting foolishly and everyone is laughing, you should have the chance to participate in something fun in the near future. This can also suggest that you should take up an unconventional opportunity, even if others disapprove.

If someone is making you look like a fool in a dream there may be a jealous family member or love rival in real life who is harbouring hidden spite towards you.

See also **clown** *or* **jester**

Foreign

Being on a holiday or living in a foreign country can be a past-life experience or a vision of the future. It is certainly an indication that any travel or holiday undertaken in the near future will be a happy and fulfilling experience.

If you are lost in a foreign land or cannot speak the language it can indicate you are worried about a future change and need to prepare yourself more thoroughly .

See also **continent** *or* **travel**

Forest

Forests represent your natural instincts and can signify that you are about to experience an exciting step into the unknown relying on intuition rather than logic.

If you are lost or pursued in the forest, it is an indication that you are uncertain about a change in your life which would involve following your heart rather than your head.

See also **tree**

Forge

To see or be a blacksmith shoeing a horse in a forge or making metal objects with fire, may be a past-life dream or simply a promise of increased wealth in the near future.

Forgery

If you are sold a forgery or given forged money, it can symbolise a hidden fear that you suspect someone close to you is deceiving you.

If you are responsible for forging money or official papers, it can be a sign that you are keen to leave a certain situation, but are being prevented from doing so, forcing you to seek other means of departure.

Forgetting

If you dream that you have forgotten a meeting, for example, it is a warning of overload in your life and a reminder that you need to double-check all of your commitments and appointments for the coming week.

See also **calendar**

Fork (road)

A fork in the road indicates a choice that you have either already made or are about to make in the immediate future. It is a warning that you should consider all of your options carefully before making a decision, even if it involves choosing between two people.

Fork (utensil)

Not having a fork when you need one or dropping a fork indicates that you have not been told all the facts about a decision that will affect you.

To be stabbed or to stab someone with a fork says that you need to be careful of what you say when speaking to people.

Fortress

What may seem to be an impenetrable institution or authority can be overcome as long as you persevere and collect together as many facts and figures as possible before you try to tackle them.

See also **castle**

Fortune

If you win a fortune it is a wish-fulfilment dream but it could also be an indication that you might have a small win in the near future.

If you lose a fortune it is a warning that you should not take risks, either financially or with a relationship, right now.

See also **gambling, lottery** *or* **money**

Fortune teller

The figure of a fortune teller is actually your unconscious mind or maybe even a special guardian in disguise. Whatever the message the fortune teller conveys (even if it is in symbols) it may help you to see your best future path.

See also **crystal ball, gypsy** *or* **tarot**

Fossil

To find a fossil in a dream is a very lucky sign as it is symbolic of long-term security and happiness.

See also **archaeologist**

Fountain

A fountain is generally symbolic of motherhood and sexual attraction between two people.

If the fountain is flowing, it signifies you will soon be inspired and will find the creative power needed to begin a new project.

If the fountain has dried up, you need to seek a new source of help or find friendship from people with new ideas.

Fox

This is an indication that you need to use subtlety and tact, rather than confrontation, in order to persuade other people to see your point of view. It can also be a warning that you should be wary of fast-talking flatterers who may not be telling you the truth.

See also **animals** *or* **wild beasts**

Freak

If you see a really strange animal or person you should not be frightened as it indicates that you will soon have a really unusual idea or plan that will be of great benefit to you.

See also **eccentric** *or* **unusual**

Friends

To dream of friends indicates that you should be able to enjoy a happy, possibly unplanned, meeting with friends in the near future. It is also a sign that your friends in your everyday life will remain loyal to you in the coming years.

To dream of absent friends means they may contact you within a few days.

To quarrel with friends can reveal a worry regarding a difference of opinion you have not talked through in real life.

See also **absent friends** *or* **hugging**

Frog

This is a wonderful symbol of fertility which is excellent if you wish to become pregnant. To see lots of hopping frogs indicates that money should come your way soon.

See also **animals** *or* **tadpoles**

Frown

If people are frowning at you, you may be worried about the disapproval of critical relations or colleagues regarding changes you wish to make.

Fruit

To dream of eating fruit or bowls of fruit is a sign of fertility and indicates that abundance will enter your life.

Fruit on trees is a promise that long-term plans and investments will be successful.

Rotten fruit can indicate a disappointment that is still bothering you regarding a relationship or project that did not work out.

See also under individual fruits, **ripe, rotting** *or* **worm**

Frustration

To feel frustration in a dream often reflects a general discontent with regards to certain issues in your life or towards someone who is causing you problems.

See also **gag**

Full moon

See **moon**

Funeral

To attend the funeral of someone important to you indicates that a particular stage in your relationship with them is coming to an end. You may also be feeling fearful that they will leave you in real life.

Your own funeral means that it is time for you to move on and leave behind the past or unresolved issues.

See also **burial, cemetery, coffin, cremation, death/dying, grave** *or* **undertaker**

Fuse

Fused lights or appliances can be an indication that you need to check your wiring as your subconscious may have noticed something that could cause a problem in the future. A fuse can also be an indication that you are feeling angry about something but have not expressed your feelings to anyone.

Fuss

If you are making a fuss about a bad service or faulty goods, it may be a symbolic rehearsal in sleep for a real-life complaint you are harbouring, possibly towards someone you know. If a person is saying you are making a fuss unnecessarily, then that person may be using emotional blackmail in real life to keep you quiet.

Gag

If a gag ties your mouth so you can't speak it is a sign that someone is trying to silence your ideas or reasonable objections.

See also **frustration**

Gain

Any gain in a dream, whether it is in the form of money, praise or a promotion, is a sign that your financial or work situation will soon show improvement.

If you gain something illegally, it could mean you are worried that an offer you have been made has hidden drawbacks.

Gale

If you or your home is being blown about by high winds, it means you need to hold firm to your principles or be patient until a temporary crisis passes.

If the gale hurts you or damages your home, it is an indication that you are fighting a hopeless situation and should withdraw or change tactics.

See also **storm** *or* **wind**

Gall bladder/gall stones

If you dream of experiencing intense pain due to gall stones or that your gall bladder is removed, it is a sign that you are swallowing a lot of resentment that you need to express.

See also **illness**

Gallows

Occasionally this is a past-life dream but it can also mean that you are worried about a friend or lover betraying you.

To escape from the gallows denotes an end to restrictions in your life.

See also **execution**

Gambling

Gambling dreams reflect risk-taking. If you win then the risk is worthwhile but if you lose then you are harbouring hidden doubts about something.

See also **cards, casino, fortune, lottery, money** *or* **roulette**

Game

If you are tracking wild animals such as deer, this is a sign that you will succeed at job-hunting or with a business venture if you continue to persevere.

To catch and kill the animal(s) says that you will need to be ruthless and single-minded to get what you want.

If you let the animals go unharmed it is an indication that you do not have the ruthlessness to succeed by force, but can win by persuasion.

See also **wild beasts**

Games

Playing team games says you will need to co-operate with others to get what you want.

To play board games can indicate the desire for a settled period in your home life.

Playing alone, if you are happy doing this, means you need more personal space.

If you are excluded from games, someone may be deliberately making you feel unwanted for their own gain.

See also **chess, playing (children), puzzle** *or* **toys**

Gangrene

To dream of gangrene means that an issue you are avoiding is starting to affect your life and inner peace.

See also **disease**

Gap

If there is a big gap between two people or objects, it means you may need to encourage compromise or act as a peacemaker to help two sides in an argument agree.

A gap between you and a partner can indicate a growing coldness in real life that you need to tackle.

Garbage

See **junk** *or* **litter**

Garden

If the garden is beautiful but wild, your natural fertility of ideas should not be held back by convention or the fear of standing alone.

A well-tended and formal garden suggests you will find fulfilment and harmony within a structured environment or situation.

A barren garden means you need to escape from the negative influences that are holding you back within some areas of your life.

See also **flowers** *or* **tree**

Gardening

If you are digging and planting in a garden, it is a sign that you are in harmony with yourself and the world. A happy, if busy, time ahead of you is promised.

If you are trying to clear weeds from a garden or are digging hard soil, you may be doing more than your fair share of hard work and trying to compensate for the lack of effort shown by other people.

Gargoyle

Hideous stone carvings on a church or cathedral can be an indication of a past-life dream. Gargoyles can represent your hidden fears about the health or safety of yourself or your family. They can also symbolise a guilty secret that you need to share with someone.

See also **church**

Garland

If you are wearing a garland of flowers it means that a happy holiday or a celebration will occur soon.

See also **flowers**

Garlic

To have garlic in your home says that your home life will be happy and that any fears about financial security are unfounded.

If you are eating garlic and are worried your breath smells, you may need to conceal future plans from someone disapproving.

See also **herbs**

Gas

A gas leak means that someone you have entrusted with a secret is gossiping about what you told them.

To cook on gas, especially outdoors, is a promise of happy times and outings with family and friends.

A gas explosion suggests a situation or confrontation you have been avoiding needs to be resolved before matters get out of hand.

See also **leak**

Gate

If you see an open gate it is a sign that you may soon have the opportunity to travel or will get a job offer in another location.

If a gate is closed it means you need to watch your possessions and finances carefully.

Geese

See **goose**

Gemstones

Precious gems indicate flattery and promises that may have ulterior motives. You should be cautious of externally attractive and exciting new friends.

If you find a single precious gem, it says that you will find the solution to a long-standing problem quite unexpectedly.

A single large jewel is a sign that you will be very fortunate throughout your life and that your efforts in a particular situation will be richly rewarded.

See also under individual gemstones **jewellery** *or* **treasure**

Geography lessons

See **academic lessons**

Ghost

If the ghost is somebody you recognise, they may have a message for you or have simply appeared to reassure you that everything will be fine.

If the ghost is frightening, then you may be afraid that an old problem or ex-lover will come back to haunt you.

See also **ethereal being, haunted house** *or* **spirits**

Giant

A giant can represent great power or a huge ambition or undertaking.

A friendly giant can be a sign that you will be offered help from a powerful source to advance your cause or overcome opposition.

A terrifying giant signifies your fear about major issues in your life that are beginning to overwhelm you. It can also be symbolic of hostility from people who seem intimidating.

See how to shrink a dream giant down to size on page 31.

Gift

To receive a gift is a sign of loving happiness from whoever presented it to you.

If you are giving something away, you may be asked to lend or give money to a friend or relative in the near future.

If you are disappointed by a gift or are not given one when you were expecting it, you may be helping others too much without expressing your own need clearly enough.

See also **tape**

Giraffe

A giraffe is a warning that you should not interfere in other people's quarrels or problems as you will only get hurt. It can also mean that someone close to you may be exaggerating the truth.

See also **animals** *or* **wild beasts**

Girl

If a woman dreams of herself as a girl, she needs to renew a past friendship or take up activities that have been cast aside. A girl generally means you should allow your spontaneous vulnerable side to emerge, regardless of whether you are male or female.

See also **children**

Gladiator

This could indicate a past-life dream. It can also mean that if you are prepared to fight a particular bully, he or she will back off.

Glass

If you are enclosed in glass you may feel that no-one is listening to your warnings. If the glass is broken, especially if you break it in the dream, your illusions about someone you care for may be shattered.

See also **window**

Globe

A globe of the world says that communication from overseas will bring you great advantage financially.

Gloves

A pair of gloves is a sign of a betrothal or wedding in the family.

A single glove warns of a petty quarrel with a lover or partner.

If a pair of gloves don't fit, you should not be worried about the opinion of a critical relation.

Gnome

This is an indication that you may receive an unexpected gift from a secret admirer. Gnomes are associated with foot and joint problems.

A malevolent gnome refers to a bad-tempered male relative who may be causing you problems.

If the gnome is one who lives entirely underground it is symbolic of buried hopes and dreams or repressed needs.

See also **dwarf**

Goat

Goats are symbolic of sexual passion and fertility. Nanny goats with kids, are a good omen for mothers or would-be mothers.

A billy goat can indicate an exciting new flirtation for women and a love rival for men.

Goats can indicate that you may need to develop your psychic or spiritual skills and suggest you would do well to seek out wise people who work in the spiritual arts.

See also **animals** *or* **wild beasts**

Goblet
See **cup**

God/goddess
To meet or talk with a god or goddess in a dream says that your psychic powers are beginning to emerge naturally and that you have the potential to take up a psychic art or learn how to become a healer.

Gold
A gold ring is symbolic that a lover is taking their relationship with you very seriously.

To dream of piles of gold says you have the power to make money within a few years.

To have gold stolen is a warning that you should take care of your financial affairs, especially if you are considering a major purchase. If you recognise the person who has stolen your gold, it could be an indication that in real-life they do not value you as much as they say they do.

A goldmine is a warning not to lend money to anyone or to take out a loan without checking the small print closely first.

See also **jewellery**

Goldfish
See **tank (fish)**

Golf
To play or watch golf means you need to relax as you have been working too hard.

To win a round of golf indicates that you will soon outsmart a business rival.

See also **sport**

Goose
This is a warning that someone is taking advantage of your hospitality. Visitors, for instance, may be staying for too long or relatives are treating your home like a hotel.

See also **animals** *or* **birds**

Government
To dream about a government indicates that the outcome to an official matter will be to your advantage.

To be working in government says that you may have to take on extra responsibilities at work.

See also **election** *or* **politician**

Grain/granary

Whether you are gathering grain during harvest-time or dream of a granary, it is a sign that money is coming your way.

If the granary is empty it means that you are giving too much of your time and possibly even your money to other people.

Grandchildren

If you dream of your own grandchildren, you may have an unexpressed worry you should discuss with their parents.

If the dream grandchildren are not your own, it is a promise of a long and happy life.

See also **children**

Grandparents

To dream of grandparents is a positive omen and promises that you will find answers to questions you may have at the moment.

If you dream of your grandparents, whether alive or deceased, it is a sign that you need advice and support from someone older and wiser.

To see a deceased grandparent or great-grandparent is a sign that they still care for you and protect you. You should feel comforted and reassured as it means you are loved.

See also **family**

Grapes

This is a symbol that your health will improve if you have been feeling unwell or, if you are already well, that you will enjoy continuing good health in the months ahead.

To grow or tread grapes to make wine is symbolic of fertility, impending pregnancy or success in a business venture.

To tread on black grapes is an indication that your enemies will soon be defeated.

See also **fruit** *or* **wine**

Grass

You may be feeling discontented and in need of a change in scene.

To run through long grass says that you may be uncertain about a path you have chosen to take and could benefit from a rethink.

Cutting grass means that you need to be firm with relations.

See also **mowing**

Grasshoppers

You should be cautious around gossips, a lover or friends who constantly change their minds and arrangements at the last minute.

See also **insects**

Grave

Like all morbid symbols, this is not an omen of an imminent death.

A grave with a lot of earth on top of it means that you will do well with a future sale or purchase.

If you see your name on a gravestone it means that you will soon have new opportunities that will change you life for the better.

If you have just left a relationship or want to do so and dream of a lover's grave, it is a sign that deep down you know the break-up would bring you relief.

See also **burial** *or* **funeral**

Green

This is a colour that represents everlasting love. Depending on the context in which you see the colour it can indicate steady growth in that area.

See also **colours**

Grey

This indicates confusion so you should take your time before making any decisions. You may have to compromise on an issue.

See also **colours** *or* **hair**

Grotto

A magic grotto or one in a beautiful location indicates that you will experience unexpected kindness from a stranger. You may also find a dear friend or lover in someone you had previously not found attractive.

See also **cave**

Groves

Groves of trees, especially exotic ones such as olives or oranges, indicate you will find happiness through the company of children. This is an excellent dream to have if you are considering a career working with children.

Guests

Unexpected guests indicate you may soon hear news from absent family or friends.

If guests are staying in your home it means you may have relations turn up unexpectedly within a week.

Guitar

To listen to a guitar indicates romance and love.

If you are playing the guitar it means that a minor scandal about a colleague or friend is not based on truth.

See also **music** *or* **musical instruments**

Gull

Seagulls flying overhead mean you should follow your heart and not your head where personal happiness is concerned. It also means that travel may result in a new romance or deepening love.

See also **birds**

Gun

If you fire the gun, you will hear news that will change your long-term plans or make you reconsider long-held opinions.

To be shot or threatened by a gun says you should not react too hastily to what may appear to be aggression at work as the person concerned will soon regret their unfair words.

See also **weapons**

Gymnastics

If you are performing gymnastics it means that you will soon need to learn a new skill, possibly a technical one, but it will be much easier than you think.

See also **sport**

Gypsy

This symbolises the need or desire for travel and to be free of unnecessary restrictions. Gypsies can sometimes represent emerging psychic abilities particulary if you dream of an older gypsy woman, as this can be symbolic of a spirit guide or guardian who may appear in other dreams to advise and guide you.

See also **fortune teller**

H

Hail

To be caught in a hailstorm says that a change you are avoiding will, after a short while, prove to be advantageous.

Hail falling on a roof is a sign that you must protect yourself from spiteful tongues at work or in the family.

Hair

Thick shining hair is a good omen as it symbolises strength, sexuality, and good health.

To dream of hair that is falling out is a sign that you are possibly feeling exhausted and stressed but are in denial of this.

If your hair is grey in a dream or you find the odd grey hair, it means that your life will get better as you get older. It is also a sign that you will always look younger than you are.

See also **grey** *or* **wig**

Hairdresser

Having your hair cut is a warning that someone is draining your energy or demanding too much of your time.

If hair is dyed or curled for either sex, it means that you may be given an opportunity to succeed via slightly dubious means.

Hallway

If the hallway is dark and narrow you may be fearful of letting your guard down in a destructive relationship and are worried that you will be trapped in that relationship as a result.

A wide and welcoming hallway promises a happy and fulfilling sexual relationship. It can also be a sign of new family members.

Halter

If a horse is willing for you to put a halter on it, it is a sign that you will persuade someone significant to agree with your point of view.

If the horse is disagreeable, it may be harder than you think to persuade others to understand your opinions.

Ham

To cook ham is a warning that you need to be careful with your money.

If you are eating ham it can be a sign that your finances should improve within a short time.

See also **pig**

Hammer

To be making or mending something with a hammer is a promise that if you are determined you will succeed.

If you drop a hammer, you may have been giving into emotional pressure which will make things harder for you in the long-term.

See also **tools**

Hammock

To lie in a hammock says you should take a step back from a situation or confrontation for a while as others need to sort out their own problems first.

Hand

If a hand is outstretched it can be a sign of a new friendship, perhaps even from someone you had considered to be indifferent or hostile.

A closed hand is a sign that a close friend or relative may soon give you a little of their time or help.

Hairy hands, whether they belong to you or someone else, suggest that you may have very strong feelings of either passion or anger that you are in denial of.

See also **handshake** *or* **palm**

Handcuffs

To be handcuffed by the police is not an omen that you will be arrested but an indication that you feel resentful toward someone who is trying to dominate you emotionally or make you take a path you do not wish to follow.

Handkerchief

To lose a handkerchief or not have one when you need one, is a warning that you should check facts and figures carefully before entering into a financial or business association.

A pile of white handkerchiefs indicates a happy marriage, either in the present if you are already married, or in the future if you are not.

Handle

To turn a handle means you will succeed through your own hard work and merits.

A handle that breaks or drops off is a warning that younger family members may become moody or uncooperative at a family gathering to be held in the future.

See also **door**

Handshake

If you are shaking hands to conclude a deal it is a sign that a new business opportunity will prove to be advantageous.

If you are shaking hands with someone it means that a stranger or new business acquaintance will become a good friend.

See also **hand**

Handwriting

If you cannot read handwriting in a dream it means that someone is hiding facts or keeping a secret from you.

If you are writing beautifully, it is an indication that you will have a chance to express yourself creatively or artistically.

See also **pen** *or* **writing**

Hanging

If you are hanging wallpaper or a picture it means that your home life will improve or that you will make a happy and profitable house move in the near future.

Happiness

This may be a wish-fulfilment dream if you are not feeling happy in your waking life but having it suggests that things will improve very shortly.

To dream of happiness in love signifies a new lover or a harmonious time in an established relationship.

Harbour

A harbour suggests you are seeking to find people who are trustworthy rather than people who offer excitement but are ultimately shallow.

See also **boats** *or* **sea**

Hare

To see a hare running fast signifies that you will complete a task or pay off a debt much quicker than you anticipated.

See also **rabbit**

Harp

If you are playing a harp it signifies a period of peace and harmony with others. It is also symbolic of betrothals and weddings.

If someone you recognise is playing the harp you should make sure that they are not taking advantage of you in real life.

A broken harp represents a troublesome relative who displays favouritism when they should not.

See also **music** *or* **musical instruments**

Harvest

If the harvest is good it means that your hard work will bear fruit before long. For the unattached, recurrent dreams of a harvest suggest that love will blossom in the autumn. This is a good fertility omen if you want to get pregnant.

Hat

If you are wearing a fancy hat it is likely that there will be a wedding or family gathering fairly soon.

A hat that does not fit or one that flies off easily is an indication that you are trying too hard to please an older member of the family.

Hate

To hate someone in a dream is an indication that you are trying too hard to be a peacemaker.

If someone hates you, there may be gossip behind your back started by a person who is extra nice to you when nobody else is around.

Haunted house

If you are trying to escape from a haunted house it is a sign that you may hear news regarding someone from your past whom you would prefer to forget.

See also **ghost**

Hawk

This is an indication that you may need to be more focused and ruthless than usual to gain the promotion or advantage you seek. You should aim high but do not confide in others about your plans.

See also **birds** *or* **wild beasts**

Headache

To dream you have a bad headache may indicate that one will develop during the following day. It can also symbolise people who are bothering you with matters that they could deal with themselves.

See also **pain**

Healing

If you are being healed it is a sign that your health will improve or that you will remain healthy in the future.

If you are the healer it could be a sign that you have healing gifts that you could develop if you wished.

Heap

A heap of money, gold or fruit indicates wealth and good health.

A heap of rubbish, clothes or washing that needs sorting is a warning that you need to sort out problems that are blighting your life.

Heart

To experience pain in your heart or dream that you have a heart problem is not a warning of imminent heart trouble but a sign that you are afraid to trust your feelings about a person in case you get hurt, although this is probably an unfounded fear.

Hearth

This is symbolic of increased domestic happiness and perhaps an indication that an absent family member will come home or someone new will soon join the family. To dream of a hearth is a good omen if you are moving house, renting or buying your first home.

Heaven

This may be an out-of-body experience. Generally it means great happiness will come your way soon.

See also **angel** *or* **saints**

Hedge

A tall hedge is an indication that someone close to you is being unnecessarily secretive.

A thorny hedge is a warning that you should try to ignore gossip from neighbours or colleagues at work.

See also **thorns**

Hell

To dream of hell means that someone is trying to manipulate you by making you feel guilty. You should ignore them.

See also **devil**

Hen

This indicates the arrival or the increasing influence of a nurturing, motherly presence. It can also be symbolic of a fussy person at work or an interfering neighbour who may annoy you but means no harm.

See also **birds**

Herbs

To dream of planting or using herbs can sometimes be a past-life dream. It can also be a sign that you or someone close to you will soon be healed of a minor illness or health worry.

See also individual herbs or **plants**

Hermit

If you meet a hermit in your dreams it means that you should listen to your intuition if you are undecided about a course of action.

If you are living as a hermit it may be that you are feeling alone and are in need of a wise friend.

Herrings

To catch or eat a herring means you need to be more economical as you may face a major expenditure in the near future. However, a shoal of herring or a pile of cooked herring indicates prosperity.

See also **fishing**

Hiding

If you are hiding from someone it may mean that you are unwilling to commit yourself to a relationship or that you are afraid to reveal your true feelings.

If you are hiding your money or valuables it can mean that an acquaintance or work colleague may be trying to damage your reputation.

Hieroglyphics

If you dream of seeing hieroglyphics that you can't understand, it foretells that you may be given conflicting advice or opinions and will need to form your own ideas.

If you are able to read the hieroglyphics it means that you will soon be told a secret or given new information that will explain the strange or difficult behaviour of someone close.

Hill

Reaching the top of a hill represents the fulfilment of a dream.

To be among hills says that you would benefit from a short holiday or some relaxation.

If you are struggling up a hill it means that you should not hesitate to ask for help with a difficult task or extra responsibility at home or work.

Hip

If a woman dreams she has big hips, she may become a mother, an aunt or a grandmother before long.

If a man dreams he has wide hips, he may take a more active role in the community. For example, he may enrol in one of the armed services or as a policemen or fireman.

A broken hip indicates someone you think will support you through a difficult time may prove unreliable.

History lesson

See **academic lessons**

Hole (ground)

If a hole appears in the ground or you fall down a hole, it is a sign that you may be worrying about losing a job, home or loved one.

To climb down into a hole and explore underground passages means you need to confront a fear or problem you have tried to bury in your mind.

Hole (objects or clothes)

This shows you need to resolve a quarrel, even if it wasn't of your own making. You should also take care when making a new and expensive purchase as it may not be all that it seems.

Holiday

If pleasurable, a dream holiday represents a desire for relaxation or travel.

To dream of a holiday coming to an end and not wanting to return home means your working or home life may have become unduly burdensome.

See also **camping, hotel, tent, travel** *or* **villa**

Home

To visit an old or childhood home is a promise that you will hear good news from someone you may have lost contact with. It can also indicate a desire to settle down.

To dream of your old home being abandoned or dilapidated means that you have lost touch with your real self.

See also **decorating, flat, house, kitchen, living room, moving (house or objects), neighbours, painting (room), property** *or* **room**

Homelessness

This is never an omen that you will lose your home. Instead, if you are experiencing money worries, to dream of being without a home is an anxiety dream. It highlights that you need to seek advice and help in order to stop worrying alone.

If you are happy at not having a home, it can mean that you are lacking spontaneity and fun in your life.

See also **beggar** *or* **tramp**

Honey

Honey is a sign of fertility and can also foretell of money coming your way. Honey can also indicate that you will receive a message from a distant friend or family member that will result in a trip to see them.

See also **bees**

Horn

Whether you dreamt of an animal or hunting horn, this is symbolic of prosperity, success and male potency. You may be tempted by an exciting sexual liaison.

Horse

To ride a horse represents harmony in marriage or love. Horses are also a symbol of fertility or an indication, if you are female, that an attractive man is interested in you.

A stampede of horses, a horse out of control and dragging the rider, or a rider falling off a horse suggests that you are feeling powerless and are being carried along by events or other people. You may be feeling rushed into a sexual partnership before you are ready.

See also **animals, neighing, riding, saddle, stable** *or* **taming**

Horse and cart

This is symbolic of a change at work or home. If the cart is full it means that a move will be an advantageous.

Horseshoe

This is a promise of good fortune. It represents a happy marriage and protection against hostility.

If a horseshoe is broken, you may be afraid of breaking up a love relationship or friendship.

Hospital

If you are a patient you may be feeling temporarily unable to cope with demands in your life and want to feel cared for.

If you are visiting a patient or are a doctor or nurse, you may be anxious to help someone close but feel as though you shouldn't interfere.

To dream of a hospital can sometimes be a telepathic call from a person who needs help.

See also **anaesthetic, doctor, illness, nurse, operation** *or* **x-ray**

Hotel

To stay in an expensive or beautiful hotel indicates that dealings overseas will bring you money.

A badly run hotel symbolises that you feel unsettled at home, perhaps because family members are taking advantage of your good nature.

See also **holiday**

House

This shows that domestic matters are at the forefront of your mind. It can be a sign that you need to devote extra time to your home and to those who live in it.

A dirty or neglected house says that you are feeling neglected by your family or partner.

See also **attic, auction, chimney, decorating, home, kitchen, living room, moving (house or objects), neighbours, painting (room), property** *or* **room**

Hugging

To hug friends or family symbolises future happiness and an unexpected gathering.

To hug a stranger means you may make new friends. If you are unattached or unhappy in a relationship, new love should come your way.

See also **family, friends** *or* **lover**

Hungry

To be hungry in a dream, unless you are on a diet, is a sign that you are lacking affection or appreciation from people around you. You need to demand more from them.

See also **food**

Hurricane

To dream of a hurricane usually indicates a desire for major change or strong feelings you should express.

See also **wind**

Hurry

If you are in a hurry it is probably a reflection of your busy life and illustrates that you need to prioritise your workload and slow down.

Husband

For an unmarried woman to dream of a husband is a sign of a future marriage.

To dream of someone else's husband can reveal a hidden attraction or indicates that your own marriage needs spicing up.

See also **lover**

Hypnotism

If you are being hypnotised it can mean that someone senior to you at work or an older member of the family is trying to deceive you.

To hypnotise people in a dream shows you have the power to influence others if you believe in yourself.

J

Ice

This can indicate you are feeling emotionally numb at the moment, perhaps because of a recent hurt or betrayal. You need to allow yourself time to come to terms with events, if necessary.

If you are trapped by ice it could be a sign that you feel that a particular situation is proving difficult to solve. You need to be patient to allow circumstances to improve.

If you fall through ice it can mean that you feel afraid you will become vulnerable if you speak out or make a move. You need to realise that your sense of security, borne from not speaking out, is based on illusion.

If you are skating and enjoying the ice, it is a positive omen that you will succeed with any delicate negotiations.

See also **icicles, snow** *or* **water**

Iceberg

This means you should check travel or business plans carefully to prevent problems that could be avoided.

Ice cream

To eat an ice cream in a dream is a very good omen of pleasure coming into your life, possibly in the form of a new lover.

If you drop an ice cream it is a sign that you may be spoiling a relationship or friendship by quarrelling over children or young people.

Icicles

Melting icicles are an indication that any recent problems should soon melt away, especially regarding property or family worries.

If icicles are forming around you, it may mean that the coldness in a relationship may be hurting you more than you care to admit. You need to take steps to resolve the matter, if necessary by expressing your displeasure.

See also **ice**

Icing

Icing on a cake is a promise that you should soon receive a gift or an unexpected treat.

If you are icing a cake it is symbolic of a family celebration.

See also **cake**

Ideal (person)

If you meet your ideal partner or lover in a dream it can be an omen that you may soon do so in reality. If you are already in a relationship this is a wish-fulfilment dream, indicating you should maybe seek to re-capture some of the romance and excitement you once had with your partner.

Ideals

See **principles**

Idea

Ideas in dreams are usually always good as your unconscious mind is drawing on all sorts of information that you may repress or not have time to think about while awake. You may well find an answer to a question or a new way of doing something while dreaming. To think up an invention or to have an original idea in a dream shows that you are in a very creative period of your life. Try to write your ideas down as soon as you wake.

Identity

If you lose your identity documents, such as a driving licence, it can be a sign that you are afraid that someone close to you with a strong personality is overpowering your own feelings.

Idle

If you dream of people in your life doing nothing while you are working, the resentment you feel and maybe express in the dream should perhaps be transferred to your waking world.

Idols (ancient)

Worshipping idols can be an indication of a past-life dream. It can also mean that you are not being realistic about a new friend or lover who may not be able to live up to your expectations.

A broken idol means that a promise someone has made you might be broken.

Idols (modern)

See **celebrities**

Igloo

You may need to withdraw for a while from a quarrel or difficult situation until matters improve naturally.

See also **snow**

Ignore

If you are ignored by someone you recognise in a dream it means that they are not taking your opinion or needs seriously in reality.

If you are ignoring a mess or problem it illustrates you need to sort out your finances or a relationship, rather than hoping the problem will go away.

Illness

If you are ill in a dream it means you need to admit you are perhaps feeling tired and unable to cope with the stresses of everyday life. You should allow other people to help you if they offer.

If you are seriously ill in the dream, you may be feeling overwhelmed by responsibility and the demands of others.

The type of illness is significant and may indicate an inner worry. A lingering infection indicates that there is a part of your body that needs special care.

See also **cancer, disease, gallstones, hospital, invalid, jaundice, measles, rabies, tumour, vomit** *or* **x-ray**

Illumination

If you dream of seeing the sky illuminated with strange lights, you may be experiencing an out-of-body dream about UFOs.

Illumination can also indicate that you will have an unexpected chance to travel with your work or that a man from overseas will become important to you.

See also **candles, light** *or* **meteor**

Imitation

To dream you are wearing imitation jewellery means that you are being offered something second-best and should not accept it, even for the sake of security.

If someone is imitating your movements or actions you need to be aware of a rival who may try to steal your ideas, or even your partner.

Imprisonment

See **prison**

Incubus (male sexual demon)

Dreams in which you are being crushed or attacked sexually by a demon of the opposite sex are surprisingly common and have nothing to do with evil. They are common for women and usually occur during the late teens until the thirties. Such a dream indicates a sense of powerlessness, concerns about awakening sexuality and identity.

See also **demons** *or* **devil**

Independence

If you are a parent with adolescent children, to dream of a teenager becoming independent and leaving the home can be a sign that any worries you have about them are unfounded.

If you become very independent within the dream it can mean that you will have a chance in the near future to travel alone or become self-employed.

See also **adolescent** *or* **travel**

Indicators

If the indicators on your vehicle are not working it can mean that you should not be pushed into making a decision. It might also be worth checking whether the indicators on your vehicle, if you own one in reality, are working properly.

See also **bus** *or* **car**

Infant

To dream of caring for a very young child whether your own or one you do not know, says that someone close to you is acting immaturely to catch your attention.

See also **children**

Infidelity

If you are enjoying an illicit relationship in a dream, it could be your subconscious experimenting sexually, as perhaps you feel inhibited during the day. If you try to overcome your inhibitions this could lead to fulfilment within a regular relationship. You might be feeling hemmed in and could benefit from some more freedom within an existing commitment.

If you are betrayed or feel very guilty about betraying someone, you may have suppressed fears about a relationship that may or may not be justified. Maybe you should discuss these with someone.

See also **cheating** *or* **lover**

Injection

If you are having an injection it is a sign that you need to protect yourself against spite or jealousy from someone who works with you or from a neighbour.

To take a child for an injection may indicate your children are being bullied in reality, even if they haven't said anything.

Injury

If you or a family member is injured, it may be a sign that you are worried about matters of safety. You may also be feeling secretly hurt by something that has been said to you, even if the person who said it did not mean to hurt you.

To inflict a wound on a dream enemy, is to indicate you need to make a break for freedom from some form of oppression or injustice.

A healing wound can symbolise the mending of wounded emotions.

See also **crutches, scabs** *or* **scar**

Ink

An old-fashioned inkpot indicates that an important matter, maybe legal, will be communicated to you in writing.

Spilled ink means you need to be sure about what you are going to write about as you may regret writing or sending it later.

Inquest

Attending an inquest after someone has died is an indication that you need to discuss past events that are still worrying you. You may have also noticed a relation or close friend going back to bad ways or habits.

Insanity

If you are trying to convince others you are not crazy, it usually means that other people are trying to persuade you that their own bad actions were harmless.

Insects

If masses of insects are crawling around your home, or even on you, it indicates that you are overwhelmed with small worries and irritations that are disturbing you more than you perhaps care to admit. Beetles, in particular, indicate a fear that hidden mistakes or omissions on your part may be discovered.

See also under individual insects

Instrument

See under individual musical instruments, **musical instruments** *or* **tools**

Insult

If someone you recognise is very rude to you in a dream or you insult them, you may have doubts about how friendly and reliable they really are in reality.

International

Anything to do with international travel or communication is generally an excellent sign that your business or finances will flourish. It can be an indication that this is a good time to plan a foreign holiday.

Internet

See **web (internet)**

Interruption

If someone keeps interrupting your conversations or stopping you from working, it represents a demanding family member or colleague who is taking up too much of your time or thoughts because of their selfish behaviour.

Interview

If the interview is going well it is a positive omen that says you should be offered a promotion or a good business deal soon.

An interview that goes badly says that you should not pay attention to an over-critical relative or friend.

Intestines

To dream of animal intestines in a butcher's shop or human intestines during an operation signifies you need to sort out a long-standing problem or family secret with older people once and for all, even if it means expressing your own resentment.

Invalid

If someone is recovering from an illness it means that any current family illness or sorrow will be short-lived.

See also **disease** *or* **illness**

Invasion

If your home or your country is invaded in a dream, you may feel that you never have time to yourself. You may also be feeling that family members are being lazy around the house. This can also be a sign that a partner or parent is being intrusive with regards to your private correspondence.

Invention

See **idea**

Invitation

To receive an invitation is very positive and means that you should be invited to a celebration or may even have cause for one yourself within the coming months.

See also **party**

Iron (clothes)

To iron clothes in a dream indicates that you are either trying too hard to stroke the ego of someone close to you or are in the middle of a family quarrel where both sides are placing blame on to you.

See also **clothes**

Iron (metal)

Iron is symbolic of protection, so you should rest assured that better times are ahead. To dream of iron can mean that you may meet someone who will take care of you.

Irritable

If a person you know is being irritable in a dream, you may be trying to please them too much in real life.

If you feel irritable, it means you should perhaps be less patient with a difficult child or relative who is acting immaturely without good reason.

Island

This is a sign that you need more rest and relaxation and would maybe benefit from a short holiday in a quiet place.

If you are trapped on an island or are in hiding, it can be an indication that you are feeling isolated. Maybe a friend or family member is being mean towards you due to their own insecurities.

Itch

If you are itching all over in a dream it means that a neighbour or work colleague is irritating you. You should try to avoid them if possible.

Ivory

To dream of a white ivory statue or ornament can be a past-life dream. Ivory is usually a good omen for improving finances.

See also **elephant**

Ivy

If you dream of this green trailing plant growing or winding around a tree, it can mean that a lover is perhaps being over-possessive and you would benefit from some space.

A single piece of ivy, or ivy in a vase, is a sign of faithful love.

See also **plants**

Jackal

A jackal is a warning that you should be cautious of a friend who may be taking advantage of you financially or asking for a lot of your time and support.

See also **animals** *or* **wild beasts**

Jackdaw

To see or catch a jackdaw is a warning that you should watch your money as others are more than willing to spend it for you. People may also be taking the credit for your ideas.

See also **animals** *or* **birds**

Jade

A green jade stone is symbolic of good health and long life, so it is a positive symbol to have if you have been feeling exhausted or unwell.

See also **gemstones** *or* **jewellery**

Jaguar

If the animal is friendly or you are able to control it, you have a great deal more power than you realise. A risk that you decide to take may pay off.

If the wild cat is attacking or chasing you, it can mean that you may be trying to battle against powerful emotions or sexual passion towards someone who has entered your life.

See also **animals** *or* **wild beasts**

Jam

If you are eating jam and getting sticky fingers, it can be a sign that someone younger or more immature than you may cause you embarrassment through their thoughtless behaviour.

To make jam or see a child eat jam represents a happy home life in the future.

See also **food**

Jar

A jar which has a tightly screwed-on lid that will not open is a warning to only tell secrets to people you can trust.

An open jar with its contents spilling out suggests that someone close to you has betrayed a confidence or is gossiping about you.

Jasmine

This foretells of an unexpected compliment from someone who would like to be more than just your friend.

See also **flowers** *or* **plants**

Jaundice

To be ill with jaundice and turn yellow is a warning that you should not let jealous work colleagues or neighbours worry you.

If a family member has jaundice it is an indication that they will try to compete for your attention in real life.

See also **illness**

Javelin

To be attacked with a javelin means that your financial affairs or private life may come under scrutiny. You should organise your paperwork in order to be prepared for a possible confrontation.

To throw a javelin in a competition signifies that you will succeed with an immediate ambition or desire.

See also **sport**

Jaws

Animal or shark jaws are a warning that you should not openly confront a boss or colleague who is being difficult.

To dream of your own jaw, whether you are eating or talking, is an indication you may receive money soon, either from a relation who may have sold property or from an advantageous property deal of your own.

Jealousy

If a partner acts jealously in a dream it may indicate problems you need to tackle within a relationship in reality.

If others are jealous of you, it is a sign that you will soon experience the success you have worked towards for years.

Jelly

Making or eating jelly indicates a forthcoming celebration. This is also an excellent omen if you want a baby or a grandchild.

See also **food**

Jester

An old-fashioned court jester or a joker can either be a past-life dream or mean that you are hiding your unhappiness behind a façade of cheerfulness. You would do well to show your true feelings as others may not realise how hurtful they are being towards you.

See also **clown, fool** *or* **royalty**

Jet plane
See aeroplane

Jewel
See individual gemstones or gemstones

Jewellery
To be given jewellery in a dream can be a sign of a forthcoming betrothal or pregnancy in the family.

If you reject the jewellery someone offers you it can indicate that you have not realised that someone you have just met means something to you.

Broken or stolen jewellery indicates that someone is trying to undermine your confidence because they feel inadequate.

See also under individual types of jewellery or gemstones

Jilted
If someone rejects you romantically, even if you are in a happy relationship in reality, you may have secret worries that you need to discuss with your partner as they are making you feel insecure.

Jinx
If you suffer bad luck in a dream or throughout a series of dreams, you may be worried that your present good fortune, whether financially or romantically, may not last. This is purely an anxiety dream so relax.

Job
To dream of changing your job indicates that you may receive a job offer or an unexpected promotion in the near future.

If you are job hunting in your waking life and dream of not having a job, you may be worrying about your lack of work and need to tackle this.

See also office, wages *or* work

Jockey
To be riding a horse in a race shows that you will need to fight off competition, whether in love or at work, to fulfil your dreams. Success is forecast if you win the race.

See also racehorse *or* rider

Jogging
To jog in a dream and not get out of breath is a sign of improving or continuing good health.

If you are exhausted from jogging, then life or events are moving too fast and you need to slow down to a manageable pace.

See also sport

Joke

If you are laughing and telling jokes in a dream it can mean that you will meet or hear from an old friend from your past who will bring you happiness.

If people are playing jokes on you it can indicate that someone at work or a neighbour, for instance, may not be as nice as they seem.

Joker

See jester

Join (fabric or wood)

If there is a huge ugly join in a garment, ornament or piece of furniture, it can represent problematical people who have recently joined your family or workplace.

A small or almost invisible join indicates that a current quarrel can be mended.

Join (organisation)

If you join a club or an organisation, it can be a sign that you will soon meet new friends who live or work locally.

To join other people in a crowd, such as a protest, means that you may be worried you will become unpopular at work or will upset your family if you voice doubts about something.

Joint (body)

If your knees, back or shoulders are aching in a dream it means you are holding back from making changes to your life because of fear.

A damaged joint shows that you are getting behind with work commitments because you are being disrupted unnecessarily by demanding children or family members.

Joint (meat)

To be cooking or serving a large piece of meat means you may be asked to give financial help to a member of your family.

A raw joint warns of a possessive friend or colleague who may try to spend more time with you than you want.

Jostle

If you are pushed or jostled by a crowd of people or by an aggressive individual, it shows that you may be being pushed into a decision before you are ready because you do not want to upset or anger the person who is pressurising you.

Journal

See magazine

Journalist

If you are a journalist carrying out interviews it indicates that you have a lot of questions you want answers to. You should persist even if it means dealing with a difficult organisation.

If you are the person being interviewed it means that you have been unfairly blamed for something and should tell your side of the story.

See also **magazine** or **newspaper**

Journey

This foretells of travel or a chance to move house in the near future.

A journey that never seems to end or one that involves a series of delays, indicates that there is too much stress in your life and you urgently need to slow down and prioritise your workload.

See also **path, road, signs** or **travel**

Joust

This can often be a past-life dream but it also indicates that you need to make your boss or colleagues more aware of your hard work in order to make an impression.

Joy

If you feel very happy in a dream it is a sign that happiness will be yours in a completely unexpected way within a month. In particular, children and animals should bring you special pleasure.

Judge

You may be feeling very guilty about trying something new, maybe because of a disapproving family member or because of past events. You should trust your own judgement.

See also **court of law** or **divorce court**

Jug

A jug that is full is a sign of good health whereas an empty jug indicates that your money may be trickling away.

Juggler

You may be trying too hard to prioritise conflicting demands, although if you manage to keep all the balls in the air it means that you will succeed.

See also **circus**

Jumping

This can be a very empowering dream, especially if you are able to leap effortlessly over objects or even buildings. It means that if you have the confidence to try something you will succeed beyond your wildest expectations.

If the objects are too high or you stumble you may be afraid of risking failure. Take your time and think carefully and you should succeed.

Jungle

If you are walking into a jungle you may be worried that a flirtation is going too far.

To be lost in the jungle says that you should watch your money carefully with regards to an uncertain venture or an expensive item you do not really need.

Junk

To clear out unwanted ornaments or furniture, especially from a cellar or attic, represents an opportunity to leave the past behind because of a new relationship, a job offer or even a house move.

To dream of piles of junk in or around your home says that you need to clear away a lot of old issues or maybe a long-standing argument to create harmony at home.

To dispose of junk means you may be left clearing up problems others have created.

See also **dump**

Jury

If a group of people are listening to a case against you, it means that you may be influenced negatively by people who believe you will fail if you decide to change your career or take up a new opportunity.

See also **court of law**

K

Kaftan

If you are wearing a kaftan or a long loose robe, you may be seeking a slower or more traditional lifestyle. You may benefit from taking some time out from the stresses of everyday living.

Kaleidoscope

Looking into a kaleidoscope represents a choice you may have to make about your future, possibly between two people or two jobs. You should wait for a few days, or even weeks, until life settles and you can make the right decision.

Kangaroo

If the kangaroo is bouncing along happily, this is a good omen for any matters connected to children or family life.

If a kangaroo attacks you it can mean that someone may be saying unpleasant things about you behind your back, although you should have the chance to discredit them soon.

If a kangaroo is caught, people you know may suddenly become judgmental or accuse you unfairly in real life. You may also be worried that something you have done underhand may be revealed to your family or colleagues.

See also **animals**

Keep

This means you need to protect your own interests and should not reveal plans or secrets for the moment, even to people you think you could trust.

See also **castle**

Keeper

If you are the keeper of, for example, animals or grounds, it represents a settled home life in which family or close friends will bring you great emotional happiness.

If a keeper is cruel or unfriendly, it may mean that you are right to be worried about a child or family member whom you suspect is having a hard time, even though they are denying it to you.

Keep-out sign

See **obstruction**

Keg

A keg of alcohol indicates that someone in your family has a secret problem, although not necessarily related to alcohol. You will need to be very tactful when asking after them if you are to discover the problem and offer help.

A keg or barrel of explosives may be a past-life dream but it could also be a warning that an older family member is feeling quarrelsome.

See also **alcohol, bomb** *or* **drinking**

Kestrel

Small hawks symbolise that you will succeed with a difficult task as long as you do not lose faith or become distracted.

See also **animals, birds** *or* **wild beasts**

Kettle

Kettles symbolise domestic discussions and family gatherings that will bring satisfaction. You may need to spend time listening to your children or partner as they may need advice or reassurance.

See also **kitchen** *or* **water**

Key

A key may materialise in your dreams if you are about to embark on a sexual relationship, especially for the first time.

The key to a home can express an underlying desire to settle down which may come as a surprise if you always saw yourself as footloose and fancy-free.

To find a key in a door represents an opportunity or an answer to a problem that may become clear to you if you open the door. Lucid dreaming may be of help in this instance.

See also **lock (door)** *or* **lucid dreaming** *(see page 37)*

Keyhole

If you dream of looking through a keyhole, you may be told a secret you will find hard to keep.

If someone is looking through your keyhole, a neighbour or acquaintance may be trying to pry into your private life.

See also **door**

Key ring

A key ring with a key attached to it indicates you will soon be welcomed into a group or organisation you want to join.

A key ring without a key is a warning that a new friendship or relationship may not lead to anything substantial.

Kid

A baby goat with its mother is a sign of the imminent arrival of a baby or child into the family.

If the kid is alone, it can symbolise that you are attracted to someone you have just met. You may have to decide whether to take it further, especially if you or they already have a partner.

See also **animals**

Kidnapper

If you or a child is kidnapped it can be an expression of fears or doubts, especially if it occurs at a distressing time, for example, when a relationship is ending or you are about to lose your home.

If you are the kidnapper, you may be harbouring feelings for someone that you cannot reveal.

See also **terrorist**

Kidneys

If your kidneys are not working properly it is not an omen for future illness but a sign that someone has been blackmailing you emotionally or swamping you with their problems.

Killing

If you are the killer this dream can be a powerful method of beginning to cleanse yourself of old guilt or regrets by rehearsing in your sleep a means of change for a destructive situation or relationship.

If you are the victim it can be symbolic of your fear that a person or situation more powerful than you is destroying your identity or personal freedom.

See also **death/dying, murder** *or* **suicide**

Kilt

This may be a past-life dream connected to your ancestors. It may also foretell that you will receive visitors or contact from afar, not necessarily from Scotland, but certainly someone with a Celtic ancestry.

Kindergarten

See **nursery (infant)**

Kindness

If someone shows kindness to you in a dream or you are kind to someone it can mean that you may soon experience unexpected kindness from a stranger or find a new acquaintance who will answer a pressing problem.

King

See **royalty**

Kingdom

If you are a King surveying your kingdom, it means that a major opportunity for promotion or for making money should come your way.

Kiss

A passionate kiss promises romance or the rekindling of passion in an existing relationship in the future.

A gentle kiss indicates that you will have, or will find, long-lasting happiness in love.

See also **lips** *or* **mouth**

Kit

An army uniform is a warning that you may have a fight on your hands to get what you want but you should win.

Sports kit represents a good time to take up a new sport or interest.

See also **army** *or* **sport**

Kitbag

Travel is forecast, either in relation to work or with regards to an interest you have. Wherever you go there will be advantageous results.

Kitchen

If the kitchen is an orderly place it means that you will find happiness at home and that any future house moves will be fortuitous.

If the kitchen is messy it is a sign that you need to tidy up clutter, whether financially or emotionally, in your life. If you have a back-log of work, a messy kitchen means you need to resolve this.

See also **home, house, kettle** *or* **pots and pans**

Kite

Flying a kite foretells that your wishes will come true. You may also go on a holiday by plane to somewhere new which will bring you happiness, maybe romantically.

See also **toys**

Kitten

A kitten represents someone vulnerable who needs a lot of nurturing. If you lose the kitten and feel sad you may be reluctant to let a family member move away because you fear they will not be able to cope properly.

If you lose a kitten and feel glad but guilty, you may secretly resent someone who plays on their helplessness.

Knife

A knife is not necessarily a bad omen but it can be an indication you need to cut through the shallow promises and vague plans suggested by others and insist on definite arrangements. This could be especially relevant if you are owed money or going into a new financial venture.

See also **dagger**

Knight

A knight in shining armour means you are looking, perhaps misguidedly, for a magical solution or ideal person to transform your life. If you ride off with the knight there may be someone in your immediate circle who, though less glamorous than your dream figure, will be able to offer you the warmth and reassurance you desire.

Knitting

To be knitting is a wonderful dream that forecasts a happy home and family life, a betrothal or a birth.

Tangled or dropped knitting indicates possible misunderstandings in communication. You should ensure you get agreements in writing or at least e-mails, as well as verbally.

Knives (crossed)

This foretells of arguments and disagreements. You need to be cautious around friends whom you suspect to be false.

Knot

A knot in your hair, in a chain or in a cord means that a current situation may not be as straightforward as you had hoped and you may need to rebook or rearrange schedules.

Tying knots is an old magical tradition so you may have had a past-life dream. It could also be a sign that your psychic powers are emerging.

Tying knots, for instance in a handkerchief, can be your subconscious reminding you to check your diary about an important date or meeting you may have forgotten about in reality.

Knowing

If you know something in a dream, write it down as soon as you wake. Answers fade quickly, but this insight could answer a major question or uncertainty in your life.

Knowledge

If in your dream you have a great deal of knowledge and are perhaps teaching others, it could be a subconscious suggestion you would benefit from some training, maybe even to become a teacher, or that you would enjoy fulfilling a creative ambition.

Know-all

If someone in your dream appears to know everything and is making you feel stupid, there is probably a know-all in your daily life who is making you feel miserable.

Label

If you are labelling objects, clothes or piles of paper it can mean that you are trying to organise someone whom you are responsible for or an area of your life that is chaotic.

Laboratory

Working in a laboratory can mean you will soon discover the answer to a problem or that you or a family member will soon recover from an illness.

See also **science**

Labour

If you or a woman in a dream is giving birth, it is an excellent omen highlighting the success of a project or financial venture. This is an especially good dream for women who are trying for a baby.

See also **baby, midwife** *or* **mother**

Labyrinth

A labyrinth has a path that leads to its centre which means you cannot get lost like you can in a maze. To dream of walking in a labyrinth therefore means that if you are patient the answers to your problems will unfold with relative ease.

See also **maze**

Lace

If you are buying or wearing lace it forecasts that you will enjoy happiness, love and plenty of money in your life.

If you are making or selling lace it means that you will have to work hard to get what you want but you will succeed.

Laces

To lose a shoe lace or have unfastened shoe laces in a dream is a warning that you need to work carefully and take time to check your written work or accounts.

See also **shoes**

Ladder

To climb a ladder is symbolic of taking steps towards achieving your ambitions, high ideals and dreams. It is a very powerful sign of imminent success.

If you feel fear from climbing a high ladder or you cling to one as it sways perilously in the wind, it suggests that you are afraid of failure.

A ladder with broken rungs means you may encounter obstacles as you try to achieve your ambitions, but you will be able to overcome these if you are patient.

Ladle

A ladle represents happiness through children, family life in general or through increased prosperity in your home.

If the ladle is broken, there may be a family dispute that is worrying you which needs to be tackled.

See also **spoon**

Lagoon

A beautiful lagoon on a tropical island often means your subconscious is trying to tell you to take a holiday, even if it is only a short local break. If you have already planned a holiday it is a sign that you will have a very happy time and, if you are unattached, may even meet someone new.

See also **boats, deep, diving, drowning, swimming, wading** *or* **water**

Lake

Swimming or boating on a lake is a very good sign of harmony in your life and of peaceful and satisfying relationships.

A stormy lake means that you may be suffering due to other people's disputes and should take a step back to ensure your own peace of mind.

See also **boats, deep, diving, drowning, swimming, wading** *or* **water**

Lamb

A small lamb playing in a field or standing by its mother foretells of a birth in the family or the addition of new younger family members, perhaps through a remarriage in the family.

To carry a lamb means you will get much happiness from caring for a small child or animal.

To cook or eat lamb represents successful DIY or building works to your home.

See also **animals, ewe** *or* **sheep**

Lame

If you, or someone you know cannot walk very well in a dream, it can signify that plans may be held back due to someone not contributing financially or failing to do their fair share of work.

A lame animal means you may acquire a new pet unexpectedly that will need lots of care initially.

Laminated flooring

See **floor**

Lamp

To find a magic lamp is an omen that your dearest wishes will come true.

If you are given or switch on a lamp it indicates that you will recover a lost possession or be paid money that you are owed.

See also **light**

Land

If you are a landowner it is an indication that any house matters or moves you make in the future will be very profitable.

If you are wandering over land it suggests that you are feeling restless and need a change, even if it is just a minor one such as a few days away or time spent redecorating your home.

See also **earth**

Landscape

Looking at or walking through a beautiful landscape represents your need for peace and harmony. You should seek the company of people who make you feel relaxed and confident.

Languages

If you are speaking in a foreign language it can mean that you may be having difficulty communicating with a family member or work colleague who is unwilling to listen to sense.

If you cannot understand people who are talking in a foreign language it indicates that you may need to change your line of argument, especially if you are trying to persuade older relations to make or accept a necessary change.

Lantern

An old-fashioned lantern is sometimes a past-life dream. It can also indicate an improvement in health for you or a close family member.

A lantern that goes out means that you may need to move on from a particular situation that is making you unhappy.

See also **light**

Lasso

If you are swinging a lasso and catching animals it is symbolic of acquiring a number of new contacts who will prove helpful to you.

To get entangled in a lasso is a warning that you should be wary of a love entanglement or hasty investment that could prove to be unwise in the future.

Laughter

If everyone is laughing, including you, it indicates that you will be invited to a celebration very soon.

If people are laughing at you, it means you may be concerned about people's reactions to a change or new venture you are planning. You should ignore your fears as they are likely to be unfounded.

Laundry

To do the laundry means you need to be careful about who you confide in regarding secrets or mistakes you have made that you wish to put behind you.

To be in a commercial laundry or to use a public washing machine means you may meet someone from your past whom you would prefer to forget.

Lavender

To dream of tending lavender means that someone will try to make amends for their previously unkind behaviour towards you.

If you are looking for a lover, lavender foretells of a gentle and kind lover who will always care for you.

See also **herbs** *or* **plants**

Lawyer

To consult a lawyer in your dream means you should read the small print or take some legal advice before signing a contract or entering into a formal verbal or written agreement.

See also **court of law**

Lazy

If you are angry with someone for being lazy, it is probably a sign of resentment towards a lazy person in real life. You need to speak out rather than simmer in silence.

Lead (animal)

If you are leading an animal by a rope or are walking a dog on a lead, it means that you will have to persuade stubborn people to look at alternatives. If you are a parent, this can often be symbolic of worry regarding teenage children making unsuitable friends.

Leader

To be a leader in a dream is an omen that you should soon be offered a promotion or a leading role in a project.

If you are following a leader you need to be sure that decisions you make are of your own reasoning and not because someone is bullying you.

Leaflets

To hand out leaflets means that you are in need of support, whether financial or practical, in order to put a plan into action.

To be given or to read a leaflet means you may have a chance to join a large organisation or be given the opportunity to have training.

Leak

If there is a gas or water leak, it can mean that someone is revealing your secrets or stirring up trouble behind your back. You should act now to avoid a major conflict in the future.

See also **floods** *or* **gas**

Leaping

To be able to leap high in a dream is a very good sign, you will succeed with a plan or dream you did not think possible. This is an especially good omen with regards to sporting activities or driving tests.

Learning

To learn something new in a dream or to master a new skill you have struggled with, indicates you may be unexpectedly offered training or extra help. It is also a sign of success with regards to a new profession or hobby.

See also **school**

Leather

This represents the chance of experiencing unexpected luxury for a day or two. It can also symbolise a very passionate time, whether with a new lover or your existing one.

Leaves

To walk beneath the leaves on a tree or to jump into a pile of leaves represents happiness, prosperity and success.

Falling leaves herald a turning point or happiness during autumn.

See also **autumn**

Leaving

If you are leaving a place or situation it can indicate that the time has come for you to move to a new job, home or situation in reality.

If someone you recognise is leaving, it can represent an unexpressed anxiety you have that you need to talk through with that person.

Legacy

To be left money in a legacy is an indication of money coming your way, not necessarily as a legacy, but maybe as a gift from a relative, the results of a past venture or from money owed to you.

Legend

To be told a legend in a dream is often a past-life experience, but it can also suggest you should perhaps try writing a book.

Legs

If you have attractive legs in a dream it means that someone will pay you a compliment and maybe flirt with you in the near future.

To have fat legs means you fear others find you unattractive.

Injured legs mean that you are being forced into a course of action or lifestyle change that you do not really want.

Lemon

A lemon tree symbolises a holiday in a warm place.

To eat lemons or to cook with them is a sign that a resentful elderly relative may try to interfere in your life.

See also **food** *or* **fruit**

Lend

To lend money or other items in a dream is an indication that you give more of yourself than you receive in return from a younger person and may need to start getting tough with them.

Leopard

This fierce swift creature represents your desire for freedom, possibly from someone who is trying to hold you back by undermining your confidence.

See also **animals** *or* **wild beasts**

Lessons

If you are taking lessons of any sort, you are ready to learn something new or to make a career change which may involve new skills.

If you cannot take in what someone is teaching you it is a sign that someone is trying to make you see life their way.

See also **musical instruments** *or* **school**

Letter

To receive a letter in a dream foretells of good news coming your way through the post within a week.

To write and send a letter says that you have something you need to say to a particular person which you have been holding back for fear of upsetting them. However, it will continue to bother you until you speak up.

See also **envelope, mail, pen, postman** *or* **writing**

Letterbox

A letterbox indicates that you need to enter into, or increase, formal correspondence regarding property negotiations or financial disputes in order to resolve the problem.

Lettuce

Picking, buying or eating lettuce is a promise of new things and people entering your life. This is an especially good symbol if you have felt stuck in a rut lately.

A limp or slug-infested lettuce is a warning you should be wary of promises made by a new acquaintance.

See also **vegetables**

Levitation

To rise above the ground in a dream may be an out-of-body experience, but it can also mean you will be successful in any venture you wish to try, whether it be a new relationship or a promotion at work.

Library

A library signifies that you know a great deal more than you think about a matter so you should trust your own judgement.

If a library building is closed it means that you should wait before making a decision or speaking out as there may be hidden factors that will emerge in due course.

See also **book**

Licence

To apply for a licence for something in a dream is a good indication that what are simply plans at the moment will become a reality.

If you dream of a marriage licence while in a relationship, it is a good indication that the relationship will be permanent.

Lie

To lie in bed feeling warm and comfortable means that you may soon get extra time off or receive unexpected help so that you can take life easy for a while.

To be exhausted or ill and forced to lie down is your body telling you to slow down in your everyday life to regain your energy and enthusiasm in order to prevent illness.

Lies

If you are lying in a dream it can merely be reflecting plans you have made which you think will be met with disapproval, thereby forcing you to keep quiet.

If someone you recognise is lying to you, it may be a warning that they are being unusually secretive in real life. Maybe you should try to find out why.

Life-belt

To be wearing a life-belt in the sea is a sign that you could sort out your current problems yourself if you stopped putting others first.

Lifeboat

To be in a lifeboat is a good omen as it forecasts that your fears of disaster, whether financial or emotional, will not be as bad as you thought. This may be because someone will come to your rescue offering you a new start.

See also **boats**

Lifeguard

If you are a lifeguard in a dream it can suggest that you may soon have to help a younger family member get out of trouble.

If a lifeguard rescues you, it is a sign of new or deepening love or happiness with someone you can trust (possibly your present partner).

Lift

To go up in a lift means that a current wish or dream will succeed.

To go down in a lift means that you shouldn't let others dampen your enthusiasm for a venture.

Being stuck in a lift reflects you are feeling trapped by a particular person or situation.

Light

To be surrounded by light represents spiritual awakening or emerging healing abilities. Sometimes ghosts of loved ones can appear within light or as light, but usually this is a positive sign.

To be blinded by lights means that someone is trying to rush you into making a decision, maybe without telling you the full implications.

See also **illumination, lamp, lantern** *or* **torch**

Lighthouse

To see a lighthouse indicates you will be able to steer an even course through the turbulent emotions of someone close. It foretells that you will be able to seek the advice of someone who is calm, reliable and detached from the situation.

Lightning

Flashes of lightning can foretell a sudden opportunity or solution to a long-standing problem.

If your house is struck by lightning you need to be wary of disruptive teenagers or difficult neighbours who may try to initiate a dispute.

See also **storm** *or* **thunder**

Lilac

Lilacs growing on a bush or arranged in a vase signify domestic happiness and indicate that family matters will bring joy. This is a good omen for older people as it suggests a long and happy life.

See also **flowers**

Lilies

These are the flowers of love and marriage and are therefore an excellent omen for you, a close friend or a family member. For those in a relationship, lilies are also a token of fidelity.

See also **flowers**

Linen

To dream of folding bed or table linen or to make a bed using clean linen, is a representation of a settled home, either now or within a few months. This dream is sometimes a sign that you are ready to settle down after frequent travelling.

Lines

Straight lines symbolise a direct course of action, a straightforward journey or a new enterprise.

Wavy or broken lines indicate uneven progress or the need to take detours to achieve an aim.

Lion

This is symbolic of power. It indicates that ambition or success will take precedence, albeit temporarily, over a relationship or domestic issue. You may be asked to lead or will find the courage to take a step towards greater independence.

To be attacked by lions indicates you are fearful of your own anger or passion and this is making you act defensively or aggressively.

See also **animals** *or* **wild beasts**

Lips

If someone's lips are moving but no sound is emitted, the person you are dreaming of may be hiding an ulterior agenda or are being insincere towards you. You should be careful of taking what they say as truthful.

See also **kiss** *or* **mouth**

Lipstick

Putting on or wearing lipstick indicates you will be noticed by someone you have always liked. This is a promising sign if you are looking for love.

Liqueur

This denotes an opportunity for passion or means you have a secret admirer who would like to be more than just a friend to you.

See also **alcohol** *or* **drinking**

Lists

This is an anxiety dream that indicates you have too much to do and don't have enough time. You should try to relax before going to bed, even for ten minutes, to avoid this kind of dream.

Litter

A place covered in litter symbolises you are becoming overwhelmed with, for example, unfinished paperwork or domestic chores. However, if you manage to clear up the litter, it shows that you have the power to maintain control of your life.

Living room

This is a sign that family or domestic matters will occupy a lot of your attention over the coming few weeks, but it will be very rewarding. This is a good omen if you are planning a family party or buying or renting a new home.

See also **home** *or* **house**

Lizard

This symbol means you should check facts carefully as the source may not be reliable. This is often an early warning signal that people may change their minds or break their promises at the last minute.

See also **animals**

Loaf

An uncut loaf indicates a future party or family celebration.

To cut a loaf and give it to other people is a warning you should not be too lavish with your hospitality.

See also **bread**

Lock (door)

If a door or gate is locked it means you may find an opportunity you had hoped for, even if the rewards do not materialise immediately.

To unlock a door is a good sign and can indicate the re-growth of love and trust after an emotional setback.

See also **door, key** *or* **padlock**

Lock (hair)

If someone gives you a lock of hair in a dream it is an indication that you may find true love soon.

If you give a lock of hair away is signifies that you may have the chance to travel, although it may cause a conflict of loyalties.

Locket

To dream of a locket is a promise of happiness in love or marriage for you or a family member. It can also indicate that someone from the past of whom you were very fond of may return.

See also **jewellery** *or* **necklace**

Logs

A pile of chopped logs promises that abundance will come and remain in your home throughout the winter.

To be cutting logs means that you should make a lot of preparations now for your future financial security.

See also **tree**

Loneliness

To feel lonely in a dream actually denotes that you will meet new friends in the near future and will be given the opportunity to enjoy a new interest.

Loom

This could be a past-life dream or a warning to avoid gossips, office plots and bitchiness, especially concerning a newcomer.

Loop

Any kind of loop in a dream is a sign that you may be temporarily diverted from your work or goal by seemingly pointless arguments and prejudices.

Loss

To lose money or a precious possession is an indication that you are worried your present success or happiness will not last.

If you have lost something in real life and dream of finding it, maybe you should look for the real-life equivalent of the dream place and you may find the missing article.

Lost

If you are in an unfamiliar place and lose your way, it can represent worries you have about a new venture such as moving house or job. This is simply an anxiety dream.

To dream of losing your child can mean that you are feeling quite naturally overwhelmed by the responsibility of caring for a child. This is also a normal reaction to the many dangers of the world. You should take extra precautions to alleviate your anxiety.

Lottery

If you win the lottery it can represent an increase in fortune, maybe in a competition, although it may well be quite a modest win.

If you dream of a friend or family member winning the lottery and not sharing it, it can show that you have hidden resentment towards them in real-life. You may feel that he or she is taking unfair advantage of you or receiving favours that you are not.

See also **fortune, gambling** *or* **money**

Love

If you are not in love at present, this dream indicates that you are receptive to love and may soon meet someone special. You may even find that particular person is literally the man or girl of your dreams.

Lover

If you dream of your present love or he/she is dreaming of you, there may be a hidden important issue that you need to talk about. Maybe you would both benefit from sharing lucid dreams (see pages 37 and 49).

If you dream that your lover is unfaithful, it can be an indication that you both have been taking each other for granted and should try to make the relationship feel special again.

To dream of a past love suggests that your present relationship is lacking in romance or passion.

See also **hugging, husband** *or* **infidelity**

Lucid dreaming

See **dreaming**

Luck

To experience good luck in a dream predicts you will have a change in your fortunes for the better.

To dream of bad luck is often an unfounded anxiety dream that your present love or happiness will not last.

Luggage

To carry a lot of luggage indicates that you are taking on too many responsibilities on behalf of others or are carrying old guilt that you need to shed.

If you lose your luggage or leave it behind somewhere, it is a sign that your mind is in overload and you need to relax more, especially before bedtime. You may also be trying to control a difficult situation.

Lungs

If you cannot breathe or are experiencing problems with your lungs, it signifies that you are holding back something you need to say or do. It can also mean that someone is suffocating you with their possessive or over-protective nature.

Luxury

To dream of living in luxury is a good omen for long-term prosperity, although your fortunes may increase gradually.

M

Macaroni

To cook or eat macaroni or other small pasta shapes is an indication that you need to be cautious with money and not make impulse buys.

See also **food**

Machinery

Machinery is a sign of prosperity and harmony. A sewing machine in particular is symbolic of domestic bliss and marriage in the family.

If machinery is broken it means you need to take care of machines at home or at work to avoid faults. This dream could be a result of your subconscious noticing a potential problem in real life.

See also **oil (engine/machine)**

Magazine

To read a magazine or a journal in a dream foretells that you will find some information you urgently need in a magazine or book. See if you recognise the publication as that will be the one which holds the answer.

See also **journalist**

Maggot

Maggots crawling on food or on a dead animal represent someone in your life who is taking a lot from you and giving nothing back. You should try to rid yourself of that person if possible.

Magical symbols

A magic circle promises that an unfinished matter will soon be completed in a way that exceeds your expectations.

Magical tools, such as wands, mean you should ignore critics as you will succeed in a way that will surprise everybody.

A pentagram is not a bad sign but a symbol of unexpected help or resolution to a difficulty you have been experiencing.

Triangles are also mystical symbols which signify unexpected possibilities and undeveloped talents that could lead to success. If the apex is facing downwards towards the earth, it is a sign that opportunities must be seized before they are missed.

Magician

If you are watching a magician perform magic tricks it means that someone at work is pretending to be more knowledgeable or competent than they actually are. You should not be fooled by their fine words and illusion of expertise.

Magic spells

To perform magic spells in a dream can be a sign that you have psychic powers and should trust your intuition more. You should maybe try to develop your clairvoyant powers.

To dream of being a victim of negative magic or witchcraft can indicate that there may be deceit or malice close to you on an earthly level which your subconscious is aware of.

Magic tricks

A box of magic tricks is a warning that you should not simply take an easier option or accept a suspiciously good offer without checking the facts properly first.

If you are demonstrating magic tricks successfully, you may get away with a risky plan. If the tricks are going wrong, however, any white lies you have told will be found out.

Magnet

A forceful attraction, either to a person or a particular course of action, means those things will bring you happiness.

If you are being drawn against your will, however, then you should try to remove yourself from a potentially destructive situation.

Magnifying glass

If you are looking at things through a magnifying glass, it is a warning that you may be worrying unnecessarily about a problem or person.

Mail

If you receive a lot of mail in a dream, it foretells that you will have lots of options that you had not expected relating to a change of job or home.

See also **envelope, letter** *or* **postman**

Mailbox

See **letterbox**

Malice

If a person is being malicious in a dream it is often a subconscious warning that a new acquaintance, who seems friendly, is in fact spiteful and gossiping about you behind your back.

Manure

To put animal manure or compost on your garden is a sign that your finances will improve gradually. This may be as a result of a new venture or investment you are planning to make or have already embarked on.

Map

This is an indication of possible travel in the near future. If you cannot find where you are on the map, you may encounter a period of indecision in your life where you will need to wait for signs to show you the best path to take.

See also **navigate** *or* **travel**

Marble

To dream of marble buildings may be a past-life dream or an indication that you will soon visit a place with ancient buildings that will bring you great pleasure.

Mare

A female horse is a positive symbol of motherhood and fertility. It signifies that dealings with your own mother or being a mother will bring you great happiness. This is an excellent omen if you are trying for a baby.

See also **animals** *or* **mother**

Market

This is a good dream to have if you are trying to sell something. It is particularly auspicious for job-hunting, especially after a period of unemployment.

Marriage

If you are getting married in the dream, even if you are already married in reality, it means that you are craving romance and security, something your present relationship might be lacking.

If you are watching other people getting married you may be feeling sidelined in a relationship, perhaps because of unfriendly or interfering relations or a love rival.

See also **engagement** *or* **wedding**

Mask

If you are wearing a mask, it can be an indication that you feel unable to show your true feelings because you are uncertain of other people's intentions or possible responses.

If someone else is wearing a mask, it can be a sign that they may have secrets from their past that they are unwilling to reveal to you or that they are playing power games with you.

Mass

To dream of attending mass, or any type of religious service, even if you do not go to church usually, is often an indication of awakening spiritual power. You may soon become aware of your guardian angel.

See also **church**

Mathematics lesson
See **academic lessons**

Maypole
This is an ancient fertility symbol which indicates the stirring of life, whether in the form of a pregnancy, a new project or delight at the onset of spring.

Maze
To be lost in a maze can be a reflection of your confusion about future plans and direction, perhaps because others have been giving you conflicting messages. You should trust your instincts with regards to the wisest path to follow and then take the course you have decided upon, dismissing doubts and doubters.
See also **labyrinth**

Meadow
To be walking or sitting in a grassy meadow is a sign of settled and harmonious times ahead of you, especially if you have been undergoing a period of change.

Meal
To enjoy a meal in a dream means that you will not lack basic resources, no matter how bad things seem financially. A family meal is an indication that domestic affairs will be happy.
See also **food**

Measles
If you or a family member suffer from measles in a dream, it is a sign that good fortune will follow an unexpected delay.
See also **disease** *or* **illness**

Measurement
To measure something indicates that any changes you make to your life at the moment will be advantageous.

Medicine
To take medicine in a dream means you need to tackle paperwork and unpleasant chores you have been avoiding.

Medicine man
To be healed or helped by a native American medicine man is usually an indication that you have a wise guardian or spirit guide looking after you. It can also indicate that you possess natural healing abilities.

Megaliths

To visit a megalithic monument in a dream may indicate a past-life experience. If you don't think it was a past-life dream, megaliths also foretell of unexpected contact with distant relatives.

Megaphone

To shout through a megaphone indicates that you are becoming impatient with a family member or boss who will not listen to your opinion or grievances.

Melon

To eat a melon is symbolic of new opportunities coming your way. This may denote a fresh start after setbacks or stagnation.

To see melons growing is a promise of future foreign travel.

See also **food** *or* **fruit**

Mermaid

A beautiful singing mermaid is a warning not to be seduced or lured by physical attractiveness and short-term gains. This dream can be a sign that you may be tempted to be unfaithful in the future or will favour temporary excitement over long-term happiness.

See also **mythical creatures**

Meteor

In the past this was believed to be a sign of a gift from the deities. The dream meteor suggests the dreamer should seize the moment as a sudden opportunity may disappear as quickly as it arrived, never to return again.

See also **illumination**

Mice

To dream of mice running about in a house represents a fear of being overwhelmed by a number of small problems that were created by other people and that are now out of control.

A mouse that runs over you indicates an invasion of your privacy at home, perhaps by a neighbour or a friend who visits too often.

See also **animals, traps** *or* **vermin**

Midwife

If the midwife is delivering your child it means that you should receive help in furthering an ambition or dream.

If you are the midwife, you may soon have to take over a job or project that someone else has abandoned, or help a younger person to get organised.

See also **labour**

Milestone

If you see old-fashioned milestones beside a road, you may be experiencing a past-life dream. Milestones can also suggest that you will succeed if you persevere.

Milk

Dreaming of pouring milk for others suggests that you are being too generous or understanding towards someone.

To drink milk or buy it is a sign of fertility. This is an excellent omen if you want a settled relationship or a child.

See also **cow, drinking** *or* **food**

Millionaire

If you marry a very rich person in your dream, it can be a sign that you may be offered a position within a big firm or large organisation.

If you are the millionaire, it can mean that your work or investments will pay off, albeit probably in a more modest way.

See also **money**

Mimic

See **imitation**

Mine (land)

To walk through an area that is full of hidden land mines reflects a potentially explosive situation at home or work that you can negotiate if you are tactful and exercise caution.

Mine (underground)

To be in an underground mine signifies that you have great potential and if you persist will succeed in any venture you choose to undertake, both financially and in terms of personal fulfilment. This is a good sign if you are learning healing or are involved in psychic work.

If you are trapped in a mine or working in one and feel exhausted, your natural optimism and enthusiasm are being suppressed by someone who would like to control you emotionally.

See also **quarry**

Mirrors

This suggests that you should learn to value your own worth and realise what a lot you have in the way of talents and charisma, especially if you are worried about getting older and less attractive.

A broken mirror, or one that reflects hideous images, expresses fears that your real self has been distorted or has disappeared due to the demands of others. This is a sign that you need to fight back.

See also **reflection**

Missing trains, appointments, etc...

This dream is usually a reaction to stress. Your body needs to slow down and you need to prioritise your commitments. It might be worth double-checking any travel arrangements and allowing extra time for keeping appointments until you feel more in control again.

Mobile phone

If a mobile is constantly ringing in your dream, it is a sign that you are feeling tense and need to find a way to relax.

If you receive a voice message, the person who sent it may appear in your life unexpectedly.

See also **dialling, telephone** *or* **text message**

Mole

This suggests that secrets will soon be revealed. It could be that someone you think of as a friend at work is undermining someone (not necessarily you) and causing discontent or disruption.

Money

If you dream of a money-making scheme write it down as soon as you wake, as it may hold the key to a successful venture in reality.

To inherit or win money can suggest you may experience unexpected prosperity in a small way.

To lose money or be overwhelmed by demands for it, suggests that you may be feeling drained due to real-life money worries. You should try to slow down so that you can deal with your problems properly.

See also **bank, counting, debt, fortune, gambling, lottery, millionaire, riches, saving, treasure** *or* **wages**

Money lender

To dream of a money lender illustrates you are worried about your finances but suggests that things will turn out fine.

If a money lender threatens you, you should avoid giving loans to unreliable people, even family members, who may never pay you back.

Monk

This is often an indication that there is a wise guardian or spirit guide in your life. It can also reflect a need within you to withdraw from the frantic pace of life.

Monkey

This is often symbolic of a mischief-maker, a fickle friend, a curious child or an immature adult. However, it can also be symbolic of ingenuity and enterprise with regards to solving problems.

A big destructive monkey represents an annoying person in your life who is quite amusing, but often at your expense.

A small cute monkey can represent suppressed maternal or paternal instincts.

See also **animals** *or* **ape**

Monster

Being chased by a monster indicates you have hidden fears which keeping growing because you keep them to yourself.

If you defeat a monster it means that you should be able to overcome even your greatest problems before the year is over.

Month

To have a dream about a particular month is a sign that any plans or dreams you have should come to fruition during the month indicated in the dream. This is often a good omen if you are looking for love.

Moon

The moon is symbolic of new beginnings, new love and increased psychic powers. It is an indication of an opportune time to learn or use the Tarot if you are interested.

Crescent or waxing moon: This is a time for wishes to come true and for new beginnings. It foretells that good things will come into your life and that existing good fortune may continue to grow within the next two weeks. This is an excellent omen if you are going for job interviews.

Decreasing or waning moon: Now is the time for you to finish a project or venture that has been stagnating but if you are planning a new venture, then you should wait and rest before undertaking it. A waning moon can also indicate that your healing powers may be naturally emerging and could be developed if you wish.

Full moon: This indicates you are ready for a big leap forward or a major change in your life, such as having children.

See also **eclipse** *or* **night**

Moth

A moth fluttering around a light suggests that something you are involved with is heading for disaster. You should fight against the destructive relationship or bad habit that is threatening to spoil your life.

See also **animals** *or* **insects**

Mother

Dreaming of your mother, whether she is alive or dead, indicates an instinctive need for reassurance and wise counsel.

To dream of your dead mother can be a very healing experience, especially if there was a bad relationship in life.

If your mother is alive and you are not getting along well in real life, a dream like this can be a subconscious way of getting through to her. This may even result in a spontaneous improvement in the everyday relationship.

If you dream that you are a mother, even if you are not in real-life, it means that you are having to care emotionally for a great deal of people at the moment. If you feel happy with this, then it is a good sign, but if you are not then you should try to spend less time with the people who are draining you emotionally.

See also **family, labour, mare** *or* **parents**

Mountains

A mountain dream is an indication that there are obstacles ahead. However, if you are running or walking effortlessly up a mountain or on the downward path, having reached the top, these problems will easily be overcome.

Mourning

To be mourning someone who has died or feel grief towards a failed relationship in a dream, even if this is not the case in real life, says that you have regrets about the loss of your personal freedom or are maybe having doubts about a relationship.

See also **death/dying**

Moustache

See **beard**

Mouth

An open mouth indicates that you have a lot of financial responsibilities and may need to prioritise your limited resources.

A closed mouth says that someone close to you will not listen to reason or persuasion so you may have to go ahead with a plan alone.

See also **kiss** *or* **lips**

Moving (house or objects)

If you are moving house and having to transport large items in a dream, it can be a sign that you are worried about a major change or upheaval that you are planning to undertake, even though it is something you really want. Try to identify the obstacles in the dream and see how these can be overcome practically.

See also **home** *or* **house**

Mowing

Mowing grass suggests you should cut your losses with regards to a particular person or reduce your expenditure on people who regularly drain your resources.

See also **grass**

Mud

Mud is a very creative dream symbol and heralds the coming of money, love and satisfaction through earthly endeavour.

To get covered in mud and hate it is an indication that you may be feeling guilty about having strong sexual feelings for someone or justifiable anger.

See also **earth** *or* **quagmire**

Murder

If you are the murderer, you may be feeling guilty about making a change in your life that will involve leaving people you love for a while.

If you witness someone being threatened with murder, it can mean that it is proving harder than you thought to, for example, stick to a diet or quit smoking. Try to persevere and it will get easier.

See also **killing** *or* **suffocation**

Mushrooms

Picking mushrooms from a field or woodland says that you may experience unexpected financial gains in the near future. If the mushrooms you pick turn out to be poisonous, you should be wary of unwise investments.

See also **food** *or* **vegetables**

Music

Beautiful music is an indication of harmonious happy times ahead and perhaps the rediscovery or development of an artistic or creative talent you last used in childhood.

Loud or discordant music indicates that quarrels with others are affecting you more than you care to admit.

See also **composer, duet, musical instruments, orchestra** *or* **quartet**

Musical instruments

If you are playing the instrument well, it indicates that your life should be without too many obstacles and setbacks.

If you cannot play an instrument or you or another person is playing it badly, then you are trying too hard to keep everyone happy.

See also individual instruments, **lessons, music, orchestra** *or* **quartet**

Mustard

Adding mustard to your plate or to food is an indication that you crave more excitement in your life or in a particular relationship.

Mutation

To see a strange being made up of different animals or people, could be indicative of an alien encounter or a fear that your life is being changed in ways you do not like.

If the form changes from one creature to another during the dream, you may have suspicions regarding a new acquaintance or lover in whom you have seen signs of a less loveable character.

Mythical creatures

To dream of mythical beings, such as unicorns, is usually a sign that a very creative period is about to begin. Sometimes these dreams can be an indication that psychic powers are beginning to emerge.

See also individual creatures

Nails (finger)

Broken fingernails foretell that a promise will be broken.

Dirty nails suggest that you should not dismiss a prospective partner simply because they are not immediately attractive.

Long nails indicate a friend may be jealous of your relationship or success in other areas.

Varnishing finger and toenails forecasts a celebration or big party. If someone you recognise is varnishing your nails they may be trying to flatter you in real life.

Nails (metal)

Banging nails into a wall or using them to make something indicates that you may need to be quite forceful in order to get your opinons heard.

Nakedness

If you are naked and feel comfortable, it suggests that you are confident in expressing your needs, emotional as well as sexual. However, if you find yourself naked in a public place or at work, you may be afraid that you are not capable of keeping your present job or that you are not attractive enough to please your lover. Usually these fears are a result of an insecure person who has tried to make you feel inadequate to make themselves feel better.

See also **undress**

Name

If someone calls your name it is an indication that you will soon get an opportunity to show off your talents.

If you change your name it suggests that there is a side to your personality you have been suppressing which would bring you great happiness if you allowed it to emerge.

To forget your name in a dream means that someone is trying to steal the credit for your ideas.

Navel

To dream of a navel is a sign of pregnancy in the family.

If your navel is swollen or infected, it means that someone has hurt your feelings deeply and you should talk about it.

Navigate

To be navigating in a car, a boat or a plane means you may need to take control of any decision-making at work or at home as others are being indecisive or arguing amongst themselves.

See also **map**

Navy

To be in the navy indicates that you are feeling restricted by your present life and need to widen your horizons.

To see a naval ship in a dockyard suggests that a relative or close friend may decide to join the uniformed services or work abroad.

See also **boats, officer, uniform, victory** *or* **war**

Neck

If you have a stiff or painful neck in a dream, it indicates that a family member or lover is being temperamental with you.

To dream of a beautiful neck is a sign that you should fall in love soon or experience a pleasant flirtation with a younger person.

Necklace

To be given or to wear a necklace symbolises emotional commitment.

A broken or lost necklace signifies that a quarrel or temporary rift is building up with someone you are fond of.

See also **gemstones, jewellery** *or* **locket**

Needle

Threading or sewing with a needle says that a quarrel or estrangement can be mended if you make the first step towards peace.

Neighbours

To dream of friendly neighbours denotes you are about to embark on a more settled phase in your life and may receive unexpected practical help from a neighbour.

If you do not recognise the neighbour in your dream, it suggests that someone new may move into your area soon and will become a good friend.

Neighbourhood disputes are an indication that you feel unsettled in your home, although not necessarily because of your neighbours.

See also **home** *or* **house**

Neighing

A neighing horse is a warning to be prepared for disruptions to your life in the form of visitors or demanding relatives. Neighing horses also reflect hidden fears about security to your home, so check your security measures are still effective to reassure yourself.

See also **horse**

Nephew

To dream of a nephew, whether your actual nephew or not, is a sign that a younger man, not necessarily a nephew, will be of assistance in bringing business your way.

See also **family**

Nest

A nest full of eggs is a sign that you will soon decorate or renovate your home.

An empty nest indicates that a younger family member, or even yourself if still living with parents, will move out.

See also **birds**

Nets

Nets full of fish foretell the success of a business or financial venture.

Nets that are empty suggest that you should maybe try further from home if you are looking for a new job or relationship.

Nettles

Nettles are a sign that you should try to protect yourself or a vulnerable family member from spite or bullying.

See also **weeds**

Newspaper

To read a newspaper forecasts good news regarding a friend or relative who is away at the moment.

If the dream newspaper has a vivid headline this can sometimes be a prediction for a national or international event.

See also **journalist**

Niece

To dream of a niece, whether or not you actually have one, refers to a young woman who will come into your life or family in the near future.

See also **family**

Night

If it is night-time in your dream, the dream is of special significance as night indicates the increase of psychic power and wisdom.

See also **moon** *or* **stars (sky)**

Nightclub

Enjoying yourself in a nightclub suggests that you will have the chance to enjoy a good night out in the near future, where you may even meet someone special if you are unattached.

To witness a fight or attack in a nightclub illustrates that you are worried that a secret affair or past mistake committed by you or someone close may be discovered.

See also **dancing** *or* **drinking**

Nightmare

A nightmare is usually an expression of your hidden fears and anxieties and can help you to overcome them when you wake.

Noises

If you dream that you are alone in a house and hear strange noises, it represents your fears for personal safety and suggests that you need to examine issues regarding security in your waking life. To hear noises can also be a warning that someone is reading your private correspondence or e-mails.

Noose

A hangman's noose says you are choking back resentment or anger at being stifled by possessiveness or criticism at home or work.

See also **execution**

North

To dream of going north indicates that new ventures are secure but you may have to persevere in order to overcome difficulties in order to make them successful.

Nose

A long pointed nose denotes interference into your personal affairs by an older relative or work colleague.

If your nose is blocked and you lose your sense of smell, it shows that you are secretly worried about the trustworthiness of someone close.

Notebook

To write things down in a notebook suggests you need to ensure you record the details of important conversations.

See also **pen**

Novel

If you are writing a novel, it indicates that you should develop your creative or artistic talents in real life.

To read a novel shows you are feeling as though you are living your life through other people and need to become more independent in order to do the things that make you happy.

See also **computer** *or* **pen**

Numbers

0   Anything is possible. You may find that your luck or money increase. This is an excellent omen for those who play the lottery or other games of chance.

1   You may soon encounter an unexpected opportunity or will enjoy the chance to shine.

2   You will need to balance the needs of two people for a while.

3   There will be a promotion or a birth in the family.

4   You need to learn to be realistic and work within restrictions.

5   You may be able to make changes in your life without creating a massive upheaval.

6   A quarrel will be resolved. This is also an indication of a new and harmonious period in your life.

7   Secrets may soon be revealed to you. You need to learn to trust your intuition.

8   This is a positive sign that highlights financial gain, a new business venture or money-making scheme. Eight is an indication that now is a good time for speculation.

9   You do not need to accept second-best. A new challenge will bring you a great advantage.

10 A long-standing dispute will come to an end or a project that you have been working on will have a successful outcome.

11 If you dream of anything grouped together into elevens or there is am emphasis on the number eleven, it means that whatever you dream about will increase in value or happiness. It is a good omen if you play the lottery or gamble.

See also **column of numbers**

Nurse

If you are a nurse working in an old-fashioned hospital it may be a past-life dream, which you could explore using lucid dreaming techniques (see page 37).

To be a nurse in the present day shows you have a talent for the caring professions and should maybe explore a career working with vulnerable people.

To be cared for by a nurse in a dream is an indication that you have too many people fighting for your attention and need to remember to take care of your own health.

See also **hospital**

Nursery (botanical)

To visit a place where plants are grown and sold means you may soon encounter a number of opportunities to make money but these will start in a small way and will take several months before you see results.

See also **flowers** *or* **plants**

Nursery (infant)

A nursery full of babies is obviously a good omen if you want to start a family, although it can also mean that you may be given or may find a young animal to keep as a pet which will bring you great happiness.

A nursery is often a pre-pregnancy dream or, if you are already pregnant, a sign that all will go well with the birth.

If the nursery is badly run, it is simply an anxiety dream (not a prediction) highlighting your fears about leaving your children or a sick family member under other peoples' supervision.

Nuts

Nuts are a traditional symbol of long-term prosperity. In particular, buried nuts indicate you may obtain an old item cheaply or will be given one as a gift that when valued in the future will be worth quite a lot of money.

Nuts are also fertility symbols and indicate healthy children, either for the dreamer or a family member.

See also **squirrel**

Nut tree

This represents long-life and health for the dreamer.

A grove of nut trees promises there will be additions to the family circle, whether by birth, marriage, remarriage or adoption, which will bring great happiness to the existing family circle.

See also **tree**

Oak tree

An oak tree is a very lucky symbol, as it forecasts a long, healthy and happy life with the prospect of a happy and long-lasting marriage.

A tree with acorns denotes a promotion and increased prosperity that will last through old age.

See also **tree**

Oar

This indicates you need to seek out your own solution to a problem or get on with a project on your own rather than waiting for other people to help. Oars also forecast a move further afield.

To lose an oar means you need to plan a future journey carefully to avoid any last minute hitches.

A broken oar indicates delays.

See also **boats**

Oasis

To dream of arriving at an oasis represents finding relief from ill-health or a long-standing problem.

If the oasis in the desert turns out to be a mirage, you should be wary of a very cheap holiday offer or a loan of money with incredibly low rates. Make sure you check the details thoroughly.

See also **desert**

Oath

To swear an oath, whether in court or a lawyer's office, indicates that a legal or official matter will soon be settled to your advantage.

To break an oath or to refuse to swear one suggests you should not be too liberal with the truth on official forms.

See also **court of law**

Oatmeal

To dream of cooking and eating oatmeal is symbolic of domestic happiness and an abundance of resources in the home. If you are worrying about older people that you know, your fears will prove to be unfounded.

Oats

A field of oats is symbolic of fertility and increased sexual happiness in a long-standing relationship. However, you should be wary if there is anyone in the dream sowing or planting oats, as you may meet someone in real-life who will prove to be fickle when it comes to love.

Obedience

To be obedient to a master or mistress in a dream could be a glimpse into a past world. Alternatively, it suggests that, for now, success lies with conforming and following official policy.

Obelisk

Originally this was an Ancient Egyptian symbol, so to see an obelisk could signify a past-life dream.

Obelisks also represent the chance to achieve an ambition in a remarkably short time so this is a good omen for those who want a career in science or technology or for men who want to father a child.

Obesity

Obesity dreams usually occur at crisis points during a diet. However, if you are fat in a dream but feel comfortable, it indicates you will enjoy an expansion in your career prospects or an awakening of sexual passion. You may also start to have a desire to become pregnant or to create a new venture.

If you are unhappy or someone is being horrible to you about your size, you may be feeling guilty about wanting too much from life or from others. You may also be worried that people will reject you if they find out what you are really like.

See also **food**

Obituary

To read about your own obituary or that of a loved one is never a premonition of death. Instead, it represents a past endeavour that will now bear fruit or be recognised. Obituaries also signal a career or life change where your past experiences will form the basis for success.

See also **death/dying**

Objections

If someone in a dream keeps making objections to your suggestions or plans, there may be someone in reality who is interfering in your life. If possible, do not let that person know your future plans.

Observatory

To dream of an observatory from which you can study the stars denotes a possibility that you will gain momentary fame or even celebrity status. Observatories can also be an indication that you have the potential to work in the media, the arts or astrology.

See also **stars (sky)** *or* **telescope**

Obstruction

To be driving along in a dream and come across an obstruction in the road can be a warning you need to check any travel plans you have made. Such obstructions or unexpected difficulties could also be your subconscious forcing you to acknowledge that you do not really want to make a planned change or leave a familiar setting. Obstructions can also suggest that you need to find more than one possible source of extra income if you need to borrow money.

If there are 'keep-out' signs everywhere, stopping you from entering a place you want to go to, this can represent people (usually family members) who are making it difficult for you to start making changes in your life or to begin a new activity or venture.

Occultist

If you dream of practising white magic or being clairvoyant, you may have psychic abilities that you could develop. To dream of watching an occultist practising magic or divination means you should listen to your own intuition when deciding whether to trust a new friend or colleague with personal information.

See also **palmistry** *or* **witch**

Ocean

See **sea**

Octopus

This symbolises a fear of being unable to disentangle yourself from an emotional situation or the possessiveness of others. An octopus also represents a desire to leave a secure, but stifling situation and can also highlight hidden worries, if you are a parent, about older children leaving home, especially if they are still very dependent emotionally on their family.

See also **animals** *or* **sea**

Offence

If you dream you commit a traffic offence or experience a minor encounter with the law in a dream, you may be feeling guilty about a minor indiscretion, not necessarily illegal, in your real life.

Offer

To receive an offer, whether of work, a loan or a bargain in a dream, is a very good omen that good luck should come your way. You may even receive a promising offer within a week or so of the dream.

Office

If you work in an office during the day and then dream of being in an office, it is simply a sign that your mind is overworked.

If you do not usually work in an office, then this is a dream which indicates that there are issues in your life that you need to sort out.

See also **boss, computer, e-mail, job** *or* **work**

Officer

To have dealings with an officer from any of the uniformed services, means you may soon have an important meeting with, for example, an employer or a bank official that will be to your advantage.

See also **army, navy, police** *or* **soldiers**

Official

To receive official communication is a guilt dream, so if you are behind with important paperwork, you should deal with it to get it off your mind.

Oil (aromatherapy)

To be buying or using aromatherapy oils can be a nudge from your body that it is in need of some extra care and relaxation.

Oil (engine/machine)

If you are oiling an engine or machine, then plans, especially concerning travel, should run smoothly.

If the oil is spilled or gets on your hands, you should take steps to ensure that you are not blamed for somebody else's mistake.

See also **machinery**

Ointment

To rub ointment on a cut or burn signifies that you may be required to act as a peacemaker, either at work or at home in the coming days.

Old (buildings)

To dream of old buildings may be a glimpse into a past-life. Old buildings can also suggest that the use of convention would be better than innovation or change at the moment.

Old (people)

See **elderly**

Olives

To eat olives denotes a holiday or a relaxed and harmonious period in your life. Olives are also a symbol of increased prosperity.

See also **food**

Olive tree

This means that a long-standing quarrel or controversy with a partner or older family member will be settled peacefully. Olive trees also represent improving health.

See also **tree**

Onions

Peeling or cooking onions indicates that any simmering domestic tension may soon bubble over, but this should help to clear the air.

Planting or eating onions suggests that a health or safety worry concerning a family member will soon disappear.

See also **vegetables**

Opal

Although many people believe opals to be unlucky, to see them in a dream is actually a sign that you could have psychic gifts.

Opals are a good omen for a betrothal or marriage in the family. They are also auspicious for younger people who may be leaving home to go to college or starting a first job.

A cracked or dull opal is an indication that your life in general is wearing you down.

See also **gemstones** *or* **jewellery**

Opalescence

If something shimmers in a dream it represents the presence of a guardian angel who will protect and guide you in the weeks and months ahead.

Open

If you come across an open door or a path through open land, it means that life will become easier for you and you may even be offered a job or promotion that you have long been seeking. This is an excellent omen for the self-employed.

Opening

If you see an opening in a fence or wall, it suggests that someone who has been hostile or unfriendly towards you will soon leave your life. Alternatively, you may be asked to join a club, a society or enter local government.

Opera

To sing in an opera denotes that your opinions will be taken seriously. This is a good omen for would-be authors, singers or broadcasters.

See also **theatre**

Operation

If you are about to undergo an operation in real life this is simply an anxiety dream. Generally, operations are a sign that you need to take decisive action to improve a situation or rid yourself of someone who brings negativity into your life.

See also **anaesthetic, doctor, hospital** *or* **plastic surgery**

Opportunity

To dream of an opportunity means that one should come your way in real life and you should be prepared to take it. The dream may suggest something you had not thought of but which would work out well if you were to put it into practice.

Opposite

If everything in a dream is the opposite way round from normal or people say the opposite from what is expected, it is a reflection of uncooperative teenagers, cranky relations or troublesome colleagues in your life who are making sensible communication difficult.

Opposition

If you are leading the opposition, whether at work or politically, you may find in real life that your principles are at odds with official policy or the majority view. You should quietly but firmly stick to what you believe in as there will be a change of heart eventually.

Optician

If you are having your eyes tested in a dream, this could be a reminder from your subconscious to book an appointment in real life.

If you are given really strong glasses it means that someone may be trying to con you or play on your sympathy.

See also **eyes**

Orange

The colour orange is symbolic of independence and self-confidence. It is a sign that you should believe in yourself more and not let others encroach your personal space.

See also **colours**

Orange blossom

This is symbolic of betrothals and marriage in the family. If you are in a relationship, it is a sign that your lover or partner will remain true to you.

Oranges

Oranges are symbolic of health and fertility. They also forecast improved finances, especially if you have the confidence to become self-employed, apply for a new job, or sign up for extra training. This is an especially good omen for people who work with children or in the travel industry.

See also **food** *or* **fruit**

Orange trees

A grove of orange trees is an indication that now is a good time to start long-term savings or investment plans for the future.

See also **tree**

Orchestra

If the orchestra is playing in harmony, it means that success may lie either in a joint venture or through cooperation with others. This is a favourable omen for partnerships of all kinds.

If the orchestra is discordant, it can mean that you are trying too hard to fit in with others and would probably be happier following your own path.

See also **music** *or* **musical instruments**

Organ

Listening to or playing organ music in a church or concert hall, is an indication that a venture or relationship will receive approval, whether from your family or an official body. This is an especially good dream for anyone submitting planning applications or trying to settle a divorce dispute.

See also **musical instruments**

Ornaments

Ornaments can be a sign of a settled home or the opportunity to settle down.

Broken ornaments can indicate you need to employ care and tact to settle an inheritance problem.

Orphan

If you rescue an orphaned child or animal in a dream, it suggests you may need to support someone close to you in the future if they are abandoned by a lover or suddenly left alone.

To be abandoned as a child and have to fend for yourself could be a reference to unresolved sorrows and hurt from childhood.

Ostrich

An ostrich symbolises someone who is ignoring a real threat or unpleasant situation in the hope that it will go away.

An ostrich's egg represents an unexpected gift.

See also **animals** *or* **birds**

Otter

This reflects a need to balance different demands on your time and priorities. You may be worrying about a new challenge at work, possibly because of new management, and are trying to adapt to the new situation as quickly as possible.

See also **animals**

Oval

To dream of anything oval is an indication that you should put long-standing plans into practice, even if only in a small way, as success could be yours. This is a good omen for college students and for anyone wishing to work in finance or banking.

Ovaries

This is symbolic of fertility and therefore an excellent omen if you are trying for a baby.

If you dream of experiencing problems with your ovaries, you should maybe wait a month before making a change or launching a new venture.

Oven

A hot oven filled with cooking food is a good indication that domestic finances will improve or remain stable.

A cold oven suggests you should not tolerate someone close to you being unfairly persistent in their cold or unloving behaviour.

Overalls

This is a good omen for all DIY, garden renovation or car maintenance work. Similarly, this is a good dream for anyone planning a more hands-on career or seeking an apprenticeship.

Overboard

To fall overboard from a boat, or to witness a family member fall overboard, reflects worries about possible changes or actions where you fear you or someone else will be taking a risk or may encounter unforeseen circumstances. This dream could also be your subconscious asking you if you are ready to embark on a new sexual relationship.

See also **boats**

Overcoat

If a man is wearing a big overcoat it can reflect a male in your life who is unwilling to express his emotions or to commit himself to a permanent relationship.

For a woman to be in an overcoat means there is a woman in your life who may be acting tougher than she really is.

Overturn

An overturned vehicle or boat is a warning not to rush into a new venture or relationship but to let events progress in their own time.

See also **boats** *or* **car**

Owl

If an owl appears in your dream just before a point of change in your real-life, it can be a warning of possible hazards and a hint that you should seek wise counsel, maybe from an expert, before taking any major steps or investments.

See also **animals** *or* **birds**

Oxen

If oxen or bulls are pulling an old-fashioned cart it could be a glimpse into a past-life. Oxen may also be a sign that you should stay with a reliable partner or firm rather than risk everything for some temporary excitement or the prospect of some fast money.

See also **animals** *or* **plough**

Oyster

An opened oyster containing a pearl heralds a sudden revelation, whether of unexpressed love or sexual awakening. Open oysters are also a sign of rewards as a result of hard work or investments.

A closed or empty oyster shell symbolises an irritating person who takes up too much of your time.

P

Packing

If you are packing in anticipation of a change in location, whether for a holiday or a new home, it is a good omen for planned changes in your real life.

If you are packing and have too much to fit in the cases, it can indicate fears or doubts about an impending change in reality. You may also be feeling guilty about leaving behind old attachments.

See also **travel**

Padlock

If the padlock is open, it suggests that you may be given the opportunity to escape from an unwanted or difficult situation.

If the padlock is closed, it reflects unvoiced worries about the security of a job or property.

See also **lock (door)**

Page (book)

An open page can offer you a solution to a problem or relay some important information. Try to record such a dream as soon as you wake so that you won't forget the message. A page is also a sign that you can trust a new friend or colleague.

See also **book**

Page (medieval boy)

To dream of an old-fashioned page can be a past-life dream or be an indication that you may have to start from the beginning in a new career or sport. Don't be disheartened by this as the signs are that you will progress rapidly if you take the time to learn the rules and details as you go along.

See also **servant**

Pagoda

To see a Chinese pagoda foretells of a long and happy journey within the next year. It can also mean that you will be given a beautiful present that will increase in value over the years, along with the affection of the giver. Occasionally, if there is a figure standing in a pagoda, it can be a sign that you have a wise Chinese spirit guide watching over you.

Pain

To feel pain in a dream can be an early warning sign that you need to take greater care of your health.

If a child or partner experiences pain, it means that in real life their unwise actions might cause them problems. If they will not listen to your advice, you can only wait and then help them if they need it.

See also **headache**

Paint

A pot of paint, whether for decorating or artistry, indicates you can expect a positive response from others, whether you are applying for a job or seeking to widen your social horizons.

To peel paint from a wall indicates that you have been neglecting your own health and wellbeing.

Painting (picture)

To paint a picture or to have your portrait painted is a good omen for all creative ventures or careers. Painting also indicates that you are presenting a very positive image of yourself to the world, however uncertain you may feel inside.

See also **drawing**

Painting (room)

This symbolises the chance to start again and to put behind you any past mistakes or guilt. If you dream of painting a room or house, it signifies a good time to buy or renovate property.

See also **home** *or* **house**

Palace

Living in a palace indicates that your financial circumstances should improve over the coming months. A house move or new mortgage may prove to be financially advantageous.

See also **royalty**

Palm

A flat palm means that you might be asked for money which you may not have, by a friend or family member.

A closed palm warns that a potential lover or employer may prove to be mean.

See also **hand**

Palmistry

To read a palm in a dream can sometimes denote an emerging psychic ability and you may find that you have a gift for palmistry or healing.

If your palm is read by a stranger, you should be wary of strangers or acquaintances in your real life who may try to persuade you to allow them into your home or invest money.

See also **occultist**

Palm tree

This represents the possibility of an exotic holiday at an unexpectedly cheap price. Palm trees also symbolise prosperity, good health and increased fertility.

A dying palm tree warns that an exciting lover or friend may prove to be shallow and fickle.

See also **tree**

Pancakes

Pancakes are symbolic of a bossy or dominant woman who may be trying to run your life or undermine your confidence.

Tossing or turning pancakes shows that you have a very determined and independent streak that will be able to overcome criticism.

See also **food**

Paper

To dream of blank paper suggests that you will come up with an original idea or solution to a problem.

A pile of papers which need to be sorted indicates that you need to reorganise your time and concentrate on the essentials.

If papers are blowing about in the wind or scattered everywhere, it means that it could be good for you occasionally to act out of character and be unconventional.

Parachute

Floating to the ground using a parachute is a good sign that if you aim high, you will not fall or fail.

If a parachute does not unfold, it means that you should not rely on others to help you with regards to your career or money issues.

See also **aeroplane**

Paralysis

If you feel unable to move in a dream it is quite normal, especially if your mind is trying to wake from a bad dream.

If you feel unable to run away from danger or formless terrors within a dream, it implies that there are frustrating issues in your life that need confronting.

Parents

To dream of your parents, whether they are alive or not, reflects that you may be feeling uncertain about taking a risk as voices from the past are influencing you.

If you and your partner are parents in a dream, even if you have no children in real life, it represents a deep commitment to each other.

See also **family, father** *or* **mother**

Parking

Parking your car represents restrictions and indicates you may need to be realistic when applying for a new job or negotiating a salary increase.

See also **car** *or* **car park**

Parking lot

See **car park**

Parking ticket

This dream suggests that past failures and criticism may be holding you back from taking a risk or making a change in your lifestyle that could be advantageous.

See also **car** *or* **fine (money)**

Parrot

This reflects any meaningless chatter that allows someone close to you to avoid discussing an important issue. It also indicates a desire for more privacy and solitude at work or at home.

See also **animals** *or* **birds**

Parsley

To see parsley growing or in a meal means you are filled with passion, either for a new love or project, and should relax and enjoy the feeling.

See also **herbs**

Party

This usually foretells that you may soon receive an invitation to a social gathering that will bring you great pleasure. You may even meet someone new who will make you happy, either as a friend or lover.

If you find yourself at a party where no-one speaks to you, you are probably feeling very isolated in your waking life and should seek support beyond your usual group of friends or close relatives.

See also **carnival, event** *or* **invitation**

Pastry

Making and baking pastry suggests that you may have to economise for a while and focus on routine but necessary tasks.

Path

A choice of clear paths or a sunny, flower-strewn path denotes opportunities that will lead to success and fulfilment, especially if the outlook is open, flat and pleasant.

A dark, overgrown path or a series of rocky uphill paths suggests that the choices ahead of you will not be easy. In particular, if the path is shrouded in mist, there will be elements of the unknown to your choice.

See also **journey, road** *or* **signs**

Patient

See **invalid**

Peacemaking

If you are negotiating a peace settlement, whether between armies or crotchety relations, it is a sign that you may be called on to act as a mediator at work or within the family. You should be careful to ensure that both sides do not end up blaming you.

Peaches

Peaches represent luxury, sensuality, beautiful surroundings and fertility. This is therefore a very positive dream symbol.

See also **fruit**

Peacock

The peacock symbolises a vain friend, relative or lover who needs to be told to reassess their priorities and attitudes. It also represents ambitious plans that may need to be modified in order to materialise.

See also **animals** *or* **birds**

Pearls

This is symbolic of romance, love and marriage, especially if you dreamt of a string of pearls. This is an excellent omen for all matters concerning babies and children. A broken string of pearls, however, can represent an unsuitable lover.

To see a pearl in an oyster when you have just embarked on a new relationship means that you should think carefully before taking that relationship to a physical level.

Broken or lost pearls are a sign that you may have shared secrets with an untrustworthy person.

See also **jewellery**

Pears

This is a good omen for all matters concerning young girls and promises joy and many rewards for the parents and child.

See also **fruit**

Peas

To see peas growing in a garden or field signifies a continuing regular income, perhaps from a hobby.

To shell, cook or eat peas indicates that your fortunes should improve but you will need to be very patient as the increase may take months to be fully felt.

Dried peas indicate you may soon receive money from an unexpected source.

See also **vegetables**

Pelican

This is a lovely symbol of mothering and unselfishness and denotes you should put aside your own needs for a while in order to care for a sick or distressed relation or friend.

See also **animals** *or* **birds**

Pen

A pen suggests that you may receive a letter from abroad before the week is through.

A leaking pen indicates you should be careful not to leave private correspondence in a place where curious eyes could read it.

See also **handwriting, letter, notebook, novel** *or* **writing**

Pendulum

If you are using a pendulum to answer questions in a dream, it means you should learn to trust your intuition more.

A clock pendulum is a reminder that time is passing, so if you are trying to come to a decision you need to make up your mind soon otherwise you may miss the window of opportunity.

See also **clock**

People

To see people we do not know in a dream is generally the different aspects of our characters projected on to various heroes, heroines or villains. Observing how they behave, and most importantly how you react to them in the dreamscape, can reveal a great deal about your current state of mind and emotions. Such dreams can sometimes be a rehearsal for scenarios that you would like to occur or fear may happen in real life.

Phoenix

This represents the renewal of a venture, friendship or past love that you thought had gone forever.

See also **ashes**

Picnic

To enjoy a picnic suggests you would benefit from a short break or a pleasurable day or weekend outdoors with friends or family.

If ants or wasps are spoiling a picnic, it indicates that there may be someone within your family or friendship circle who feels left out and may try to make trouble at a social event.

See also **event** *or* **food**

Pig

A pig is a warning against overindulgence in any way, although a lovely pink pig can represent a person who is generous, especially with regards to hospitality.

See also **animals** *or* **ham**

Pigeon

This represents a trustworthy messenger. You may receive unexpected communication from afar.

See also **birds**

Pilgrim

An old-fashioned pilgrim can be an indication of a past-life dream or an indication that you have a wise spiritual guide who will protect you, especially when you travel.

Pin cushion

If the cushion is full of pins it suggests that your wishes will come true very soon. This also represents new love and romance.

See also **pins**

Pine tree

Pine trees are a symbol of domestic happiness and family celebration. They are also a sign that money will come into the home.

See also **tree**

Pink

This colour is symbolic of gentle love and is a positive colour regarding matters to do with children, families or mothers.

See also **colours**

Pins

To have a large collection of pins is an indication of impending good luck. If you drop them it means you should be careful not to break anything the following day which may be of value.

See also **pin cushion**

Pipe (metal)

An electric, gas or water pipe says that you may have to spend time on essential repairs or house maintenance in the near future.

A broken pipe is an indication of communication breakdown, maybe with a difficult teenager, but if you are patient you will be able to restore equilibrium.

Pipe (smoking)

This refers to a comforting presence in your life and suggests you should consult a wise older person before making a decision.

See also **smoking** *or* **tobacco**

Plane

See **aeroplane**

Plants

Healthy plants are a sign of good or improving health.

Dying or wilting plants means you need to take care of yourself as this can sometimes be a sign of impending ill health that you can avoid if you improve your health care immediately.

See also **cactus, flowers, herbs, ivy** *or* **nursery (botanical)**

Plastic surgery

If you are having reconstructive surgery, it can be a sign of low self-esteem or worry about how you present yourself to others. This is a common dream for those who have come to the end of a love affair. Try to believe in yourself and then others should see you differently.

If someone you know is having plastic surgery in a dream, it can be a sign that they are trying to hide something.

See also **operation**

Play

To act in a play is an indication that your talents and hard work will gain you much deserved recognition.

To watch a play suggests that you may be feeling sidelined at work at the moment, but if the play ends happily, this is a good omen for the future.

See also **actor or actress** *or* **theatre**

Playing (children)

To watch children playing suggests that you need to take a break from your responsibilities and have some fun.

If you are a child again, it is an indication that you need to allow your true personality to shine through, especially if events in life or certain people have taken your smile away.

See also **dolls, games, puzzle, swing** *or* **toys**

Playing (sports)
See sport

Plough
To be ploughing a field suggests that you will have to work very hard to get a new project off the ground, but it is a good omen, particularly for anyone who is self-employed. An old-fashioned plough may be an indication of a past-life dream.

See also oxen

Plums
To pick, cook or eat plums is a sign of increased money as a result of hard work. You may find that a job share or collective effort proves to be advantageous.

Plums in generally are a good omen for people who play games of chance, as plums are symbolic of money, especially inherited wealth. They also symbolise burgeoning love and consummation.

See also fruit

Poison
Poison represents spite and malice, maybe at work or at home. Try to avoid the source of this 'poison' if possible.

Police
If you call the police for help in a dream, it can be a reflection on how you may be feeling in real life, particularly if you are being threatened by a bully or are afraid you cannot protect a child from being bullied.

If the police chase or arrest you, it may be your subconscious reminding you, for example, to check whether your vehicle documents or taxes are up-to-date.

See also officer, uniform *or* wail

Polished flooring
See floor

Politician
If you are listening to a politician you should be wary of someone who is trying to persuade you to change your mind about an issue, as they may be doing this for their own gain.

If you are the politician in a dream, it means that you want your voice to be heard.

See also election *or* government

Pool

A garden pool means your home life should soon enter a very peaceful phase.

To be at a public swimming pool means that you should soon have the chance to relax with friends whom you feel particularly close to.

To experience an accident of any kind in a pool indicates a fear that deep emotions or sexual desire will overwhelm you.

See also **swimming** *or* **water**

Popcorn

See **corn**

Postman

This suggests that positive correspondence or an unexpected cheque will arrive through the post in the near future.

See also **envelope, letter** *or* **mail**

Potatoes

Potatoes that are still growing or picked and covered in dirt, represent impending money.

To cook or eat potatoes means that there may be an unexpected household expense in the near future.

See also **food** *or* **vegetables**

Pots and pans

Pots and pans in a kitchen signify a period of hard work ahead with many domestic responsibilities. However, this is a good omen for all who work in catering or the hospitality trade.

See also **kitchen**

Precipice

This warns that you may have to negotiate a potentially awkward situation with officials. Alternatively, you may be asked to take sides in an argument.

Pregnancy

This is obviously an excellent omen if you want a child.

If you are already pregnant, you may dream of your unborn child and be able to talk to him or her.

Pregnancy dreams at other times usually represent a yearning for deep unconditional love and acceptance. If you do not want a child but are having sex, whether you are a man or woman, it is an indication you need to be careful as you or your partner could be entering a very fertile period.

See also **baby, birth** *or* **family**

Present
See **gift**

Price
If you are buying an item in a dream and the price is very high, it could be a reference to the price you are being asked to pay in some other aspect of your life, maybe in terms of emotional stress, in return for security or approval.

Priest
This suggests that you might benefit from advice regarding a very personal or spiritual matter. You may also be seeking forgiveness for a less than kind action.
See also **church**

Principles
If you are being asked in a dream to go against your principles, someone in real life may offer you cheap renovation work or the chance to make some fast money. You should perhaps ignore the offer as it may not be of any real benefit to you.

Prison
Usually this type of dream is a result of temporary deprivation, such as dieting, or an attempt, for example, to give up alcohol or cigarettes.

If you are not depriving yourself in real life and dream that you are imprisoned, especially in a dark dungeon, it can indicate you are feeling stifled and unable to speak or act freely, possibly because of a bully or a controlling boss, partner or parent. If someone you recognise is imprisoned, you may be secretly worrying that they are keeping bad company.
See also **captivity** *or* **criminal**

Prize
To win a prize in a dream can be a prediction that you will win a competition or gain an award for work you have completed.

Procession
To take part in a procession says that you should be given credit for the successful completion of a project or for winning an important order at work. It also denotes success in examinations, tests or interviews.
See also **carnival**

Property

To buy or sell property in a dream suggests that it is a good time for you to initiate any house moves, redecoration, DIY or major renovations to your home or work premises. This is a good omen regarding the expansion of small businesses.

See also **flat, home** *or* **house**

Pump

Pumping clean clear water says that any communication, whether verbal or written, will be successful, especially concerning applications of any kind.

Dirty water suggests there may be a troublemaker in your waking life who would like to see you quarrel with a friend or lover.

Purple

This colour is linked with all things spiritual. It can be a sign that you have many psychic gifts.

See also **colours**

Purse

If the purse belongs to you, you may encounter an unexpected expense in the near future.

If the dream purse belongs to someone you recognise, it can indicate that person is perhaps over-cautious with their money. This may not be a quality you want in a future partner.

Puzzle

If you can solve the puzzle or fit the pieces of a jigsaw together, you should shortly resolve any outstanding problems.

If there is a missing piece to the puzzle, it can indicate that someone is not telling you the whole truth or are telling white lies about a financial difficulty.

See also **games, playing (children)** *or* **toys**

Pyramid

If you are inside a pyramid it may be a past-life dream. Pyramids in general are an indication of healing and psychic abilities that could be developed if desired.

Quacking

If you can hear ducks quacking then your subconscious mind is warning you of a possible hazard. For instance, you maybe trusting someone unwisely with your money.

Quad bikes

Racing a quad bike is an indication you need to include more spontaneity and fun in your life.

Quadrangle

If you are walking round a grassy outdoor quadrangle in a school or college, it means you could benefit from learning something new or from joining a class. Ignore any fears you may have about not being clever enough to do this as they are unfounded.

Quads

If you dream of giving birth to four babies at once or of having four identical children, it can be a sign that you may have taken on more than you can cope with, although the rewards could be numerous if you manage. This is obviously a good omen for people who want a big family although the children may not be all born at once.

See also **baby**

Quagmire

If you dream of being trapped in a muddy quagmire, it means you are getting too caught up with small details and are missing the wider issues and more urgent matters in your life. You need to forget about what cannot be changed in order for your energy to return.

See also **mud**

Quaint

If you are in a charming old-fashioned town or building, it may be a past-life dream, especially if the dream recurs. However, the dream may be telling you that you need to go back to your own roots and maybe contact family or friends in the place where you were born.

Quality

If you are given something that is of poor quality or, for example, are eating poor quality food in a restaurant, it is an indication that a present friendship may be good fun but will probably not stand the test of time.

To be given something of high quality means that you may be offered something that is very valuable in the near future or could meet someone very special soon.

See also **useless**

Quantity

To have or be given a large quantity of something represents a rapid increase in the area referred to in the dream. Therefore, this is a good omen if the dream is about money but obviously not so good if the dream is about work or chores.

Quarantine

To be placed in quarantine in a dream because you are sick or carrying an illness, means that you may feel helpless regarding gossip someone is spreading about you and are worried that other people will believe them.

Quarrel

Quarrelling in a dream is a reflection of resentment building up within you. You should express your feelings strongly as you have the power and energy to win any quarrels in reality, even if you do not do so in a dream.

Quarry

Dreaming of a stone quarry indicates you will have to work harder than you think to succeed, whether in an examination, at work or in learning something new, but do not give up.

A closed or empty quarry suggests you should not waste any more effort into trying to please or mend a quarrel with a particular person as you have exhausted all possibilities.

See also **mine (underground)**

Quarter

If anything, whether food, treasure or money is divided into quarters, it signifies that you may have to share your success or profits, even if you did most of the work or contributed the most financially.

Quartet

If you are playing or singing in a quartet it is a sign that you are entering a more harmonious period. In particular, joint ventures and small family gatherings are favoured.

See also **music** *or* **musical instruments**

Quay

To stand on a quayside watching boats arrive and depart is an indication that you will get the opportunity to put long-wished-for travel plans into action.

If you see fishing boats unloading their catch it is an indication that money or perhaps a wealthy relation may arrive unexpectedly from overseas.

See also **boats**

Queen

See **royalty**

Queries

To be answering queries for the general public or sorting through work and documents is a sign that you need to attend to unfinished business in your waking life. This is a good omen for all who work in the public sector, in retail or public relations.

Quest

To embark on a quest, either to find hidden treasure or to help people in need, signifies you need to fulfil an ambition before you settle down and commit your life to a particular path for a number of years.

Question

If you are asking questions and not getting answers, you may have unvoiced doubts about the reliability of an offer or the trustworthiness of a person.

If an individual or group of people are questioning you, you may have to justify a decision or expenditure in your own mind before going ahead.

Quick

If events happen very quickly in a dream, you should be prepared for events to happen equally quickly in your waking life. This dream denotes a period of positive change ahead with lots of new people coming into your life.

Quicksand

If you or someone else is trapped in quicksand but manage to escape, it is a sign that you will have the chance to move away from a potentially destructive situation involving an over-possessive or treacherous friend.

If you or someone else is trapped and can't escape the quicksand, it is a reference to worries regarding money or debt. You should maybe consult an expert for advice.

Quicksilver

If you dream of quicksilver or mercury in a thermometer or barometer, you should seek the opinions of people you trust before making a decision. You should also try to avoid temperamental people for a while.

Quiet

If everything is quiet in a dream or usually talkative people are silent, it indicates you may need to wait for others to initiate action or communication. Silence can also suggest that you would benefit from a period of rest away from your frantic and noisy lifestyle.

If a person is telling you to be quiet it means you should not allow others to override your opinions.

Quilt

If your bed has an elaborate quilt covering the duvet, you may have to try and make an impression on someone influential or present plans formally in order to get funding or an offer you want. This can also be a sign of a person who wishes to be celibate for a while.

See also **bed/bedroom**

Quintuplets

Five babies or identical children are usually a reference to a number of commitments you have at the moment that must all be juggled until you are in a position to concentrate on only one. This is obviously a very good omen for fertility.

See also **baby**

Quips

If someone keeps making stupid remarks that are meant to be funny, it can reflect a sarcastic colleague or family member in real life who needs putting in their place.

If you keep thinking of funny quips, write them down when you wake as you could make use of them in your daily life.

Quit
If you quit something, your subconscious may be trying to tell you to tackle issues that are irritating you before you end up quitting a situation. If you are miserable about something in real life, this dream could give you the impetus to leave the source of your unhappiness.

Quitter
If someone in your dream accuses you of giving up too easily, ask yourself if that is true or whether you have stayed too long in an unsatisfactory situation to stop someone claiming you are a quitter.

Quiver
To carry arrows in a quiver can be a past-life dream. It could also be an indication that you may need to defend yourself against unfair criticism forcefully, even if you are usually a gentle person.
See also **arrow**

Quotation
If you see or hear a quotation in a dream, try to locate it the next morning as the passage may hold the answer to an important question you could be harbouring.

If you are given a quotation, for example, for car insurance or house repairs, it may be an indication you need to seek more actual quotes or options in real-life before making a decision.

Quotient
If you are struggling to remember mathematical formulae in a dream, you may have become bogged down by details in your everyday life and need to take a step back.

R

Rabbit

This is the ultimate fertility symbol and is therefore an excellent dream for all matters concerning babies, children and family life. White rabbits in particular are a sign of faithful love. Rabbits also indicate the need for speed, whether in applying for a job, finishing an overdue project or moving away from a potentially explosive situation.

See also **hare**

Rabies

To dream of yourself or a family member being bitten by an animal with rabies symbolises the destructive influence of a person in your life who has no scruples or restraints.

See also **disease** *or* **illness**

Race (athletic)

An athletic race represents a deadline you have to meet or a number of pressing commitments. You need to pace yourself rather than rush. If you win or manage to complete the race it is a good omen suggesting you will meet your deadline.

Racehorse

This is symbolic of a temperamental but talented individual, perhaps one of your children, if you have any, who would benefit from some gentle coaxing in order to achieve their potential.

If you are racing it means you could benefit from taking a chance on a venture as this dream is a good omen for all matters of chance, such as gambling, especially if your dream horse comes first.

See also **jockey** *or* **riding**

Race (motor)

This indicates that rivals may cause you problems, but you have the power to outpace them if you do not hold back or worry about offending them too much.

See also **car**

Radiation

To be caught up in a radioactive leak is a warning that your ideas or work may be copied by a rival who will claim credit for them unless you are careful. You should also be vigilant to prevent people gaining access to your e-mails and confidential documents.

Radiator

A radiator warming a room suggests that you will welcome many people into your home over the coming weeks.

A leaking radiator is a warning that money is trickling away on a project that is ultimately not going to be profitable.

Raffle

If you dream of winning a raffle, it suggests that you may win a prize or be selected out of a large number of applicants or competitors for a desired position. This is an especially good omen if you have already entered a competition or applied for a job.

Raft

To make or sail a raft suggests you may find success in another part of the country or overseas. This is therefore a good sign for anyone leaving the country to work elsewhere.

A dream about being cast adrift in a raft may occur after a loss or betrayal and suggests that for now you should allow events to take their course.

Rage

If someone is very angry with you, it is a sign that you should not allow yourself to be bullied in real life, whether from children, teenagers, your partner or your boss.

If you are in a rage, especially if you are normally a placid person, it indicates that you should not compromise your integrity for someone else, no matter how powerful the adversary is.

Rags

This is one of those dreams that mean the opposite, as it represents restored hopes, projects and dreams.

Rail

Railway track suggests that both daily and long-distance travel will be straightforward and problem free so this is good for anyone who works in transport or travels regularly.

See also **train**

Railings

Railings around a porch or the boundaries of a house are generally a sign that your home and family will be safe and that you should not worry about them.

Railings around a public or official building indicate that you may have to be persistent in order to gain access to a less than helpful official or department.

See also **fence**

Railway ticket

The destination on the ticket means it could be beneficial for you to travel there for a holiday – you may meet someone special there. If the destination is unusual, someone who lives there may make contact with you in the future.

See also **train**

Rain

This is actually a powerful symbol of fertility and male potency in many cultures. It is also an excellent omen for the success of new ideas, new beginnings and the growth of a business.

If rain spoils an outdoor event it can indicate that you are focusing your efforts too narrowly.

See also **storm** *or* **umbrella**

Rainbow

The rainbow is a universal image of new beginnings, joy after sorrow, the mending of quarrels and the reconciliation of parted lovers. It is a good omen to dream of a rainbow as it represents good luck and the chance to fulfil a secret dream.

Rainforest

See **jungle**

Rake

If you are raking through leaves or weeds in a garden it means that you need to sift carefully through conflicting advice and be very wary of accepting gossip as truth.

Ram

This is symbolic of male sexual potency and also of power. For both men and women the ram means that if you forge ahead for what you want you will succeed.

See also **animals** *or* **sheep**

Rape

This is never a prediction of a future sexual assault but a symbol of an essential part of yourself that has been taken away, perhaps by a controlling partner or domineering employer. Rape dreams can also occur during a custody battle when you fear an ex-partner may try to take your children away from you. Occasionally this dream is a sign that you are being emotionally pressurised into a sexual relationship that your subconscious knows is unwise.

See also **sex**

Raspberries

To pick or eat raspberries is a sign that you will experience happiness in the summer. This is a good symbol for anyone who is pregnant and also for those who work in horticulture or herbalism.

See also **food** *or* **fruit**

Rats

If the rats are in large numbers, it symbolises a fear of disease.

If you dream of being overrun by these small rodents, it can mean that you are feeling overwhelmed by demands that seem to multiply by the day. You may be worrying about mounting debts or unresolved minor health worries and should maybe seek advice to help put your mind at rest.

See also **animals, traps** *or* **vermin**

Raven

Odin, the main deity in the Norse pantheon, was the god of wisdom, divination and prophecy who owned two tame ravens, Hugin and Mugin, who were symbolic of mind and memory. The raven is therefore a symbol of wisdom and if you listen to its croaking, the bird may impart some of his knowledge to you.

See also **animals** *or* **birds**

Razor

A sharp razor is symbolic of a sharp-tongued colleague or neighbour who does not realise the hurt he or she is causing you.

Reading

If you are reading, you may discover the answer to a question you have been harbouring within the pages of the dream book or in the real book if you own it. If you are unable to read the words or they fade away, it can mean that you are possibly disregarding good advice.

See also **book**

Recurring dreams

Any recurring dream suggests you should pay close attention to it as it may be a subconscious warning. Your inner voice will often use recurring dreams if you are not listening to it in real-life. If you dream repeatedly of a particular place, try to locate it and go there as you may learn something or meet someone of significance.

Red

This is the colour of courage and action and suggests you should act rather than wait, and speak rather than remain silent. This is a particularly pertinent dream if you have experienced an injustice as, if you take some decisive action, your courage may pay dividends. Red is also the colour of passion and can indicate a sudden increase in desire for someone you previously regarded as a friend.

See also **colours**

Reflection

To see your reflection in a mirror suggests that you may be worrying about the opinions of others too much and should allow your own originality and initiative to shine through.

See also **mirrors**

Relations

To dream about your relations usually indicates an unexpected visit from relatives in the near future.

See also **family**

Religious studies lesson

See **academic lessons**

Removal van

A removal van carrying away your possessions means that it may be time to transfer your loyalties to a more deserving cause. This is also a good omen for an imminent house move or job relocation.

See also **vehicle**

Repeat

To watch programmes you have seen before on the television suggests you may be about to repeat an old mistake in a relationship.

Reptile

A reptile is a warning that you should not trust an over-charming colleague at work or a new financial or business adviser who offers you an easy solution or a get-rich-quick scheme.

See also **animals, snake, tortoise** *or* **turtle**

Ribbons

This is symbolic of fun and festivities, such as a family get together or celebration. Ribbons also indicate that a younger female family member may unexpectedly decide to get married.

Rice

Rice is symbolic of births, marriages and growing prosperity. It is a good dream for all matters concerning small children and relationships.

See also **food** *or* **wedding**

Riches

To inherit or acquire great riches in a dream tends to refer to emotional or spiritual happiness rather than material wealth. Riches also suggest that additions to the family, whether through remarriage, adoption or birth, will bring great happiness.

See also **money**

Rider

If you see an unknown rider in the distance it foretells that a new and positive influence should soon enter your life.

If you recognise the rider it means that he or she may seek a closer relationship with you or will become more co-operative if they have been difficult in the past.

See also **jockey**

Riding

Riding a horse is symbolic of increased harmony, whether in a love or business partnership. This is a good omen if you are seeking a more permanent relationship or work with animals.

See also **animals, horse** *or* **racehorse**

Ring

Rings symbolise betrothals and marriages. If you have been doubtful whether your partner is being faithful, rings represent true love so you should put your fears aside.

Ripe

If fruit or vegetables are ripe, it means that now is the right time to take decisive action, take up an opportunity or cash in investments.

See also **food, fruit** *or* **vegetables**

Rival

To dream of a real-life rival indicates that he or she is more successful than you because you are allowing them to undermine your confidence regularly.

An unknown rival suggests you should follow your instincts.

River

A fast-flowing river is indicative of powerful emotions and perhaps a change of location to be with a lover.

A stagnant or weed-choked river can reflect the emotions from a past betrayal which are making a new commitment difficult.

A dried-up river can confirm that a love affair has run its course and sometimes appears when the dreamer is thinking about a separation or divorce.

See also **boats, deep, drowning, swimming, wading** *or* **water**

Road

A road represents your path through life so you can tell a lot from its form, both of hidden influences and coming opportunities.

A road with a fork represents choices. If one has a dead end or is full of potholes it naturally reflects a wrong decision, whereas a clear path indicates the right journey through life.

An uphill road suggests that you may need extra help for a while.

A gentle incline represents a gradual increase in luck.

See also **journey, path** *or* **signs**

Rocket

This is symbolic of a very ambitious plan that will need a tremendous amount of impetus to launch, but will have far-reaching effects.

Rocks

This is symbolic of potential hazards which with time can be surmounted and used to scale even greater heights.

Jagged rocks represent jealousy and spite.

Rocks that are covered by the sea suggest that you will need to wait for the right moment before going ahead without hesitation.

Roof

Sitting or climbing on a roof is a warning that an ambition you wish to fulfil may involve some risk but will open a whole new world to you if you succeed.

Room

An unfamiliar room is one that you may visit which will become familiar before too long.

A warm and welcoming room says that your domestic life will become or remain settled. This is also symbolic of a first home.

An empty room reflects regret about a lost opportunity or a broken relationship that could still be mended.

See also **home** *or* **house**

Rope

This represents security and the binding of people in love and trust.

However, a frayed or twisted rope is a warning that one person in the relationship may be less willing to settle than the other person.

Rose

This is symbolic of love, kindness, trust and fidelity. Roses represent the healing of old sorrows and pain but a garden of roses is the best omen of all as it indicates lasting love and happiness.

See also **flowers** *or* **plants**

Rosemary

This represents the rekindling of passion within an existing relationship and happy memories that could be used to revive a friendship or marriage that has faded into indifference.

See also **herbs**

Rota

If you or somebody else draws up a rota, it may be a sign that you are doing more than your fair share of work or contributing more financially or in terms of time towards a venture.

Rotting

Rotting or rotten food indicates that it is now time to abandon a fruitless effort or an unsatisfactory way of life. It can also suggest that it is unwise to enter into a new commitment or contract without checking its reliability first.

See also **food, fruit** *or* **vegetables**

Roulette

This is a good omen for all who play games of chance.

A turning roulette wheel suggests that you should take a risk and not worry about tomorrow. If you win at roulette it means you may receive some unexpected money.

See also **casino** *or* **gambling**

Rowing

Rowing a boat alone indicates a desire and need for independence.

If you are rowing in a team it means it is important to co-operate with others and go along with group policy, even if it is not exactly what you wanted.

See also **boats**

Royalty

Kings and Queens, according to Freud, stand for the dreamer's parents or parental figures while Princes and Princesses are the dreamer, his or her brothers and sisters or people of the same age.

Kings represent fathers or authority figures. Kings can denote that a wise old man or someone in authority will help you to succeed. This is a good omen to experience if you are dealing with officials.

If the King is hostile you may be assuming, through a lack of confidence, the role of child or subject to a critical authority figure. You need to rebel against this.

A queen represents your mother or an older or more powerful woman and your feelings towards them. If the queen is unfriendly or domineering, you may need to stand up to your mother or the other woman over a decision of which she does not approve. If your mother or the woman is no longer alive, you need to try to come to terms with her different opinions.

If you see yourself as royalty, you may be feeling discontented with familiar faces and places and need to extend your horizons.

If you are mixing with royalty and talking to them on intimate terms, you may have a desire for promotion or public recognition.

See also **castle, court of royalty, crown, jester, palace, throne** *or* **usurper**

Rubbish

See **junk**

Rubies

Rubies symbolise faithful love and can also be a sign that someone feels very passionately about you. If you are suspicious regarding a lover's actions, this dream can sometimes be an indication that your suspicions are not justified.

If a ruby loses its colour in a dream, it is a warning that you are feeling tired and should rest.

See also **gemstones** *or* **jewellery**

Ruins

Ruins reflect a need to rebuild and learn from the past. You may also be secretly yearning to get intouch with childhood friends or family you have not seen for many years.

Running away

To run away represents escapism and reflects that there is something or someone you want to avoid.

If you are being pursued and find that you cannot run, fear may be holding you back from tackling a problem head-on. Alternatively, you may be keeping yourself in a destructive or emotionally draining situation or relationship because you fear the consequences of leaving.

Rust

Rusty metal symbolises health worries and a disappointment that has temporarily clouded your enthusiasm for life.

Saccubus (female sexual demon)

See incubus (male sexual demon)

Sack

A full sack means you may soon receive a surprise gift or an unexpected additional source of income.

An empty or ripped sack suggests that you may be feeling exhausted and would benefit from some rest to replenish your energy.

Sacrifice

If you are making a willing sacrifice at an altar this could be a past-life dream or simply a representation of awareness that certain paths in your life may involve the temporary sacrifice of comfort and security to allow for permanent gain. This dream can sometimes occur if you are entering a new sexual relationship.

If the sacrifice is unwilling or a human sacrifice, it can indicate that you are resentful for sacrificing your own needs and happiness, perhaps for an ungrateful family.

See also altar

Saddle

A saddle or a saddled horse is an indication that you may be given an opportunity to work in a new location or area of expertise.

If you are sitting in a saddle it suggests that you will gain a position of authority.

To saddle a horse means you may have an increase in prosperity.

See also horse

Safe

To dream of a safe means you need not worry about money as you are entering a stable financial period.

An empty safe suggests you may be worried about a lack of savings or long-term security.

To rob a safe indicates that you may have an opportunity to profit from someone else's mistake or carelessness.

See also bank

Sage

Whether the herb is growing or being used in cooking, it symbolises improved or improving health. This is an excellent dream image if you have been worried about the health of an older person.

See also **herbs**

Sailing

Sailing in calm waters represents future harmony in every aspect of your life.

If a sail is filled with a breezy wind, it is symbolic of the chance to make money by travelling.

A ripped or broken sail can foretell temporary delays to travel plans and is a warning that you should maybe check details carefully to avoid problems whilst away.

See also **boats**

Sailor

To dream of a sailor can mean that you or one of your family will marry someone from overseas.

If you are the sailor it means that your business horizons will expand.

Saints

If you dream of meeting saints it is usually a sign of emerging spiritual and healing powers. If you have recently been feeling in despair, you may experience a near miracle in your real-life very soon.

See also **heaven**

Salad

Eating salad is a sign of good health and increased strength and enthusiasm for life. Salad is also indicative of an unexpected weekend trip to the countryside.

See also **vegetables**

Salmon

This is a sign that you may have the chance to visit your childhood home or will renew contact with elderly distant relatives who will be able to tell you about your family history.

See also **animals** *or* **fishing**

Salt

This is a universal symbol of life, health and healing. Salt may appear in a dream when your healing powers are beginning to evolve.

Spilled salt is a traditional sign of treachery from someone who is pretending to be a friend. You may also be feeling unwell but have tried to ignore it.

Samples

If you are being given samples of material, food or beauty products, it can be a sign that your business or future plans will grow and prosper.

A family member may need to try several jobs or forms of training before they are able to settle, but eventually will find the right career.

Sand

An expanse of sand is a sign that you would benefit from a period of rest, perhaps in the form of a holiday where you will be able to reflect on the future and recover some energy.

See also **desert** *or* **dunes**

Sand hill

See **dune**

Sandstorm

This represents a number of minor irritations at work or with family members that may result in a bitter exchange that could be difficult to heal if you fail to tackle the problem straight away.

Sapphire

This beautiful blue gem is symbolic of fidelity so it often appears in dreams when a betrothal in the family is imminent. Sapphires can also be a sign that you will be recognised in your career and may even be offered a chance to lead or manage other people.

A cracked sapphire means that you should not waste time grieving over an unworthy lover who may have left you.

See also **gemstones** *or* **jewellery**

Satin

To be wearing satin or to sleep between satin sheets is an indication that you would like more romance and excitement in your life.

Sauna

To sit in a vapour bath or sauna indicates that you will have the chance to leave old problems behind you. To dream of making love in a sauna is a powerful sign of fertility and promises a lot of passionate love and babies.

Sausages

This is often a sign of simmering resentment that may end in a minor domestic upheaval. You may find that a disappointing present proves to be useful.

See also **food**

Saving

To be saving money in a dream is an indication that your finances will improve because of a wise investment you have made or because you have a useful skill.

See also **bank** *or* **money**

Sawing

Sawing wood or trees is symbolic of a new home and a trustworthy partner. This is a good omen for all who work with their hands.

See also **tree**

Scabs

To dream about being covered in scabs is an expression of worry about your imperfections, usually as a result of an over-critical ex-lover or spiteful ex-friend.

A child covered in scabs is a common parental anxiety dream and simply indicates that you are worrying about your child's welfare.

See also **injury**

Scar

To have a scar or scars in a dream is a representation of deep inner hurt that you may have tried to hide about a past betrayal or injustice. This is also a sign that a bad experience could be used as the basis for growth and future success.

See also **injury**

School

A happy return to childhood school days indicates that you will have the chance to study or learn a new skill. This is a good omen if you are worried about your children's education or if you work as a teacher or in childcare.

To return to unhappy or humiliating school scenes can indicate that you may be lacking in confidence regarding your abilities and have been listening to unjustifiable criticism from a current authority figure such as a boss or in-law.

See also **academic lessons, classroom, desk, examination, exclusion, learning, lessons** *or* **teacher**

Science

Learning science in a dream means you should follow your head and not your heart. You need to find out what someone is really asking you.

See also **laboratory**

Science lesson
See **academic lessons**

Scissors
Cutting with scissors means you need to cut through other people's inertia or indecisiveness and be proactive.

If scissors are dropped or broken it can represent two people who are quarrelling as they compete for your attention.

Sea
The sea generally represents the opportunity to travel or to learn new skills. It can also be a sign that you are acknowledging deep emotions towards someone that will offer new levels of commitment and intimacy.

A calm sea indicates a peaceful time in a relationship or in your life, perhaps after a turbulent period.

A stormy sea says that you should try to avoid being drawn into the disputes of other family members or work colleagues.

See also **boats, deep, diving, drowning, ebb, fishing, harbour, octopus, swimming, wading, water** *or* **whale**

See-saw
Fluctuations in your circumstances and opinions mean that it will be important for you to try and keep level-headed. You may be finding other people's mood swings difficult to gauge and deal with.

Servant
To dream of being a servant may be a glimpse into a past-life world. It can also indicate that you are doing rather too much for someone who acts helpless or is a hypochondriac.

To have servants is an indication that you will take on a managerial role or will have to organise other people in an activity.

See also **page (medieval boy)** *or* **waiter/waitress**

Sex
This can be a wish fulfilment dream if you are not currently involved in a sexual relationship or are experiencing less than satisfactory sex with a partner. Sexual dreams can, however, help to initiate a rich and fulfilling sex life and are often a good way of getting in touch with your instinctual feelings.

If you dream of having sex with someone you are not in a relationship with, it can indicate a sexual interest that you may not have acknowledged.

See also **rape, vice, virgin** *or* **x-rated**

Shacks

To see old derelict wooden buildings is a sign you have inner fears that your stressful and unhealthy lifestyle may result in ill health and premature ageing.

Shark

You need to be wary of emotional predators who will play on your natural kindness in order to gain sympathy. Sharks also symbolise spiteful and gossiping neighbours or co-workers whom you need to warn off.

See also **animals**

Sheep

This is a sign that others may be imitating your ideas or always relying on you to take the initiative. Sheep are also symbolic of reliable friends whom you should treasure for their loyalty even if they may not be very dynamic.

See also **animals, ewe, lamb** *or* **ram**

Shell

You need to listen to your inner voice before making a decision. Shells also represent emerging sexual passion and deep feelings that you perhaps need to keep hidden until the right time.

Ship

See **boats**

Shipwreck

Be careful of others who may try to sabotage a plan or financial arrangement through their ineptitude or lack of commitment. A shipwreck can also represent a disruptive influence in your family life.

See also **boats**

Shoes

New shoes can indicate a new job or business opportunity.

If the shoes are uncomfortable you may find it difficult to settle in one place.

Worn-out shoes suggest you should stop using the same approach when dealing with a difficult person. Maybe you need to stop arguing and walk away.

To lose a shoe is a warning that you may be making excuses in order to avoid a change in your life that deep down you do not want.

See also **feet** *or* **laces**

Signs

Signposts mean that you need to be aware and ready for situations in your life which could lead to an advantageous change of direction.

Signs are also a good omen for those who are planning a holiday, a house move or are embarking on a new career or course of study.

See also **journey, path** *or* **road**

Silver

To be given silver jewellery or items is a sign that your true love may be someone who might not be very prosperous but who will cherish you deeply.

Silver coins signify lasting money.

A silver shimmer is another method through which guardian angels may make their presence felt.

Tarnished silver means that you have not been listening to your intuition as much as you should have.

See also **jewellery**

Singing

If you are singing it can be a sign of great future happiness.

If a group of people are singing together it means there will be harmony at a family gathering or important meeting at work.

See also **duet**

Sister

To dream of a real-life sister is often proof of a telepathic bond. You may find that your sister telephones you the following day.

If you do not have a sister, the dream can indicate that a new female friend will become very close to you and will prove to be a long-term and trustworthy confidante.

See also **family**

Skeleton

People or memories from the past may return but you will find that they have lost their power to trouble you.

See also **bones** *or* **death/dying**

Sky

A blue and cloudless sky is a fortunate omen for any planned holidays. This is also symbolic of a trouble-free period.

A cloudy or stormy sky means that people may try to spoil your happiness but you should ignore them.

See also **clouds** *or* **dawn**

Smoke

Smoke that is rising upwards is a good omen for instant results whereas smoke that is travelling horizontally can indicate delays.

If a room is filled with smoke, it is a warning that you should not let your attention be diverted by people who are causing an uproar.

See also **chimney**

Smoking

If a person who does not usually smoke has a cigarette in a dream it can mean they may be feeling very tense but are unwilling to talk about a problem or secret.

If you are smoking it is a sign that your needs are not being met or that you are not speaking your mind. You may also have a hidden worry about your health.

Cigarettes are a symbol of forthcoming money and opportunities.

See also **pipe (smoking), tobacco** *or* **vice**

Snail

Snails suggest that you will need to tackle a problem or piece of work very slowly in order to avoid mistakes and misunderstandings. You should not rush into making any decisions.

See also **animals**

Snake

This is symbolic of rebirth and new beginnings which will probably manifest themselves in the early spring. The snake is also an image which is associated with male sexuality and female fertility.

If you are afraid of or are bitten by a snake, it can represent fears of a betrayal or your own temptations.

See also **animals** *or* **reptile**

Snow

Dreaming of snow that prevents you travelling, for example, is often an indication that deep down you do not want to do something.

To play in the snow is a promise that you will find happiness in the winter.

If you are stranded or trapped by snow, it is a sign that you must wait for the right moment before making a move or a change. The right time might be when the snow melts.

See also **ice, igloo, water** *or* **white**

Soil

See **earth**

Soldiers

You may need to devise a strategy in order to outmanoeuvre someone devious who is forcing his or her way to the top at work.

Soldiers can also indicate the importance of defending your boundaries at home from interfering or difficult neighbours.

See also **army** *or* **officer**

South

This is a promise of sunshine entering your life, either in the form of a holiday or as happiness due to your efforts finally bearing fruit.

Space

This is usually an out-of-body experience. If you made contact with an extra-terrestrial or angel think about what happened. Was it a positive or negative encounter? Did they tell you anything that relates to your life at the moment?

See also **alien, comet, stars (sky)** *or* **universe**

Spiders

Spiders are a very lucky omen as they indicate good fortune and money, especially if they crawl over you in a dream. Take note of the size as the bigger the spider, the greater the benefits.

A spider's web indicates that a number of different factors in your life will come together and you may be able to work from home or turn an interest into a career. A spider's web is also a universal symbol for the web of fate as a web indicates that your destiny is very much your own creation.

To be trapped in a web with a giant spider symbolises that you are feeling trapped by fate or the actions of others.

See also **animals**

Spinning wheel

See **loom**

Spirits

To be spooked in a dream by an unknown spirit is usually a sign that your natural clairvoyant powers are developing. If you recognise the spirit it can indicate that there is a matter from your past which needs to be resolved and laid to rest in your mind. To talk to a spirit you recognise in a dream is a sign that your endeavours will succeed and be rewarded.

See also **ethereal being** *or* **ghost**

Spoon

A full spoon suggests that you would benefit from a little indulgence, especially if you have been on a strict diet.

A dirty spoon means that you don't want someone who is new to your circle of friends to get too close to you.

An empty spoon represents your subconscious fears about financial security.

See also **ladle**

Sport

To take part in a sport represents a side of you that is seeking a more active role in life. You may also be living or working in a very competitive atmosphere and are finding it hard to set your own pace.

To take part and win in a sport is a good omen that suggests that you will succeed with a new venture.

If you take part and lose it can be a sign that you feel like a failure unnecessarily in your waking life and should not be so hard on yourself.

See also individual sports, **kit, team** *or* **victory**

Spots

A spot on your face represents resentment that someone close to you is too overly concerned with physical and material perfection.

Spring

This is an excellent omen indicating that now is a good time to start something new.

Squirrel

This represents the need to conserve resources and time, as you may suddenly receive a great deal of unexpected work or a number of urgent demands.

See also **animals** *or* **nuts**

Stable

Security is probably more important than excitement in a relationship right now so you should stick with a person or people you can trust. An open or empty stable can also indicate a subconscious worry about personal or house security.

See also **horse**

Stag

This is symbolic of male potency and courage. It can mean that you could become a leader or win a promotion if you are competitive and show a willingness to fight for your beliefs and take pride in your personal strengths and talents.

See also **animals, deer** *or* **wild beasts**

Stairs

Walking upstairs is a promise of increased finances or a promotion.

To go downstairs indicates that you may decide to downsize in property, perhaps for a rural lifestyle, or will choose fulfilment rather than material gain in your next career move.

A wide carpeted staircase symbolises increased opportunities while a dark and narrow staircase represents family secrets.

See also **escalator**

Stars (screen)

To meet famous people in a dream means you need more excitement and romance in your life. To mingle with the stars can also be an indication that a creative project will become successful.

Stars (sky)

To see a starry sky or to journey to the stars can be an out-of-body dream which can also represent your psychic powers. Stars also indicate the possibility of making a wish or dream come true if you allow yourself to aim high. They are also a symbol of love and a sign that you may soon meet your soulmate if you have not already.

See also **night, observatory, space** *or* **zodiac**

Stomach

Dreams of stomachs are an indication that you should trust your gut feelings about the reliability of a person or offer.

A fat stomach is a good omen if you wish to get pregnant. It can also relate to fears of asking too much from others and life which can be a throwback to childhood.

A flat stomach is a wish-fulfilment dream if your stomach is not flat in reality.

Stork

This is an excellent sign of impending pregnancy or a birth, either for you, someone in your family or for someone in your circle of friends. The stork can sometimes mean you will hear about a birth from an overseas relative. This is a wonderful dream to experience if you are trying for a baby.

See also **animals** *or* **birds**

Storm

A storm can be a good omen as it predicts the end of a period of tension and frustration. Storms also mean that you should speak your mind regarding a matter that has been annoying you.

See also **gale, lightning, rain, thunder, tornado** *or* **wind**

Stranger

A friendly stranger in a dream means someone new will enter your life and bring happiness with them.

An unpleasant or frightening stranger is a warning that a new person in your life should be treated with caution initially.

Straw

Straw in any form is a fertility symbol and also promises early autumn joy. A straw hat foretells of a holiday.

Strawberries

To pick or eat strawberries is an indication of summer happiness. Strawberries are also a sign that you should allow yourself a few indulgences and relax if you have been working hard recently or have been on a strict diet.

See also **food** *or* **fruit**

Stress

See **anxiety**

Success

Success dreams sometimes occur when things are going badly in order to encourage you to persevere as your subconscious knows you will succeed eventually.

Suffocation

Although it is upsetting to dream of suffocation, it is usually just a sign that you need a short break away from the demands of others. It can also indicate that someone is being possessive towards you and although this may not be malicious, it is nevertheless stifling. Parents can experience anxiety dreams of suffocation when their children are about to leave home for the first time.

See also **asthma, death/dying, murder** *or* **suicide**

Suicide

If you are about to commit suicide in your dream, it means you are deeply unhappy with your life and need the support of your friends and family.

If a relative commits suicide it can mean that in reality they are trying to make you feel guilty unfairly.

See also **death/dying, killing** *or* **suffocation**

Summer

If you dream of summer, whatever the season really is, it means you need a holiday to recharge your batteries, preferably somewhere warm. Summertime is sometimes an indication of future success.

Sun

To enjoy the sunshine is a universal symbol of coming joy, renewed health and energy. It also a reminder that you should enjoy each day rather than worry too much about tomorrow.

If a burning hot sun is scorching the land or an open plain which has no shade, it can be symbolic of emotional or physical exhaustion as a result of intense pressures.

See also **eclipse**

Swan

This is a sign of inner stillness and harmony and also indicates a spiritual or inner transformation that will enable you to move forward. Swans are a good omen for anyone who works in artistic and creative fields.

See also **animals** *or* **birds**

Sweetcorn

See **corn**

Sweets

To enjoy eating sweets is a sign that you are comfortable with yourself and are not afraid to enjoy your body, especially sexually.

If you experience guilt about eating sweets it can mean that you are afraid to let go of your inhibitions and indulge your desires.

See also **chocolate** *or* **food**

Swimming

Swimming, like floating, is an excellent dream omen as it indicates that your life should flow happily with fortuitous events happening quite naturally. To swim to shore is an especially good omen if you have been struggling or worrying about the your future. Swimming can also be symbolic of a fulfilling sexual relationship.

See also **lagoon, lake, pool, river, sea** *or* **water**

Swing

This indicates a more carefree period ahead involving lots of fun, relaxation and days spent with friends and family. Swings are also a good omen for all matters to do with children and represent the resolution of problems left over from childhood.

See also **playing (children)**

Sword

This may be a past-life dream but a sword also symbolises the need to cut through inertia, indecisiveness, gossip or bickering before it takes hold. Swords also represent new beginnings after difficulties or loss.

See also **weapons**

T

Table

To eat a meal at a table is a sign that you will receive abundance or that abundance will remain in your home.

To set a table ready for a meal signifies that you may have unexpected visitors within the week.

Tadpoles

If you are experiencing problems with children, these difficulties will be resolved in time. Tadpoles also signal a transformation in your life, such as reinventing your image. Tadpoles are an excellent symbol for male potency and this dream is therefore a good omen for anyone wishing to become a father.

See also **frog**

Tail

The tail of an animal is symbolic of distractions caused by an immature person and can also symbolise an incompetent boss who will not listen to reason.

If a dog is wagging its tail it denotes there will be a welcome homecoming of an absent family member or someone you thought had left your life forever.

See also **animals** *or* **dog**

Tailor

If you are the tailor measuring someone for a suit, you may have to adapt your plans to fit in with others who are not so well prepared. You should also trust your own judgement regarding someone at work who asks for your help.

See also **clothes** *or* **costume**

Talisman

To wear or carry a good luck charm in a dream is a sign that you will experience good fortune and perhaps even a small win on the lottery or some other game of chance.

If you make a talisman it means that your luck will improve through your own efforts.

Talking

If you are conversing in a dream try to remember what you and other people said as your dream may be trying to convey an important message from your subconscious. Try to write down what happened as soon as you wake as the words may be of significance.

Taming

To be taming wild beasts or breaking in a horse is a sign that you have had to curb your own desires and impulses but still need to express your free spirit sometimes. The dream can also represent defeating a tyrannical boss or talking down a domineering relative.

See also **horse** *or* **wild beasts**

Tank (army)

An army tank indicates someone is disregarding your feelings and trying to force you to accept their ideas or follow a course of action about which you are uncertain. You should follow your own judgement. Tanks can also appear in dreams if a local piece of land that you love is under threat or you are battling with someone over a property dispute.

See also **army** *or* **war**

Tank (fish)

Fish in a tank, especially goldfish, are a sign of money coming into your business or home.

An empty fish tank means you are in denial about the fact you are no longer enthusiastic towards a person or project.

See also **fishing**

Tank (water)

A domestic or industrial water tank is a good omen if it is full of water as it indicates you will have plentiful and continuing resources in your life, especially if you own a business.

A leaking tank is a warning that someone is draining you emotionally or financially.

See also **water**

Tape

Mending a broken object with tape is a sign that you can recover from a setback or betrayal, although it may take time.

To buy tape is a sign that you should check your diary as a missed appointment in the near future could result in a loss.

To tape up a parcel for the post means you should not put all your hopes or resources into one place or project.

See also **gift**

Tarot

If during a reading you are shown negative cards such as the death/dying card, this is never a bad omen but an indication that deep down you are fearful that your life is out of control.

If you are the person reading the cards it can mean that you have hidden talents in this field and maybe you should try reading the cards in reality.

See also **cards** *or* **fortune teller**

Tattoo

If you are a tattoo artist you may be feeling very strongly about somebody and are anxious for a formal commitment to symbolise your love or loyalty.

If you are being tattooed you should be careful to ensure that a close friend or lover does not become over-possessive.

See also **artist**

Tea

Making or drinking tea signifies the need to confide in an older or wiser friend or relation so that you can talk over any sorrows and worries you have. Tea can also be a sign that you may have a visitor from England in the near future.

See also **drinking**

Teacher

If you are a pupil in a dream, your teacher may be a spirit guide who is trying to impart advice.

If you see a teacher from your past then it is a sign that you need to seek support and guidance in your present life

If you are teaching, it means that you need to express your valid opinions more openly and regularly at work or at home.

See also **academic lessons** *or* **school**

Team

To be part of a team is a sign that you may be asked to join a committee or group to help push through a joint project or pool resources. If you are self-employed in real life you may get an offer to merge with another company.

See also **sport**

Tears

If you are crying it means you need to share a sorrow that you have been trying to cope with alone with a trusted friend.

If a relative or friend is in tears it can be a sign that they may need your help but are unwilling to appear weak and ask for it.

Technology lesson
See **academic lessons**

Teenager
See **adolescent**

Teeth
This is a common dream and usually reflects worries and problems regarding teeth and gums in real life. To lose teeth also highlights fears about ageing and losing your grasp on work or life. Teeth also represent words so you should be wary of someone in a dream who has bad teeth, even if they do not in real life, as they may be lying to you.

See also **decay**

Telephone
This represents important communication via a phone. Sometimes this dream can be a premonition of a phone call from a person you think a great deal of who has not been in touch for a while.

Being unable to dial a number correctly in an emergency, being unable to hear the speaker or be heard yourself or to constantly get the engaged tone are common anxiety dreams about needing help but not receiving it or not being able to get people to take your worries seriously.

See also **dialling**, **engaged** *or* **mobile phone**

Telescope
This means that answers or opportunities lie beyond your immediate environment so you need to look further away, possibly on the internet, to gain a long-term solution.

See also **observatory**

Television
If you are watching television in a dream it can mean that you may have become too involved with the problems of a friend or relation.

If you are appearing on the television it is a sign that your talents and achievements will soon be recognised.

Temple
To dream of a temple may be a past-life dream but it can also indicate emerging spiritual and healing powers and perhaps the chance to develop them. Temples also signify a desire for silence and solitude away from the frantic world.

Temptation
If you are tempted in a dream to do something wrong this can be a wish-fulfilment, especially if you have been denying yourself the odd indulgence or expression of resentment or desire.

Tent

Living or sleeping in a tent represents your free spirit and indicates you have perhaps become too weighed down with routine. Tents are a good omen for anyone about to change to a simpler lifestyle, those who have children who are backpacking around the world or for those planning to have a long holiday.

See also **camping, holiday** *or* **travel**

Terror

A terrifying dream is your subconscious mind trying to rid itself of all the anxieties and free-floating fears you may be harbouring such as all the dreadful things that could happen to you and your family. Although such dreams are unpleasant, usually people feel better the following day.

Terrorist

With the increase of global terrorism, dreams about terrorists have also increased. They tend to symbolise fears about aspects of our lives where safety is beyond our control. Nevertheless, if you do experience a very vivid dream with specific details that stays with you all the next day, for example, of a terrorist threat to a place you are planning to visit, it would do no harm to take extra precautions.

See also **bomb, kidnapper** *or* **war**

Text message

A pleasant message from someone you know in real life could be a sign that the person is thinking or dreaming of you.

If you receive a nasty text message, it means that your privacy is being invaded.

See also **mobile phone**

Theatre

This symbolises someone in your family or a friend who behaves over-dramatically in order to get their own way. You should refuse to be a willing audience.

See also **actor or actress, drama, opera** *or* **play**

Thieves

If thieves break into your home or workplace, it means you need to watch out for people stealing your ideas, or even your partner. Dreams about thieves are sometimes a subconscious reminder that your security measures need checking or updating.

See also **criminal**

Thirsty

To be thirsty in a dream is a sign that you are not receiving enough affection or gratitude. Thirst can also be a warning that a source of income may dry up so you should think about new financial ventures.

See also **drinking**

Thorns

A thorny hedge is a traditional symbol of magic and protection so this dream can represent ideas or feelings that are half-formed and need time to develop before being revealed. Thorns also provide a necessary barrier from those who are critical or draining your self-confidence and so are also symbolic of difficult neighbours or in-laws.

See also **hedge**

Threat

If you are threatened in a dream, it can be a reflection of your fears in the real world about a particular person or situation.

Throat

A sore throat means you have been trying to soothe other people's quarrels and complaints but should now voice your own thoughts.

Throne

To be sitting on a throne indicates that you are aiming high in your job and should be offered a promotion or pay rise soon.

See also **royalty** *or* **usurper**

Thumb

A swollen or bandaged thumb means that petty and irritating people are making you feel stressed and you need to confront them before they make you feel ill.

To hold your thumbs or raise them up is a sign that all will turn out very well, no matter how uncertain your life seems at the moment.

Thunder

Thunder without lightning is symbolic of a person who is making a fuss but unlikely to carry out their threats.

See also **lightning** *or* **storm**

Tidal waves

See **floods**

Tiger

Tigers represent luck with regards to money and speculation. If the tiger attacks you it represents your own justifiable anger bursting out, maybe with regards to somebody who is bullying a child.

See also **animals** *or* **wild beasts**

Time

This is a common anxiety dream. If you run out of time in a dream or are rushing to catch a train or plane, you need to slow down in real life and concentrate on your priorities. Your subconscious is probably trying to tell you to include some form of relaxation in your life.

See also **train** *or* **watch**

Toad

A toad is a very lucky omen for all matters concerning money, health and fertility. Toads are creatures of the moon and signify an improvement in circumstances before the moon cycle has ended.

Tobacco

Rolling tobacco to make a cigarette is an indication that you should take your time before making a decision or commitment.

See also **pipe (smoking)** *or* **smoking**

Tongue

A tongue, especially a swollen one, is a warning that any gossip and rumours you hear during the next week should be ignored as they are totally untrue.

Tools

If you are fixing something it is an indication that you have the power to solve a current problem that is troubling you.

If your tools are broken, it can mean that you are not getting the support or service you need and should perhaps look elsewhere.

See also **hammer**

Torch

A beam of light being emitted from a torch means that you will suddenly discover the solution to a problem or will master a skill with which you have been struggling.

A torch that does not work is a warning that you need to keep a careful watch over your finances.

See also **light**

Tornado

This can reflect emotional turmoil or fears that yours or the life of someone close to you is spinning out of control. You should wait for things to calm down before speaking or acting. Tornadoes can also represent a person who would benefit from your calming influence as they have a habit of rushing through life creating chaos.

See also **storm** *or* **wind**

Tortoise

This is symbolic of longevity, the past and traditions. If you are embarking on a new venture, a tortoise means that you will have to be patient before you can enjoy success. You may receive good news from older relations.

See also **animals** *or* **reptile**

Tower

A watchtower represents your subconscious mind overseeing a situation. What you see from the watchtower can help you with any future plans as it can either bring an opportunity to your attention or warn you of an avoidable problem.

Being locked in a tower suggests you are suffering from isolation due to restrictions, overwork, a recent betrayal or a loss. You should try to go out and meet other people.

Toys

If you have become a child and are playing with toys, it is a sign that you are unhappy at the moment and need to seek some fun.

If you are an adult playing with toys or the toys become animated, it could be a sign that someone from your childhood may try to contact you in the near future.

See also **dolls, games, kite, playing (children)** *or* **puzzle**

Trailer

If your car is pulling a trailer, you may be offered a large but cheap item that you have been searching for in the near future. This is a good omen for bargain hunters and for people who trade in antiques.

Train

Travelling by train suggests you should follow through a plan logically and methodically in order to achieve a set goal or reach a chosen destination in life.

If the train journey goes well, it is a good omen for the days ahead. If the train journey takes you through lovely scenery it indicates that your current path through life is harmonious.

If you miss a train or your stop, or the train is late, it reflects your fears that matters are out of your control.

See also **rail, railway ticket, time, travel** *or* **vehicle**

Training

If you are taking a course or training for a sporting event, it can be a sign that you may get an opportunity to turn an interest into a profitable career.

If you are turned down for a course, you should try another route in order to fulfil your ambition.

Tramp

If you are frightened by a tramp, it can highlight that you are feeling insecure at the moment.

If you give something to a tramp, it can reflect a desire to have more freedom in your life.

If you are a tramp then it means you are not happy with your life at the moment and should try to make some changes.

See also **beggar** *or* **homelessness**

Traps

Animal traps are a warning that you should not confide any secrets or confidential work to people you do not know very well, and even if you do know them you should exercise caution.

Vermin traps are an omen that a spiteful colleague will be caught out through their own lies.

See also **animals, mice, rats** *or* **vermin**

Travel

Travel dreams are usually a form of wish fulfilment when you would like to go on holiday, move house or change your job. Sometimes the dream can nudge you in the right direction

Very vivid travel dreams to a specific place may be a premonition that before long you may get the chance to visit the place in the dream.

See also **aeroplane, boat, car, carriage (horse and), carriage (train), continent, cruise, delays, driving, foreign, holiday, journey, packing, tent** *or* **train**

Treasure

To find treasure is an excellent omen for finances and the development of new talents.

To bury treasure is a warning that you should not give too many good ideas away for free.

See also **gemstones** *or* **money**

Tree

This is always a good omen if the tree is growing or in a forest as it symbolises health, healing, strength, protection and gradual growth in areas of your life that are most significant to you. Forests or woods are also positive signs if you want children as it represents the possibility of extending your own family tree.

Falling trees represent fears about family catastrophes and are usually just anxiety dreams.

See also *individual trees*, **forest, garden, logs, sawing, wood** *or* **woods**

Triangle

See **magical symbols** *or* **musical instruments**

Trumpet

Playing a trumpet is usually an indication of promises that cannot be kept. Trumpets also mean that you should not be intimidated by boastful people.

See also **music** *or* **musical instruments**

Tumour

To dream of a tumour is not a premonition but a reflection of fears that are building up in your mind regarding your health or that of someone close. Tumours can also represent resentment that may be building up inside you about unfair treatment.

See also **illness**

Tunnel

Tunnels symbolise temporary confusion or setbacks that will soon clear if you forge ahead nevertheless.

Light at the end of a tunnel signifies that things in your life will improve and you will find happiness.

Turtle

This is an ancient symbol for Mother Earth as turtles symbolise security and illustrate that you should value your home and what you have.

See also **animals** *or* **reptile**

Twins

If you are pregnant or trying to conceive a child and dream of twins it is usually an omen that you will have twin babies. Twins can also represent two sides of your personality or of new talents which may be beginning to emerge.

If you dream of having a twin, it can foretell that you may soon find your soulmate or at least someone with whom you are totally at ease. Fighting twins indicate rivals in love.

See also **baby**

U

UFO
See **alien**

Ugly
An ugly person represents negative emotions that have been attached to a dream figure.

To dream you are ugly means you are worried about expressing an opinion or revealing your true self in case you are rejected, either by a new lover or by somebody you admire.

An ugly young woman traditionally indicates a forthcoming inheritance.

Ulcer
Mouth ulcers represent angry words that you are trying hard not to express.

Stomach ulcers signify a long-standing grievance or injustice that is gnawing away at you and needs resolving.

Umbrella
An open umbrella in the rain is a lucky omen as it indicates that you will be protected from harm and malice.

A leaky or broken umbrella represents constant pressure from a child or your parents, which is beginning to wear you down.

See also **rain**

Uncle
An uncle in a dream, whether or not you have an uncle in reality, represents a wise older man, perhaps an older male relation, whether living or deceased. If the uncle figure gives you advice in the dream you should try to remember what he says and act on it.

See also **family**

Underground
An underground world is an ancient symbol in many cultures of a parallel world in which ancestors and wise people live. Any person or talking animal you meet in this fairy-tale dream should answer your questions truthfully.

If you are buried alive or find yourself trapped underground, whether in a mine or a cavern, it is a sign that a vital part of yourself has been buried beneath the demands of everyday life.

Undertaker

This is never a premonition of death but symbolic of someone who will shortly come into your life, if they are not known to you already, who could help you to leave the past behind.

See also **burial, coffin, cremation** *or* **funeral**

Underwear

If you see a friend or relation in just their underwear in a public place it can indicate they may be caught out in a compromising or embarrassing situation in the future.

If you find yourself out in public in just your underwear it can mean that you are worried about a minor indiscretion or mistake becoming public knowledge.

See also **clothes**

Undress

If you feel comfortable taking your clothes off in a dream, it means that you are ready to shed your inhibitions either emotionally or sexually with a new partner.

If you are embarrassed to undress or feel shy, you may be worried about your privacy being invaded or feel that someone is trying to become too close to you.

See also **nakedness**

Unfaithful

See **infidelity**

Unicorn

This foretells of a rare opportunity or unusual experience coming your way which will bring you happiness. You may also have emerging psychic powers as the unicorn is symbolic of healing. This is a good omen for men wishing to become fathers as unicorns also represent male potency.

See also **mythical creatures**

Uniform

Any uniform means the loss of your unique identity. If you dream of wearing a uniform you may be feeling that your family don't appreciate what you do for them or that your contributions at work are being overlooked.

If you are involved in a job which requires you to wear a uniform in real life, this dream is a good omen for the future.

See also **army, navy** *or* **police**

Union

To be a member of a union in a dream means you should be more proactive and perhaps join with others to demand improvements at work or protest against an issue you feel strongly about.

Universe

To glimpse the universe and feel at peace is what is called 'a peak experience'. Although we may only have one or two of these special dreams in a lifetime, they are a reminder that we are all unique and special and that there is more than this earthly life.

See also **space**

Unlucky

This dream actually has the opposite meaning in reality as it is an excellent omen for any new venture where luck plays a part.

Unusual

Unusual symbols or really strange dreams are often the first sign that you are experiencing lucid dreaming (see page 37). Any symbols and messages which you see or hear are usually significant and may help to answer questions you might have in real life.

See also **eccentric** *or* **freak**

Upside down

A subverted dream world means you may be feeling as though your life has taken a wrong turn. If your dream rights itself, you should stick with your chosen path as it means your life should go back on track. Sometimes this dream can be a sign that you are about to fall madly in love with someone.

Urge

If you have a strong urge to do or say something in a dream, you should perhaps act upon it in reality.

Urgent

Whether the dream refers to a letter marked urgent or an urgent job, it is usually your subconscious reminding you of an important matter that you have not yet addressed in your waking life.

Urinate

At its most basic this is a wake-up call from your bladder. If you cannot find anywhere to urinate in the dream it means that you are afraid of your true nature being exposed in reality, maybe as a result of low self-esteem caused by a spiteful person.

Useless

If something you buy is useless it symbolises the doubts you may have about an investment or purchase.

If someone says that you are useless, the dream persona is probably reflecting your own thoughts about yourself.

See also **quality**

Usurper

If someone takes the throne or someone else's job in a dream it is a sign that you need to watch out for someone at work who would like a promotion at any cost.

See also **royalty** *or* **throne**

V

Vacation
See holiday

Vaccination
To dream of getting a vaccination means you are trying to resist the charms of someone you suspect is not reliable. This is also an indication of imminent travel to a hot destination and can also be a sign that you are worried about a child's health.

Valentine
To dream of receiving a special Valentine, whether or not you are in a relationship, is a promise of romance and excitement in the spring.

To send a Valentine card in a dream means that you are looking for someone special. If you are already in a relationship and experience this dream, it means that your relationship needs spicing up.

A box of old Valentine cards indicates that you may meet an old lover or hear from them unexpectedly.

Valley
A beautiful green valley represents a happy future, perhaps as a result of moving to a place surrounded by hills or mountains which you may identify as the location seen in the dream.

A barren valley means you need to spend time with your partner if you are to revive a relationship.

Vapour bath
See sauna

Varnishing (furniture)
Varnishing furniture suggests that people close to you may be distorting the truth. Similarly, you may be asked to avert your eyes to a person's less-than-honest practices, perhaps at work. However, this dream is a good omen for DIY work or house restoration that you may be about to undertake and for people who work with wood such as wood carvers and furniture-makers.

Varnishing (nails)
See nails

Vault
See bank *or* church

Vegetables

If you are eating a particular vegetable, your subconscious mind may be telling you that your body needs the nutrients from that type of vegetable. Generally, to see vegetables growing represents the potential of a financial venture. When cooked and eaten, vegetables signify rewards for past efforts.

See also under individual vegetables, **ripe, rotting** or **salad**

Vehicle

Any vehicle represents some form of movement. In particular, works vehicles represent business travel while luxurious vehicles represent your mode of travel in the future.

A broken-down vehicle can be a subconscious alert that you need to check your own vehicle for faults.

See also **bus, car, removal van, train** or **wheel**

Veil

A bridal veil can be an omen for a wedding in the family.

A nun's veil suggests you would benefit from some solitude and a withdrawal from the frantic pace of life for a while.

Any other type of veil symbolises secrecy.

See also **bride**

Velvet

To wear velvet or sit on velvet chairs is a promise of profit, recognition and happiness. Velvet is also a symbol of sensual love and beauty and points towards a future considerate (and prosperous) lover.

Vendetta

If someone you recognise is waging a vendetta against you in a dream, that person may be talking about you behind your back in reality, even if they seem friendly towards you.

A gangland vendetta is a reflection of major rivalries in your world, whether in the form of office politics or disputes in the family. You should try to keep your distance.

See also **violence**

Venison

Preparing or eating venison means you will be rewarded if you put a lot of effort into hunting out lots of new opportunities to either find a job, a new lover or a new item that you need.

See also **deer** or **food**

Vermin

Dreaming of vermin such as fleas or head lice suggests that you are frustrated at being invaded by a host of irritating people, perhaps your partner's friends or relatives. If you have animals or small children, your subconscious may be warning you to check them for infestations that they may have picked up outside the home.

See also **mice, rats** *or* **traps**

Vicar

To dream of the local clergyman is a sign that there may soon be an announcement of a wedding or birth in the family.

See also **church**

Vice

To dream of a vice or prostitution can mean you are feeling as though a lover or partner is not giving you the respect you deserve or is pressurising you to have sex more often than you want to.

See also **drinking, sex** *or* **smoking**

Victory

To dream of a victorious army, sports team or a victory parade is an excellent omen of success if you have been struggling for some time to make a business profitable or to make headway with a legal matter.

See also **army, navy** *or* **sport**

Villa

To dream of a holiday villa in a hot country can be a wish-fulfilment if you are finding life dull and boring and the weather cold. However, the dream may represent the chance to rent a cheap villa, perhaps through a friend or relative, for a holiday.

See also **holiday**

Vinegar

Sour vinegar is symbolic of a spiteful neighbour or relative.

Apple vinegar is a sign of improving health and if you are on a diet it is an omen for success.

Vineyard

A vineyard in a dream promises an improvement regarding matters of health and prosperity. Vineyards are also a very ancient symbol of fertility and are therefore a good omen for both satisfying sex and the conception of children.

See also **wine**

Violence

If you are the victim of a violent attack or act violently in a dream, you may be repressing strong feelings in real-life so your mind is expressing them in an uncontrolled way in the dream. You should try to channel your energy to create a positive change in reality.

See also **criminal, vendetta** *or* **war**

Violets

These tiny purple bud-like flowers are symbolic of secret love and secrets in general.

If someone you recognise gives you violets in a dream, that person may secretly be in love with you in real life.

If you pick violets you may need to keep your feelings for someone or something a secret until you are sure they will be respected, especially if you or a would-be lover are already in a relationship.

See also **flowers** *or* **plants**

Violin

If there is beautiful violin music in a dream, it represents an harmonious relationship between lovers, marriage partners or a particular employee with whom there have been past problems.

If you are playing the violin well, it means that you are in tune with yourself and can trust your judgement.

If someone is playing a violin badly it means that you should be cautious around someone who acts as though they are your friend but may actually be a troublemaker.

See also **music** *or* **musical instruments**

Virgin

To dream of losing your virginity, whatever your age, indicates the flowering of innocent love and the desire to give yourself emotionally as well as physically to a new love.

See also **sex**

Virgin Mary

Women often dream of the Virgin Mary either just before they become pregnant or when they are pregnant. This is a very special dream which denotes that blessings will fall on your home and your life. This is an excellent and comforting omen for all mothers, grandmothers and would-be mothers.

Visitors

If you recognise the visitors in the dream it may be advance warning that they will come to you unexpectedly in real life.

If you do not recognise the visitors, it can be a sign that you may be given the opportunity to meet new people who will eventually become close friends.

Vivid

A very vivid dream is always of great significance. If the dream contained advice, good news or a warning you should take it seriously.

See also page 37 for more details on lucid dreaming

Volcano

A volcano can refer to a permanently angry or irritable person who often uses their bubbling fury to bully others. However, volcanoes can also be positive healing symbols which signify the release of old emotions or the consummation of love.

See also **eruption**

Vomit

Vomiting in a dream means you have been swallowing angry words and painful feelings.

A vomiting child can sometimes be a subconscious alert that a child close to you is unwell.

See also **illness**

Vulture

A vulture represents someone who rejoices in other's misfortune. It also means that you should be cautious as to whom you tell your problems and fears, as a new-found friend or recent addition to the workplace may be a gossip.

See also **animals, birds** *or* **wild beasts**

Wading

Wading through clear water is a good omen for rapid and easy progress with a venture, especially if it involves dealing with people who may have been difficult in the past.

Wading in muddy or weed-choked water is a warning of tangled communication or love affairs.

To wade out of your depth means you should not get involved in a quarrel between lovers or a married couple as there are issues you do not know about.

See also **floods, lagoon, lake, river, sea** *or* **water**

Wages

Dreams regarding wages are good omens for the unemployed, for those beginning work for the first time or for those returning to work after a break.

To pay other people's wages reflects a need to spend money on work you cannot do yourself, such as house renovations, extra office staff or domestic help.

To receive an increased wage means you may soon get a better paid job or a promotion.

See also **job, money** *or* **work**

Wagon

A wagon is sometimes an indication of a past-life dream, especially if you live in a city. If you dream of a wagon loaded full of hay or harvest crops, it is a sign that your life will be filled with happiness.

There may even be additions to the family whether through birth, marriage, remarriage or adoption.

Wail

Wailing in a dream, whether from a child or an adult you recognise can sometimes be your subconscious alerting you to the fact that the person is suffering in real life.

If you are wailing it may be a reflection of your feelings in real life. Maybe you should try harder to ensure your voice is heard.

The wailing of an emergency vehicle siren is another subconscious call to check your house or personal safety and maybe test any fire alarms. A police siren can be an indication that a family member has had a minor encounter with the law and are trying to keep quiet about it.

See also **police**

Waist

A tiny waist can either be wish fulfilment if you long to be slim or it can represent a female who acts as though they are helpless in order to gain sympathy and avoid responsibility or hard work.

A large waist is a symbol of abundance, physical health and strength and symbolises a reliable person.

Waiter/waitress

If you are the waiter or waitress, this may reflect how you see your role at work or at home.

To be waited on may be a wish fulfilment but it can also be a sign that you could soon be invited out for a meal during which you may receive an offer from your host or hostess.

See also **servant**

Waiting

If you are waiting in a dream for a person or an event, you may be feeling frustrated in reality or feel that a relationship is not progressing.

Walking

To dream of enjoying a walk denotes an easier time ahead. If you are a workaholic, this dream is a reminder that you should relax and enjoy life more. The people you are walking with can reflect the type of people who will make you happy and with whom you should make an effort to contact.

To walk alone is an indication that you have your own agenda at the moment.

Wallet

See **purse**

Walls

High walls can symbolise either protection or exclusion depending on whether you are inside or outside them and whether you want to be there or are trying to escape. Walls represent a barrier between two places or two states, for example, captivity or freedom. Your feelings in the dream are therefore crucial as to whether the walls are a positive factor in your life and should be strengthened or whether they are negative and should be knocked down.

Wandering

To wander aimlessly across land means that there is a great deal of indecision in your life, possibly caused by other people who refuse to finalise plans or make a decision. You may need to make a decision for them if you are not to lose your impetus.

War

If you are in the middle of a battlefield you may be standing between warring factions in your everyday life and should take a few steps backwards.

If you dream of living in a war zone, it means that you are secretly afraid that someone, such as an ex-partner, will resent your happiness or current relationship, and will try to spoil things.

See also **army, battle, fighting, navy, tank (army), terrorist** *or* **violence**

Warts

To be covered with warts represents an image problem. You may be worried about your appearance or your ability to make friends as a result of a change that has made you temporarily insecure.

Warts on hands belonging to somebody you recognise is a warning that the person may not be trustworthy in real life.

Washing

Washing yourself or clothes can indicate that you feel guilty about an omission or minor misdemeanour.

To wash dirty dishes suggests that you feel disappointed by the outcome of a celebration or family gathering.

See also **clothes**

Wasps

You should be wary of a vicious-tongued colleague or neighbour and avoid contact with them where possible.

To kill wasps is a good indication you are ready to stand up to a critical relative.

See also **insects**

Waste

To waste food or money in a dream means an opportunity will be wasted unless you are ready to take a chance.

Watch

To keep checking a watch means you are worried that your plans in real life might go wrong. Maybe you should prioritise and allow yourself some extra time.

A broken watch means you are wasting time and energy dwelling about past events that cannot be altered.

See also **time**

Water

All water dreams are associated with emotions, both your own and those of other people.

Deep water can indicate buried emotions while fast-flowing water denotes an unexpected declaration of love. Still and sunlit waters are a sign of harmony but you should take note of a dream containing polluted waters as these can indicate that there are bad influences on your children.

See also **drowning, floods, ice, kettle, lagoon, lake, pool, river, sea, snow, swimming, tank (water), wading** *or* **well**

Wax

Wax dripping from a hot candle is a warning that you should be careful not to get hurt.

Wax images are not symbols of evil but indicate that you have subconsciously noticed someone at work or socially is jealous of you.

See also **candles**

Waxing moon

See **moon**

Weapons

If you are wielding a weapon it is a sign that you need to be more assertive, especially if you are being bullied emotionally in real life. If someone is threatening you with a weapon, it can illustrate that you are concerned about a bully in your waking life. You should maybe seek support and advice.

See also **gun** *or* **sword**

Weather vane

This symbolises an inconsistent and indecisive person. You should also watch out for signs of change so that you can act appropriately at the right moment.

Web (internet)

To be connected to the internet suggests that information or contacts you need will be found on the web. Try to recall which pages you saw in your dream as these will be key to finding what you want.

To catch a virus whilst surfing the net indicates that someone in your life is trying to invade your privacy, maybe by reading your confidential e-mails or by stealing your ideas.

See also **computer**

Web (spider)

See **spiders**

Wedding

Any wedding celebration in a dream represents a deep commitment or a desire for a permanent relationship. The identity of the bride or groom may be a prediction of the person who could make you happy.

Sorrow at a wedding indicates you may be afraid you are with the wrong partner or have unfulfilled desires for love.

See also **bride and/or bridegroom, marriage** *or* **rice**

Weeds

Weeds indicate that you have neglected a particular aspect of your life or not kept up an interest or skill that you need to practice regularly.

Weeds also represent an unresolved issue that is upsetting a current relationship.

See also **nettles**

Weighing

If you are weighing food, you need to consider the relative merits of two courses of action that will affect your home.

To weigh yourself can indicate a dissatisfaction with your appearance or current performance, either at home or work.

Well

This is a universal symbol of life, health and fertility. Wells also symbolise the entrance to the womb of Mother Earth. Dreaming of a well full of water suggests that you have within you the ability to heal a situation or person or to tap into a deep source of wisdom that will bring harmony into your life.

A dried up, abandoned or polluted well represents a loss of vitality, optimism, creativity and sore throats.

See also **water**

West

To go or look to the west is an indication that after a period of stagnation or setbacks, things should begin to move forward, maybe as a result of some unexpected help. Sometimes, this dream can mean that you would benefit from some relaxation to allow life to pass you by for a while.

Whale

This is symbolic of a huge undertaking that can be successfully fulfilled and of success, particularly in the fields of commerce, accountancy, banking or administration.

See also **animals** *or* **sea**

Wheel

This denotes a period of travel and change. A turning wheel indicates new opportunities or challenges and heralds the end of a period of stagnation. A broken wheel warns of travel delays or missed trains, ferries or planes so you should double-check any travel plans and allow yourself extra time.

See also **vehicle**

Wheelbarrow

To be using a wheelbarrow means you may need to adapt plans and maybe even relocate your home or work.

If a man or woman you recognise is pushing a wheelbarrow, they will prove to be a trustworthy person who keeps their promises.

Whispering

To whisper in a dream or hear whispers is a hint towards intrigue and secrets in your waking life that can lead to disputes within the family or workplace.

White

This colour represents new beginnings and indicates that unexpected opportunities should present themselves to you soon.

See also **colours** *or* **snow**

Widowed

If your real-life partner dies in a dream, it is never an omen of physical death, but a representation of a new phase in the relationship, such as marriage, childbirth or retirement. If such events haven't happened in real life, the dream can be a sign that major adjustments need to be made if the relationship is to continue and thrive.

See also **death/dying**

Wig

To be wearing a wig or hairpiece means you wish to keep your feelings private for now.

If someone you recognise is wearing a wig, it indicates that their personality may be very different to the façade they present to the world. They may even be much friendlier than you think. However, if the wig slips or falls off, you should be cautious around them as they may have a secret past.

See also **hair**

Wild beasts

These are very instinctive symbols. If you feel excited at the sight of them it is reflective of your own power and passion.

If you feel threatened by a wild beast it means that you are allowing someone to intimidate you, even though they are making you angry and want to retaliate.

See also individual animals or **taming**

Wind

A strong wind can represent the blowing away of inertia and stagnation.

A warm wind promises happier and more prosperous times.

A cold or cruel wind indicates disillusionment, coldness and criticism from others and a sense of being vulnerable.

If a wind is blowing leaves, travel and house moves are well favoured as it shows that you have the energy for embracing change and new opportunities.

See also **gale, hurricane, storm** *or* **tornado**

Windmill/windfarm

This is a hint that you should wait for the right time before you embark on a new venture.

Window

This denotes a new insight or a period of freedom.

A curtained window can symbolise narrow-mindedness in others or an unwelcoming older family member or in-law.

See also **glass**

Wine

Drinking wine is a sign of forthcoming celebrations. To be drinking wine with someone you are having a relationship with indicates the deepening of love and attraction.

See also **alcohol, drinking, grapes** *or* **vineyard**

Winter

You may be feeling as though you are on the periphery of your social circle. It could be that the person or people who are excluding you are generally unfriendly and you should maybe seek out the company of kindlier people.

Wish

To make a wish in a dream is a good sign that it will come true.

Witch

A wise white witch denotes that you can achieve your dreams and desires if you believe in yourself.

A wicked witch represents the negative side of your personality or a troublesome older woman.

See also **occultist**

Wolf

This is symbolic of nurture and represents your family and other people you care for. If the dream featured a pack of wolves, it indicates that a lover will always be loyal to you. If a lover is being unfaithful to you at the moment and you experience this dream, loyalty is obviously important to you and so you should seek a new and more faithful partner.

Being attacked by a pack of wolves can represent a sense of being torn apart by family or relationship conflicts. You may be feeling as though you are having to compromise with a situation that feels wrong to you.

See also **animals** *or* **wild beasts**

Women

If a woman is talking in your dream, it denotes that you will receive a warm welcome into a group within your community.

A crowd of women can be a warning not to join in with gossip, either at a party or at work, as a particularly treacherous woman there may accuse you of being the one who instigated any rumours.

Wood

A wooden carving or a beautifully carved piece of wooden furniture is a sign of durability and indicates that you will enjoy long-term domestic happiness and security. You may be given or will acquire a wooden carving that will bring you good luck.

See also **tree**

Woods

Green healthy trees growing in a wood are symbolic of family life and denote that your family will grow over the next few years through marriage or remarriage. These events will bring great joy to older relatives, who may be feeling isolated at the moment.

See also **tree**

Work

If you dream of being at work it is a sign that you are either working too hard and need to switch off or that there is a problem at work that is bothering you and maybe you should seek advice to solve it.

If you find yourself working in a new job, your subconscious may be trying to tell you that it is time to leave your current occupation and try something different.

See also **boss, job, office** *or* **wages**

Workshop

A workshop of any kind denotes the achievement of practical aims and realistic projects. This is also a good omen for people who work in manufacturing or craft work.

Worm

A worm on a fishing line indicates that you will need to coax others to agree with your ideas. You may have to demonstrate any advantages and if necessary offer incentives for cooperation.

A worm inside fruit represents a treacherous person, either at home or at work, who is encouraging others to complain and then reporting their dissension.

See also **animals, birds, fishing** *or* **fruit**

Wound

See **injury**

Wreath

Dreams of wreaths foretell of christenings and weddings in the family, not funerals.

Writing

Written communication in dreams have great significance, more so than spoken words, as they often contain information from deep within the psyche.

If you are writing in a dream you may have something very important to communicate; you may even have to acknowledge something to yourself.

Indistinct or unintelligible writing can denote that you are uncertain of your feelings towards someone or can't decide whether someone is telling you their real feelings regarding an issue.

See also **handwriting, letter** *or* **pen**

X

If you dream of an x beside a paragraph of writing or a calculation, perhaps in a classroom environment, you may be secretly afraid that a decision you have made will be criticised or judged as wrong by someone of importance and you will be made to feel inadequate.

If you are crossing someone's name out, it shows that you wish to remove their presence or influence from your life.

See also **classroom** *or* **examination**

Xenophobia

If you are hostile towards or feel afraid of foreign people in a dream, you may be feeling isolated by a recent house move or change in career which has meant mixing socially with a new set of people.

X-rated

If you are enjoying an x-rated film or experience in your dream, your subconscious is telling you that you need to shed your inhibitions or adapt a more spontaneous and sensual outlook. If you feel guilty or disgusted in the dream, it can denote that you may be feeling pressurised to become more physical in a new relationship. Sometimes a dream such as this can be warning that a secret liaison may not be such a good idea.

See also **sex**

X-ray

To have an X-ray generally denotes that you are worried people will find out what you are really like.

If you dream that an X-ray reveals an illness, this is generally an anxiety dream that can sometimes occur if you feel that you have no right to be happy. Only if you have a persistent health problem and experience the dream regularly, should you see a doctor for some reassurance or advice.

See also **doctor, hospital** *or* **illness**

Xylophone

If you are playing the xylophone well, it is a sign that your life will become more harmonious and any quarrels you may have been involved in recently will be resolved.

If you cannot play but are trying, it means that you are attempting to act as a peacemaker between people who have no intention of being reconciled.

To listen to a xylophone indicates that you need to become more proactive in life.

See also **music** *or* **musical instruments**

Yacht
See **boats**

Yam
This fruit symbolises fertility and may indicate that there is a pregnancy in the family. For older women, yams signify a new phase in their lives, in which they may make radical but welcome changes to their lifestyle.

See also **food** *or* **fruit**

Yard
A backyard or chicken yard represents your territory and shows that you are unwilling to share your home just yet with another person or to allow others to dictate changes to your lifestyle. If your family are quarrelling in real life, this dream suggests that you should try to keep problems within the family circle. In particular, if two families have come together through remarriage, it may take time before they accept and feel comfortable with one another.

Yawning
Yawning in a dream signifies discontentment with a present lifestyle. You should maybe think about cutting ties with people whom you have known for years but who bore you.

Yellow
This colour is often associated with future travel but can also be an indication that you will need to be logical in order to resolve a personal matter.

See also **colours**

Yellow bird
A yellow bird in a dream traditionally represents marriage to a wealthy partner or an increase in joint marital wealth, maybe through an inheritance. A yellow bird also denotes personal success through overseas ventures or contacts.

See also **animals** *or* **birds**

Yew tree

Yew trees can live for two thousand years and are often found in churchyards as they represent immortality. Yew trees in dreams are, therefore, symbolic of long life and health in old age and are a good omen if you have been worrying about the health of an older person. They are also symbolic of faithful love.

See also **tree**

Young

To dream that you are young again or of your adult children as babies, represents the need to leave the past behind instead of trying to recapture it. You will probably find that the future will seem much better if you look forward to it positively. Occasionally, this dream can sometimes be an indication of the arrival of grandchildren.

See also **children**

Z

Zealous

If you are being zealous pursuing something in a dream, it would probably be of your advantage to follow it up in real life.

Zealot

If someone you recognise is being fanatical, it indicates that you are being pressurised into making decisions you would rather avoid.

If you do not recognise the zealot, you need to be wary around a newcomer who may try to persuade you to sign away more money than you can afford.

Zebra

To dream of a zebra is a sign that you are losing interest with a particular activity or person.

A zebra in the wild indicates that you need more personal space and freedom.

See also **animals** *or* **wild beasts**

Zero

See **numbers**

Zest

If you feel full of zest or enthusiasm in a dream, it is a positive sign that you will soon enter a happy and energetic phase in your life complete with new opportunities .

If you are lacking zest it indicates that you are not as enthusiastic about a new project as you say.

Zinc

This metal refers to relatives who live abroad and indicates that they may ask you to join them. Maybe you should go on holiday and see how you like living abroad. Sometimes this is also a subconscious alert that you need to increase your vitamin and mineral intake.

Zip

If a zip will not fasten in a dream or it keeps coming undone, it means that you are afraid a secret you have been keeping will be revealed.

A broken zip indicates that you feel more hurt than you care to admit about a close person's indiscretion or tactless remark.

Zip file

To dream of a zip or concentrated file of information on a computer says that there is a lot more to a current situation than you have been told.

A zip file that will not open indicates you are feeling frustrated with someone close to you who is refusing to share their feelings or trust you regarding a problem.

Zit

See spots

Zodiac

To dream of studying the zodiac means that you are worrying too much about the future and need to relax and let life take its natural course. Sometimes this dream can be an indication that you could be a gifted astrologer if you were to study it. This dream is always an omen for good luck.

See also stars (sky)

Zodiac wheel

A painted zodiac wheel or a wheel of stars is an excellent omen that promises a fulfilling year ahead. It is also an indication that your psychic gifts are developing spontaneously.

Zoo

If enclosures are large and the animals are well cared for, it means that you are blessed with energy, intuition, logic and common sense.

If the animals in your dream are trapped in tiny, bare cages, it means that your intuition is telling you that a present situation is destructive or a proposed action unwise.

See also animals

Zoologist

If you are studying animals in a dream you may need to listen to your instincts and possibly take a chance on love. This dream can also be a sign that you are hiding passionate feelings.

Index

Adams, Kaye 25
advice in dreams 31–3
angels in dreams 54–7
anxiety dreams 12–13, 24, 25, 28–9
    maternal 25, 29

bad dreams
    importance of 28–9
    turning into good ones 29–31
    see also night terrors; nightmares
Bast 17–18
Big Brother 23–5
Burns, Robert

cars, runaway 22
catastrophes, enacting 12–13
cats 17–18
celebrities 23–26, 42
children
    night terrors 9, 29–31
Christmas ritual 46
coincidences, meaningful 17, 43
controlling dreams 23, 35–8
crystals and angels 56–7

daydreaming 16, 38
dead relatives 57–9
decision-making 11–12
dream catchers 7, 9
dream fantasies 42–3
dream giants, shrinking 31
dream journals 15, 16
dream journeys 35
dream lovers 9, 42–50
    identifying 43–5
    modern rituals 48
    traditional rituals 46–48
dreaming true 31–3
dreams
    and advice 31–3
    controlling 23, 35–8
    and daily life 37–8
    erotic 42
    frequency 11
    inducing 9–10, 27–8
    lucid 37–8,
    past-life 38–41, 42
    positive purpose of 35

predictive 51–4
psychic 51–60
recording 15
recurring 17–18
remembering 14–15
shared 49–50
traditions surrounding 7, 35
understanding 7–8, 16

Egyptians, ancient 27, 31–3
erotic dreams 42
essential oils 27–8

falling 29
family traditions, following 21
fantasies 42–3
financial problems 22
flashbulb memory 14
floating 29

ghosts 57–9
giants 30–1
    shrinking 31
gods, knowledge of 31–3
Grandmother Spider Woman 7, 9
grandmothers 13–14, 34
guardian angels 54–5
    calling 55–7

happiness, finding 36–7
Hawaiian ritual for remembering
    dreams 14–15
Hewson, Sherrie 25
home and security 13–14, 34

images, personal 17–18
    see also symbols
inner voice *see* subconscious
insomnia 15, 27
intuition 11, 16, 52

journals 15, 16
Jung, Carl Gustav 17, 39
    synchronicity 17, 43

Loose Women 25–6
lovers 9, 42
    see also dream lovers; shared dreams

lucid dreaming 37–8, 42

McGiffin, Carole 25
maternal anxiety 25, 29
memory 14–15
Messenger, Melinda 23, 35
monsters 29–31
mothers
  in dreams 33–4
  and predictive dreams 52–3

naps 9
native North Americans 7
night terrors 9, 29–31
nightmares 9, 15

past life dreams 38–40
  creating and inducing 40–1
perfume
  use to create harmonious dreams 27–8
pictures and dreams 13–14
pillows, scented 28
power naps 9
predictive dreams 51–4
  and mothers 52–3
psychic dreams 51–60
  trusting 53–4

remembering dreams 14–15

sex 9, 42
shared dreams 49–50
siestas 9
sleep
  disturbance 8–9
  paralysis 9
  pillows 28
  prioritising 9
  promoting 9–10, 27–8
stress 8–9
subconscious 11, 13–14
  and bad dreams 28
Sweeney, Claire 25–6
symbols 15
  interpreting 16, 17
synchronicity 17, 43

telepathy 43, 53
tiredness 8–9
traditions surrounding dreams 7, 35

understanding dreams 7–8, 16

war dreams 20–1
water ritual 47
wedding cake ritual 47
wedding ritual 47
well rituals 47–8
wolf dream, The 19–20